Haitian Vodou

Haitian Vodou

Spirit, Myth, and Reality

Edited by Patrick Bellegarde-Smith
and Claudine Michel

Indiana University Press
BLOOMINGTON | INDIANAPOLIS

Chapter 4, "Of Worlds Seen and Unseen: The Educational Character
of Haitian Vodou," was originally published in *Comparative Educational
Review,* vol. 40 (August 1996), pp. 194–280. © 1996 by the Comparative
and International Education Society. All rights reserved.

This book is a publication of

Indiana University Press
601 North Morton Street
Bloomington, IN 47404-3797 USA

http://iupress.indiana.edu

Telephone orders   800-842-6796
Fax orders   812-855-7931
Orders by e-mail   iuporder@indiana.edu

The paper used in this publication meets the minimum requirements
of American National Standard for Information Sciences—Permanence
of Paper for Printed Library Materials, ANSI Z39.48-1984.

Manufactured in the United States of America

Library of Congress Cataloging-in-Publication Data

Haitian vodou : spirit, myth, and reality / edited by Patrick Bellegarde-
Smith and Claudine Michel.
     p. cm.
   Includes bibliographical references (p.   ) and index.
   ISBN 0-253-34756-4 (cloth : alk. paper) — ISBN 0-253-21853-5
(pbk. : alk. paper)   1. Voodooism.   I. Bellegarde-Smith, Patrick.
II. Michel, Claudine.
   BL2490.H35 2006
   299.6'75097294—dc22   2006006213

2 3 4 5   17 16 15 14

Published under the auspices of KOSANBA,
A Scholarly Association for the Study of Haitian Vodou,
and the Center for Black Studies, University of California, Santa Barbara.

The authors dedicate their work to the elders who pioneered in the enterprise of presenting a new *visage* of the Haitian religion to the world. Among them we cite Milo Rigaud, Odette Menesson-Rigaud, Suzanne Comhaire-Sylvain, Katherine Dunham, Guérin Montilus, Marilyn Houlberg, Charles H. Long, Karen McCarthy Brown, and LeGrace Benson. To them we say: "Ayibobo!"

And we wish to acknowledge the work of all *gason ak fanm vanyan,* the *houngan* and *manbo* who perpetuate well-founded traditions against all odds. We salute in particular André Pierre, Thérèse Roumer, Jacqueline Epingle, Max Beauvoir, Alourdes Champagne (Mama Lola), and Rose Richard (Manman Yaya). To them and to their many children, the young *manbo* and *hougan* who are continuing the ways of our ancestors, we say: "Mèsi anpil! Kenbe rèd pa lage!"

Development, when real and successful, always comes from the modernization of ancestral traditions, anchored in the rich cultural expressions of a nation. *Declaration,* KOSANBA (1997)

Contents

Acknowledgments

We wish to thank the Center for Black Studies at the University of California, Santa Barbara for hosting the first International Colloquium of the Congress of Santa Barbara (KOSANBA) in April 1997, and for unwavering and critical support in the intervening years. The Center for Black Studies (CBS) has acquired a towering presence in recent years in fostering scholarly activities concerning the whole of the Black world, and we are grateful to the Center for serving as host for KOSANBA, the only scholarly organization in the world dedicated to the academic study of Haitian Vodou. We are also grateful for the support we received from the Office of Research and the Division of Social Sciences of the College of Letters and Science at the University of California, Santa Barbara.

The editors would like to acknowledge by name a few people who have given extraordinary support to this project. Chryss Yost, Managing Editor of the *Journal of Haitian Studies* and Publications Director at the Center for Black Studies, located publishers, painters, and art collectors on three continents to scan photos of rare paintings and secure the permissions we needed for the images to be included in this volume. She had a three-inch-thick folder of correspondence for the requests alone; those of us who do work in Haiti and know the lay of the land view this as a *tour de force,* as it is simply not easy to get this kind of work done with Haitians overseas. Chryss also oversaw the permission process with the authors themselves. *Tour de force* is also what we need to call what Amber Wallace, Managing Editor for *Screening Noir* at the Center, did to help secure the permissions for the individuals appearing in the photographs of the Vodou ceremonies. Both Chryss and Amber assisted with multiple other tasks—emailing authors and our sponsoring editors often to ensure that we would get the work done in time. Erin Edmonds, former Managing Editor of the *Harvard Law Review* and Ph.D. candidate in history at UCSB, worked diligently to change our original footnote style which did not conform to the Indiana University Press style. Her editing was most useful, as was her thorough review of our bibliographical entries. Mahsheed Ayoub, Business Officer at the Center for Black Studies, gave her time and skills to this project by overseeing the budget accounts for the Center which funded the research for this book. She also offered support for other administrative matters related to the KOSANBA research. These four individuals were crucial to the completion and success of this project. We are most grateful to them for their commitment and dedication.

We also wish to thank Richard Brent Turner, a reviewer for Indiana University Press, whose constructive comments where most useful in revising this manuscript. We thank Professor Roberto Strongman of the Department of Black Studies at UCSB for the translation of a difficult (literary) passage that needed to be done at a time when we could not reach one of our authors. We are grateful to painter Hërsza Barjon for the use of her artwork on the cover of this book; we also acknowledge Hërsza for asking KOSANBA to oversee the circulation of the *Legend of the Lwa,* a collection of 121 paintings on the Haitian pantheon. Nancy Sterlin, a friend of the Center, was of extraordinary help when we needed to reach her uncle, Rénald Clérismé, and *Ati-Houngan* Max Beauvoir in Haiti and also, during field work in Canada. Paulette Poujol-Oriol helped with transmitting phone messages and distributing packages on multiple occasions to authors residing in Haiti; we also thank her for her unconditional support of the Center's publication projects.

At Indiana University Press, we were fortunate to have a very supportive team. Robert Sloan showed interest in the project and put us in contact immediately with our sponsoring editor, Michael Lundell. Michael was enthusiastic about the project from the moment we submitted the manuscript and worked diligently to secure proper reviewers within an incredibly short timeframe. Clearly he wanted to see this book done and done quickly, as he was eager to add it to the Indiana religion list. We are grateful for his support. Beth Marsh, assistant sponsoring editor, worked with us on every aspect of the project. Simply put, this book could not have been done without her diligence and expertise. She guided us throughout the process and oversaw all the details of the manuscript, from text and footnote style to photo quality, permissions, and deadlines. In fact, we stayed in such close contact with Beth that we referred to her as "a member of the Center's team." She displayed utmost patience and understanding whenever deadlines where hard to meet due to difficulties in locating authors or securing photo permissions. We are truly appreciative for all Beth gave to the project throughout this entire process.

We were fortunate to have had as copy editor someone as talented as Kate Babbitt. Her skillful yet sensitive comments and corrections made the manuscript stronger; she double checked every footnote, every source, every detail to ensure the accuracy of the material (this even includes Max Beauvoir's chapter on medicinal plants for which Kate consulted medical dictionaries and web sources to ensure that all Latin, English, and Kreyol spellings were correct). Kate also sent warm and uplifting emails letting us know how much she was enjoying the manuscript and the concepts that we were advancing. We clearly connected; we felt positive energy on both ends. The copyediting process which is often quite a challenging task turned out to be a blessing: for Kate, as she shared with us, but certainly, for us as well.

Kevin Marsh and Greg Domber, project managers, were a pleasure to work with. They were instrumental in overseeing all the later phases of the project. We are grateful for all their efforts on our behalf. The work of managing editor Miki Bird, and of designer Matt Williamson, are also to be acknowledged. Miki oversaw administrative matters while Matt designed the book's beautiful cover. Together, the Indiana University Press team was wonderful to work with. We appreciate all their contributions to make this project a reality.

We also thank all the contributors—Guérin Montilus, Max Beauvoir, Marc A. Christophe, Marlène Racine-Toussaint, Florence Bellande-Robertson, Gerdès Fleurant, Reginald Crosley and Rénald Clérismé—for their first-rate research which allowed us to produce a very strong volume—the first of its kind by Haitian contributors writing on Vodou from an emic perspective in a book published by a leading university press in the field of religion. Our appreciation also goes out to the other members of KOSANBA's executive board for their work on behalf of the group, including hosting the organization's subsequent conferences. In particular, we note the efforts of our KOSANBA and HSA colleagues Régine Latortue, Marc Prou, Leslie Desmangles, Kathy Balutansky, Roberto Strongman, Karen McCarthy Brown, and LeGrace Benson; board members Florienne Saintil, Viviane Nicolas, Laennec Hurbon, and Nancy Mikelson; colleagues Bamidele Demerson, Lois Wilken, Margaret Mitchell Armand, Elizabeth McAlister, Jacob Olupona, Richard Turner, Don Cosentino, Patrick Polk, Melvin Oliver, George Lipsitz, Ingrid Banks, and Gaye Johnson.

Words of sincere appreciation are to be extended to two *manbo,* both renowned vodou priestesses, Jacqueline Epingle of Montreal, Canada, and Mama Lola of Brooklyn, New York, who opened their houses to us for research purposes in addition to offering—always—perfect Haitian hospitality. Special kudos to Maggie and Marsha and to Jacqueline Epingle's many *pitit fey* who also welcomed our (intrusive) cameras and note pads. The women who gave us permission to print their photographs in this volume deserve our heartfelt thanks for allowing us to capture and reproduce these very special encounters with the spirits. We offer our appreciation to Jacqueline Epingle, Minou Placide, Mamoune Placide, Paulette Denis, Nirva Chérasard, and Myrtha St. Louis, who was furthermore of special assistance in getting signatures and releases for us in Canada. The tables for the Lwa were meticulously prepared by a master of the craft—Nanny Placide. The women we interviewed for chapter seven—*From the Horses' Mouths*—spoke candidly about being practitioners of the Vodou religion and allowed us to write firsthand about their experience as female priests. For some, it was a sort of coming out, and we salute their courage; for others it was yet another opportunity to speak in support of their religion. We express our sincere appreciation to all of them: Carole Lalanne De Lynch, Anastasia De Lynch, Margaret Mitchell Armand, Evelyn Carthright, Georgette Roger, Elizabeth Beauvoir, Nicole Miller Thomas, Jacqueline Epingle, Marthe Bauzile Charles, Carole Desmesmin, and one other *manbo* who chose to remain anonymous.

We also wish to thank family and friends for supporting this project. A special note of appreciation goes to Viviane Nicolas who made many trips from Haiti to attend the KOSANBA meetings; to Douglas H. Daniels for his personal support and his recording of the early KOSANBA conferences and lecture demonstrations; to Kyrah Daniels who served as a research assistant for this project, including during two research trips in Montreal where she video-taped over fourteen hours of ceremonies. This youngest member of our group, still a high school student about to embark on a study of comparative world religions in college, has been and continues to be an inspiration. She might well be a member of the next generation of scholars to whom we will pass not only Haiti's rich cultural heritage but also the *ason*.

Enkò nap di tout moun sila yo ki ede nou mèsi anpil pour akolad sa yo yo bay Vodou, yo bay Haiti. Nou voye yon gro kout chapo pou nou tout.
May this project serve Haiti and its people well!
To all, Honè! Respè!
Ayibobo!

Introduction

PATRICK BELLEGARDE-SMITH AND CLAUDINE MICHEL

This volume brings together, for the first time, a collection of original essays by Haitian scholars on the subject of Haitian Vodou. It was long in coming. The discovery of Vodou by Hollywood in the 1930s, 1940s, and 1950s, years that coincided partially with the U.S. military occupation of Haiti (1915–1934), was accompanied by the first bona fide academic studies, by ethnologists, ethnographers, anthropologists, and sociologists in Haiti and abroad. Among the Haitians, we must mention the pioneering work of Jacques Roumain and his followers in the Ecole d'Ethnologie, founded in 1941. In this scholarly constellation, Jean Price-Mars appeared as the brightest star, an appreciated elder. In the foreign camp, we cite Melville J. Herskovits, James G. Leyburn, Harold Courlander, Alfred Métraux, Sidney W. Mintz, Maya Deren, Zora Neale Hurston, and Katherine Dunham. Their works were respectful of Haitian culture, a world far away from the Western tradition in which they had their grounding.

The cataclysm of foreign military intervention was the backdrop which provided the impetus for some Haitian intellectuals to explore a world somewhat alien to Western-educated Haitians, steeped as they were in the unexamined scholarly assumptions of Western Europe and North America. Dismayed by what they perceived as the recolonization of the Republic of Haiti by the Americans, some Haitians questioned long-held assumptions about a whole range of subjects, but few requestioned the paradigmatic frameworks that had established the Haitian state. Because these Haitians were first and foremost intellectuals, their literary schools of thought did not shake the ideological foundations of the Haitian state. Jean Price-Mars, seen by many as the father of worldwide *négritude;* Jacques Roumain; Suzanne Comhaire-Sylvain, Haiti's first woman anthropologist; and precursors Théodore Holly and Georges Sylvain (Sylvain edited the first major poetic work in the Creole language) created the psychological and scholarly spaces from which important literary movements and, to some extent, social movements, would take hold. They were among the first Haitians of the upper or middle classes to venture *publicly* into Vodou ceremonies.

The *indigénisme* movement, which later transmogrified into worldwide *négritude,* was largely literary; it was a reformulation of an earlier Pan-Africanism. It was nevertheless an affirmation on the part of these scholars, who were eager to examine Haiti's social system and its cultures, to explore both the self and collectivity. Soon thereafter, *indigénisme* crossed over from literature into a broad effort by the middle classes to achieve full participation in the political arena, which they achieved under the presidency of Dumarsais Estimé (1946) and, later, under President François Duvalier (1957). The exploration of Haiti's African-ness was no less than a willful and conscious intellectual realignment toward what was in fact the hitherto-unrecognized cultural core of the country, mediated by centuries of dislocations and historical experience. Haiti was one of several nations in Latin America that found themselves in such circumstances. They were, in effect, discovering neocolonialism. Haitian *indigénisme* evolved in tandem with Mexican *indigenismo*, Afrocubanismo, and Western European modernist thought and art, with its *engouement*, its love affair with "African primitivism."

Earlier, in 1915, the Haitian peasantry had taken up arms against the United States Marines in guerrilla warfare, a struggle it continued until its defeat in 1929. The leaders of the popular uprising had often come from the ranks of Vodou practitioners and the lower echelon of regional armed bands, labeled bandits and gooks by the Americans. But between the peasant insurgents and members of the Haitian elite, there existed only a most tenuous link, since they had come from antagonistic social classes and ostensibly different cultural worlds. These literary and peasant movements did not merge. One would have to await the overthrow of Duvalierism in 1987 and the emergence of active popular resistance to the dictatorship to begin to see a reconciliation between intellectuals and the nation at large.

While Haitian scholars had adopted pro-Western and especially pro-French philosophies throughout the nineteenth and early twentieth centuries, those associated with *indigénisme* and *négritude* were unabashedly more Africanist. Yet their intellectual paradigms and societal models remained nonetheless Western, strongly rooted in the philosophy of positivism. This was also true of those who later espoused Marxism. More-recent developments in Haiti and in the French Antilles, France's Départements d'Outre-Mer, have led to a further cultural reassessment that has led to a conception of a creole culture, *créolité*, which also represents a rejection of earlier thought, a necessary "rectification," some argued, of the view of a solely African genesis of Haitian culture. Nevertheless, *créolité* remains a conservative reaction to *négritude*, which was read as politically radical but clearly was not. It is now left to contemporary scholars, such as the contributors of this book, to go beyond previous analytical and philosophical categories, to show the potentially radical and transformative possibilities of religio-philosophical systems such as Vodou, to move away from European and American heuristic models toward a new formulation rooted in an African ethos in a conversation with the West that is nevertheless divorced from it. Scholarship published in this direction in Haiti, France, Brazil, the United States, and elsewhere includes works by Milo Rigaud, Odette Mennesson-Rigaud, Maya Deren, Roger Bastide, Pierre Verger, and, more recently, Robert Farris Thompson, Karen McCarthy Brown, Laënnec Hurbon, Leslie G. Desmangles, Michel S. Laguerre, Gerdès Fleurant, Erika Bourguignon, Patrick Bellegarde-Smith, Patrick D. M. Taylor, Paul Browdwin, Lilas Desquiron, Claudine Michel, Claude Dauphin, LeGrace Benson, Marilyn Houlberg, Elizabeth McAlister, Wade Davis, Lois Wilken, Gage Averill, Donald J. Cosentino, and Mercedes Guignard (Déita).

The perception of Vodou remains extraordinarily negative for most Westerners, as can be seen from media images. However, Vodou has come full circle in the minds of some educated observers, from an equation of the practice with minstrelsy and satanism with a black face to folklore that might attract American tourists in search of forbidden eroticized exotica or exotic eroticism to a national religion with a proven revolutionary past and a capacity for further radicalism. Of course, to its adepts, Vodou has always remained true to itself, whether as a collective ethos that transcended self or as a rational explanation for the universe that is rooted in its own logic. Unlike the mighty oak in the fable of the French writer Jean de La Fontaine that broke like a twig under severe winds, Vodou has bent and survived the hurricane, as blades of grass are wont to do.

What Is Vodou?

Haitian Vodou seems to be a compendium of a deliberate amalgam of Dahomean traditions, those of the Kongo basin and surrounding ethnic nations in both West and Central Africa. But the origins of Vodou lie in Dahomey (present-day Benin), either because that population provided a critical mass to that of colonial Saint Domingue over a historical period of time or because Dahomean tradition offered a theological sophistication found throughout that region of Africa in Yoruba, Dogon, Dagara peoples and others. Furthermore, because Islam spread to the African continent from its inception in the seventh century CE, a few Muslim practices became integrated into the ritual. The impact of Christianity came much later and under a different set of circumstances—a colonial imposition upon societies that then fought for their physical and cultural survival. But in most of the Caribbean colonies, the effort to christianize enslaved Africans could not be completed because of the large numbers involved and because of the disinterest typically shown by French colonial authority and slaveowners. Meanwhile, the Roman Catholic church and most other Christian denominations justified and sustained slavery.

Haitian Vodou remains arguably the most maligned African-based religion in the Americas. Its revolutionary potential was clear in its opposition to the U.S. occupation of Haiti and in the consequent American reactions to that politico-religious phenomenon. Hollywood and the film industry followed suit and obliged, denigrating the religion in accordance with U.S. governmental policy. Patrick Bellegarde-Smith's essay addresses the importance of Vodou in the Haitian Revolution of 1791, a revolution that was simultaneously radical and conservative, a reaction against potential europeanization by a half-million slaves, two-thirds of whom had been born in Africa. The evolution of Haitian Vodou, as distinct from traditional Dahomean and present-day Beninois Vodun, was shaped by the confluence of contentious forces Haiti encountered in the international system, the history of colonialism, and "race" as defined in northern Europe and North America, and all these structural elements clearly went beyond what had established Dahomean Vodun in West Africa. But whether inside or outside Dahomey in an earlier time or inside or outside Haiti in the modern and contemporary periods, the interactions of diverse populations, the unequal dynamic relationships among social classes in the political arena, clearly had an impact on the development of Vodou. Religions are created by men and women (but mostly by men); they are institutions that remain sensitive to their human environs and other prevailing conditions.

What is of paramount significance in a book about religion is religion itself, its cosmology and cosmogony, its hermeneutics and theology. These areas have not been touched upon yet—anthropologists have dominated the study of religion in Haiti. These are some of the fields we hope to research in the future. This may seem elitist, but it is nevertheless essential if Vodou is to be given its place alongside all religions, on a par with all others.

There are various interpretations of the word Vodun as it erupted from the experience of the Fon people of Dahomey and as it changed when it was transposed to another but similar tropical geographic locale. The word Vodun can be interpreted as "Spirits"; another interpretation emphasizes the particles Vo and du—introspection into the unknown. In the first instance, it bears some resemblance to the Yoruban vocable *ile aye,* house of Spirits. Of great significance in the religious perspectives of peoples of primary African origin is that Spirits are powerful yet invisible forces that can materialize easily into the visible world, the physical dimension.

But Vodou can have other meanings between these two poles, reflecting the religion's propensity for fluidity in marrying ostensibly opposite constructs, sometimes making them more apparent than real and other times more real than apparent. Clearly it has a transformative capacity. The original Dahomean concepts remained valid for Haiti, although the word Vodun did not label the religion, as the circumlocution *sèvi Lwa,* to serve the Spirits, came to be used. Partly because of Hollywood, partly because Haiti faced new realities of competing religions in its midst after sixty years of isolation between 1804 and 1862, Vodun, Vodou, Vodoun, or Vaudou have come to designate the national religion of Haiti. Thus far, in French or English, there is no correct way to spell the name of Haiti's national religion. The establishment of a Haitian Language Academy, as mandated by the Constitution of 1987, will surely reinforce the official Creole orthography—Vodou. In fairly closed social systems, there is no need to name a religion because it encompasses all reality and all persons as part of that reality. For example, the (ancient) Israelites and (modern) Israelis shared and still share that reality, of one defining religion in a system open to the world. Haitians do not. The world has changed for us who suffered the brunt of colonialism and its attendant proselytism.

In the Caribbean colonial crucible called Saint Domingue, or Haiti, dozens of discrete African ethnic formations met, often for the first time. They spoke a large variety of languages and dialects. They met the French with their array of regional differences. The ratio between whites and others in the colony was 18 to 1, yet Blacks were still the Other. This was the backdrop from which Haitian Vodou evolved and thrived. But in contradistinction to the continued use of Yoruba as the liturgical language in both Cuban Santería and Brazilian Candomblé, Haitian Creole, the lingua franca spoken by all by the time of Independence in 1804, took hold. But because most Haitians were born in Africa, they retained the knowledge of their languages well into the first quarter of the nineteenth century. In Cuba and Brazil, slavery lasted formally until 1886 and 1888; emancipation in Haiti had come five generations earlier in 1793. The date at which colonialism ended in these different regions had a lasting impact on the extent of retention of African-based cultural practices in the Americas.

The political values and norms recognized by the religion are discussed in the chapters by Guérin C. Montilus and Patrick Bellegarde-Smith. In his chapter, "Vodun and Social Transformation in African Diasporic Experience: The Concept of Personhood in Haitian Vodun Religion," Dr. Montilus, a veteran of research on African-based and African-derived religions in Benin and Nigeria in West Africa and in Cuba, Haiti, and Brazil, argues that the transformation that took place in the diaspora from *within* millenarian constructs of the person and his or her world in relationship to the whole. Enslaved Africans brought to Haiti worldviews, a "world sense," myths, rituals, and beliefs rooted largely, but not exclusively, in Benin and Togo, in Yoruban Nigeria, and in southeastern Ghana. In a brief essay rooted in his experience, Montilus traces the Haitian articulation of personhood, which allows for useful contrasts and comparisons with Judeo-Christian and Islamic notions.

In Bellegarde-Smith's chapter, "Broken Mirrors: Mythos, Memories, and National History," he attempts to view Vodou as a spiritual discipline and a paradigmatic framework for a possible social, economic, and political transformation of Haiti. "Vodou economics," communal economics, becomes a tangible reality. The Haitian national religion, he argues, has been singularly important over the entire span of the country's existence. Haitian elites who were trying to justify their existence in a hostile international environment pursued the same policies of assimilation after Independence that France had imposed under slavery; this created dynamic interactions within the lenses of social class at home and power abroad. Bellegarde-Smith brings to the study of Vodou his training in political science and international relations and his status as an *oungan,* a male priest in the Haitian Vodou tradition.

The *courroie de transmission,* the conveyor belt which teaches norms, values, and standards in social systems, is found in Claudine Michel's "Of Worlds Seen and Unseen: The Educational Character of Haitian Vodou." Currently, the transmission of ancient and esoteric *konesans* (knowledge), as amended by the experience of slavery, neocolonialism, and diverse forms of cultural imperialism, is found in the homes of millions of Haitians, or in the *hounfò,* the temples they attend. Michel's chapter discusses options and possibilities that might benefit larger portions of the population and the hope that their worlds might be reflected profitably in the educational system and new/old processes of a reinvigorated Haitian nation. She analyzes how principles are passed down within education writ large and how respect for cultural core values might lead to conscientization and empowerment. The state as presently established has much to fear from the implementation of some of these ideas. She argues for a restructuring of the educational system and pedagogical techniques in ways that are truer to Haitian culture.

In a chapter entitled "Vodoun, Peasant Songs and Political Organizing," Rénald Clérismé—a Haitian diplomat and anthropologist but foremost a grassroots organizer—describes the role of Vodou in organized resistance in rural communities. This role has been central through the course of Haitian history, though it went largely unrecognized. Clérismé's specific illustrations demonstrate the existence of political messages in the lyrics of Vodou songs, circumstances seen as tendentiously radical by Haiti's power structure and its foreign allies: Vodou as consensual politics.

Vodou pervades and permeates all systems and fields in Haitian culture. Marc A. Christophe's "Rainbow over Water: Art, Vodou Aestheticism, and Philosophy," situates itself in the melding of harmonious, mutually penetrating systems via the instrument of Haitian art, in this case, painting. Haitian "outsider" art, once labeled "primitive," is arguably Haiti's best-known contribution to the international art world. Haitian painters, born mostly in the peasantry and in the urban working class, sometimes paint while in a religious trance. Removing the source of their inspiration might well obliterate the art. Christophe, himself a poet and painter, speaks to the notion of re-creating a world in which balance is inherently sought in order to live well, a cardinal point in African metaphysics that has been reconceptualized in the context of a Caribbean society as creole culture, as thesis, antithesis, and synthesis.

What Christophe does for painting, Gerdès Fleurant does for music. In his "Vodun, Music, and Society in Haiti: Affirmation and Identity," he discusses Vodou's musical styles and their provenance and evolution. He also describes their distinct and distinguishing character—complex rhythms, dialectical melodies, and patterns of call and response. Fleurant notes that understanding the musical idioms properly is associated with the rank one has achieved in his or her spiritual evolution.

From Clérismé's content and Fleurant's form to Montilus's essence, we situate Réginald O. Crosley's "Shadow-Matter Universes in Haitian and Dagara Ontologies," which questions the rapports between content, form, and essence. He addresses the marriage of philosophy and science, the unicity of two apparently different systems that are both profoundly ingrained in African worldviews. Crosley, who is a physician, views Haitian cultural systems and those of the Dagara of Burkina Faso from a vantage point derived from physics—quantum mechanics, chaos theory, and the theory of relativity. He wishes to advance the study of alternate realities which, in some sense, can be said to parallel parallel universes. Afro-Haitian and, by extension, African ontologies seem to be a reservoir of parallel universes where ordinary and extraordinary perceptual realities coexist in both a composite and complementary fashion. Crosley argues that while Western thinkers have seen the African weltanschauung as imaginary or even psychoid, Haitians seem to have discovered the means of controlling forces that issue from the shadow-matter dimension, the superposition state between the Euclidean-Newtonian dimension and the realities of quantum and shadow matter.

More a spiritual discipline than a mere religion, Vodou encompasses science and technology, the healing sciences, kinship and kingship, and familial and gender relations. Though the various levels of sophistication are not readily apparent or available to all, they can be made so as levels of initiations (*grades initiatiques*) are achieved, one person at a time, at one's own pace, over a lifetime.

Max-G. Beauvoir, who trained in chemistry at the Sorbonne and New York University, is a *houngan* with two *hounfò,* one outside Port-au-Prince, Haiti, and the other in Washington, D.C., in the United States. In "Herbs and Energy: The Holistic Medical System of the Haitian People," Beauvoir describes the scientific and philosophical underpinnings of the healing arts and the context in which they thrive. He speaks of the basic element in healing practices in which the fundamental and overarching concept of energy/ies is indeed essential. He categorizes the holistic healing system of Haiti in three broad areas: a phytotherapeutic social system, a phytotherapeutic medical system, and the masterly medical system. Because Haiti has few Western-trained physicians (barely a few thousand), few nurses, and few hospital beds for its 8 million citizens, most Haitians have relied on traditional medicine over the centuries and will continue to do so in the foreseeable future.

Psychology in the Haitian context is worlds apart from Western psychological constructs. In fact, the fields as presently defined are antagonistic in essential ways. Haitian psychologists and sociologists trained in the West are accused sometimes of "whitening" Haitian children, their culture having been defined a priori as defective, in the name of progress (in the nineteenth century) and development (in the twentieth century). To counteract this trend, it might be important to turn to the foundational principles underpinning Haitian society and its national religion. These principles are best enunciated by *manbo,* female priests, mothers and keepers of these traditions and values in Vodou communities in Haiti and outside Haiti.

A collective piece by Claudine Michel, Patrick Bellegarde-Smith, and Marlène Racine-Toussaint explores the thought and roles of Haitian *manbo* in the religious world they inhabit. "From the Horses' Mouths: Women's Words/Women's Worlds" selects several priests from a variety of class backgrounds in Haiti, the United States, and Canada, from *bourgeoises* to members of the middle class and the urban working class. Their visions and perspectives are informed by the myths, legends, ontologies, and theology of their religion, yet the impact of the contemporary world seems to hinder them as women. The world of deities in the metaphysical plane may be half female and the majority of priests may be women, but the Haitian scene in the physical plane remains unapologetically macho and sexist.

The chapter by Florence Bellande-Robertson, "A Reading of the *Marasa* Concept in Lilas Desquiron's *Les Chemins de Loco-Miroir*" attempts to deconstruct the

Haitian universe and Haitian realities in a different way. It deals with upper-class society and offers just one example of that class's numerous literary achievements. While the chapter by Rénald Clérismé specifically addresses the efforts by the Haitian peasantry to transform their country and improve their life chances in ways that have eluded them for the better part of two centuries, Bellande-Robertson discusses the contribution of a novelist who is an anthropologist, an educated member of the Haitian upper classes, to that conversation.

Written literature, as distinct from oral literature, demands literacy and a lifestyle and enough wealth to provide leisure time to engage in these creative pursuits. It requires a room of one's own and the luxury of domestic servants. In examining Desquiron's novel, which was recently translated into English, Bellande-Robertson analyzes the concept of twin-ness, or *marasa*, which is a fundamental Vodou metaphysical concept of polarity that resolves within itself. At the pedestrian level, *marasa*-ness seems to indicate that both the privileged and the downtrodden in Haiti partake of the same essence. The common ground between the *mulâtre* and the *noir* in Desquiron's novel, which is defined contextually in terms of class and culture, is an African mother, but the two protagonists have different fathers, one African, one French. Bellande-Robertson's essay augurs well for a future in which Haitians from antagonistic classes may wish to work for Haiti's reconstruction. However, the upper-class protagonist in the novel is destroyed in the process. Martyrs are thus created. Human suffering and sacrifice would seem to be the requirements for social change and personal transformation.

The systematic study of what one calls traditional, natural, or neotraditional religious systems by academics outside anthropology is still fairly new. This is especially true for indigenous scholars trained in the academy. Besides the aforementioned pioneers, Suzanne Comhaire-Sylvain, Jean Price-Mars, and Lorimer Denis, one must await the likes of Michel S. Laguerre and Leslie G. Desmangles to bring these studies into the contemporary period. But these religious systems, particularly if they derived from peoples of primary African descent, went unrecognized or were disparaged by early travelers, explorers, and conquerors. Both Asia and Native America have transcended these burdens, their thought fully acceptable now in the world of polite academic discourse. Indeed, programs of religious studies at many American universities make room for the study of religions other than the Judeo-Christian-Islamic complex, but it bears repeating that such programs largely involve Asian religions rather than those whose anchors are on the African continent. Early works that were largely descriptive popularized disobliging concepts such as animism, fetishism, or black magic. The analysis, when it occurred at all, inferred that these religions were spirituality *remis en enfance*, religion in its infancy.

Another devastating blow came with the imposition of the concept of syncretism, as if not all human systems demonstrated borrowing and adaptation and as if Africans were unable to produce an original thought. They were capable of both and did both. This changed with the advent of scholars in religious studies who worked away from earlier forms of anthropology and the advent of educated adepts who had begun to speak for themselves. One could appreciate the travails of Western scholars who, by peering into their own cultural past, inadvertently helped us re-create our present as people of African descent. Scholarship has always played itself out against the backdrop of European imperialism—always. But things do change.

One illustration of what precedes is found in the naming of the religion, and this is significant. The power to name and define is an awesome responsibility and the appanage of power. The West has largely defined the world. Typically in Africa, on a continent where each ethnonational group devised a religion suited to its human and physical environs, naming a belief system which was not in competition with others became superfluous. The context was one in which only one religion and one worldview dominated the terrain. The introduction of different beliefs through interaction with others—cultures from Africa, the Middle East, and Western Europe—usually by force of arms, brought forth dimensions that had hitherto been unnecessary.

Traditionally, Haitians had referred to their religion by the circumlocution *sèvi Lwa*. Serving the Spirits did not prevent them from satisfying the demands of other belief systems, primarily Roman Catholicism. However, it became increasingly necessary to differentiate Haiti's indigenous religion from other religions—Catholicism and Protestantism—that were vying for space in the country. Vodou seems to have become the favored name.

In this volume, three scholars named the religion Vodun. Seven have opted for the frenchified and most commonly used Vodou, while another two chose Vodoun. Still in usage are Vaudou, Voudoun, Vodu, and the colloquial vocable preferred in the United States, voodoo. No agreement could be reached among the twelve Haitian scholars in this book at the time the work was done. Some preferred the nasalization inherent in Fon and Haitian Creole—Vodun or Vodoun; some, the mellifluous French version—Vodou. We tried. But we also felt that it was important to reflect in a first volume of its kind the different spellings currently used as well as the reasoning behind the particular choices made by the authors. One anticipates that at some not-too-distant future the spelling for the religion of those who *sèvi Lwa* will gel and set, just as the relatively new official Haitian (Kreyòl) language orthography has.

In fact, KOSANBA (the Congress of Santa Barbara, the Scholarly Association for the Study of Haitian Vodou, which was created in 1997 after a colloquium at the University of California, Santa Barbara) organized a roundtable on the question of a standardized spelling for the Haitian national religion at its fourth conference in Vermont in October 2001. The Congress chose "Vodou" as the standard spelling that we plan to adopt in our future writings. The group is currently working on a position statement explaining its recommendation.

The authors of this book are all Haitians. Some of us are faculty members at various universities, others are engaged in their communities as activists or are in the professions. We hail from a multiplicity of disciplines and are all scholars. We are in the social sciences and the humanities; we are professors, poets, and

painters; we are specialists in rural development, education, or international politics. Some of us are priests and healers. We are women and men who know Haiti,
have studied it their entire adult lives, and are conversant with their country's
culture in ways few have bothered to become. Haiti, after all, even by the standards of the world, is a small country, just a bit larger than Israel; it is the size of
the states of Maryland and Rhode Island. We are widely traveled and—in Haitian metaphysical terms—have also taken the less traveled road, that of presenting to the world aspects of a Haitian religious system that are unheard of, or generally ignored. We hail from all social positionings in terms of origins, but as
intellectuals we find ourselves somewhat *déclassé,* outside the boundaries of strict
class observances, neither fish nor fowl.

We are both insiders and outsiders, and our work reflects this. As insiders, we
have a lifelong participation in things Haitian. We are outsiders because our doc-
torates and other diplomas place us in a rarefied intellectual atmosphere achieved
by few, even in the United States. But we are still inside looking out. We chose
to translate one world—ours—into the language of another. In this capacity, we
are like the Deity Legba, the gatekeepers, the translators, the linguists. Some are
writing on this subject in English for the first time, away from our native Kreyòl
or French languages. We present scholarly perspectives and analyses of Haitian
Vodou, finally, as entities that are sui generis, as is done routinely for the "religions of the Book" or for Buddhism and Shinto and as was done earlier for Ifa in
Yoruban Nigeria by Nigerians and by native-born Cuban and Brazilian scholars
for their religious practices and systems. We are animated by the desire to introduce the Vodou religion from our own perspectives in our own words and on
our own terms to the rest of world. We are at a crossroads in scholarly research
on Haitian Vodou.

Nomenclature is important and, in this case, a challenge. As specified earlier,
there was no agreement possible at the time that we wrote these chapters on the
spelling of the world "Vodou." If spelling, which can be viewed by some as a
straightforward exercise, hides unresolved conflicts beyond etymology and geographic provenance in the guise of the dimension of proper and improper French
or the proper way to express our *créolitude,* other awesome concepts, names, and
words can encounter a similar or even worse fate. Can thoughts that do not readily occur in a given culture and give rise to alien concepts be readily expressed
in a foreign tongue, translated, transposed, and transported into a wildly different universe? Those who study Asian religions have had to apply themselves, re-
solving the dilemma by using a large number of specialized words instead of opt-
ing for inappropriate translations. The authors of this book have had a similar
problem. The elliptical translations we give only approximate what is meant, and
a full paragraph still would not suffice. A *houngan* is far more than a priest, or a
manbo, a female priest—their calling involves far more and the preparation for
sacerdotal functions lasts a lifetime . . . and beyond. Similarly, the *hounfò,* a temple in the *lakou,* simulates the heart of a West African family compound, as does

the Brazilian Candomblé *terreiro* and many functions observed therein. All manner of things can happen there, and more.

Words do challenge the reader, but that reader must take on some responsibility as well. And the ride can still be exhilarating and enjoyable, even as the rider becomes puzzled and full of wonderment. In one sense, it is like that other realization of Black genius, jazz, like the blue notes that cannot quite be produced if one lacks the particular sensitivity or musical scale. Hidden but still real, Vodou can give off vibrations that resonate in all who share a common human origin.

Haítían Vodou

1

Vodun and Social Transformation in the African Diasporic Experience: The Concept of Personhood in Haitian Vodun Religion

GUÉRIN C. MONTILUS

African slaves came into a "New World" naked, but their minds were clothed and wrapped up with myths, rituals, customs, traditions, cultures, and civilizations—in essence, a worldview, as Roger Bastide argued.[1] Such worldviews are what has survived everywhere in the Americas. They have given northern, central, and southern African America cultures, art, religion, pharmacology, aesthetics, and linguistic institutions such as the Creole languages of Haiti, Martinique, Guadeloupe, and New Orleans. They have included extended family structures and socioeconomic structures such as the typical African Caribbean markets that are much like their counterparts in West Africa. Sociopolitical institutions housed in African American religious temples can be found everywhere: in Brazilian Candomblé and Umbanda; in Cuban Santería and Palo Monte; in African American Protestant churches in North America; and in the Vodun of Haiti, Cuba, the Dominican Republic, the Bahamas, New Orleans, Florida, Chicago, New York, and Canada—in short, wherever peoples of African descent have found territories that lend themselves to human habitation.[2] In all these geographic areas, African and neo-African ethics and morals permeate personal and collective behavior and give people norms they are expected to follow. They are embedded in minds and intelligences, in the languages and arts such as songs, poetry, proverbs, and sayings that are the legacy of ancient African wisdom.

This chapter focuses upon one aspect of this African heritage in Haitian Vodun—the concept of personhood. It retraces its heritage and provenance among the Adja Fon of West Africa and points to cultural and semantic continuities and discontinuities despite present-day linguistic differences.

The concept of the person is central to any human understanding and conceptualization of the world. "Person," in this context, refers to the human being's ability to have a consciousness of the relationship of oneself to oneself and an awareness of the existence of the external world of beings, objects, events, and facts—all of which intersect. While Christian theologians were discussing whether Africans have souls, these people were carrying on with the African meanings of personhood through their religion. While Christian catechisms made sinister associations with the color black as sinful, connecting it with death and mourning, enslaved Africans were defining their Black bodies as the centerpiece of personhood. And while European moralists were focusing on the myth of Noah and its curse of servitude on all the descendants of Ham in the book of Genesis, Africans were rebuking that form of racism in their own theories of personhood, for the definition of person in each culture and society is contingent on the limitations of language as a vehicle for thinking and perceiving and on the elocutionary act itself, which leads to the individuation of the myth as social heritage. All cultures have their own notions of person and each such notion is a coded symbol that carries specific semantic value.[3]

The notion of person as a symbol of and for human consciousness, as it is inherited through the Vodun religion, is distributed throughout the body as a whole, but it places special emphasis upon some special constituent parts of that body, such as the head or the foot. Symbolically the head is the most important part of the body. It carries the four most significant senses: sight, hearing, smell, and taste. The African ritual of initiation among the Adja Fon gives special unction to the head. In this tradition, the crown of a person's head is never touched because it contains the principle that conditions human consciousness. This belief also exists in Haiti. One should never touch the crown of newborn babies, infants, or children; a most vital part of human consciousness is located there. This might take away their psychic reality and they could die. Doing this kind of touching can be seen as an act of sorcery and witchcraft.

The missionaries in slaveholding societies attempted to teach the slaves that a soul lived in their Black bodies and that slavery was good because it could redeem this soul from the sins that Blacks had committed.[4] The Vodun religion of the Adja taught these same Africans that their psychic reality and source of human life was metaphorically symbolized by the shadow of the body. This principle, represented by the shadow, is called *ye*. There are two of these. The first is the inner, the internal and dark part of the shadow, which is called the *ye gli;* that is, a short *ye*. The second, the external and light part of the same shadow, is called the *ye gaga;* that is, long *ye*. The first, *ye gli*, is the principle of physical life, which vanishes at death. The second, *ye gaga*, is the principle of consciousness and psychic life. The *ye gaga* survives death and illustrates the principle of immortality. It has a metaphysical mobility that allows human beings to travel far away at night (through dreams) or remain eternally alive after the banishment of the *ye gli*. After death, the *ye gaga* goes to meet the community of Ancestors, which constitutes the extended family and the clan in their spiritual dimensions.

Although the Haitians have lost both lexemes (*ye gli* and *ye gaga*), these concepts and principles of classification remain. They are embodied in the Haitian (Creole) and French-inherited expressions *gwo bon anj* and *ti bon anj,* which refer respectively to the *ye gaga* and *ye gli*. The Haitian-language expressions have kept "shadow" as the semantic basis of these metaphysical realities. They are not the equivalent of two souls, as some anthropologists have mistakenly claimed. They are rather two symbolic renditions that explain the physical (material) and metaphysical (psychic) life. They have become a part of the Haitian language and beliefs that serve the substratum of Vodun culture, Haitian medicine and the healing arts. For example, it is common in the Haitian countryside for a person to ask others not to walk on his or her shadow for fear that they will walk over his

Lwa touching *manbo/*head. Individuals in photo: Jacqueline Epingle and Nostalie (Minou) Placide. Photograph by Claudine Michel.

or her *ti bon anj* or *gwo bon anj.* Thus, while the missionaries from the slavehold-ing society were preaching solely an internal soul, the slaves retained their belief that *ye* was the center of human personhood, residing in the crown and the shadow.

These two principles, the *ye gli* and the *ye gaga,* allow Haitian Vodun to con-ceptualize and give a rational and logical explanation to the phenomenon of the epiphany of the Lwa as an extension of the Adja tradition. The Lwa manifest them-selves in the body of their devotees, the *hounsi.* The word Lwa itself is a lexeme borrowed from the Yoruba term *oluwa* (lord). The enslaved retained the word Lwa to name the spirits of their pantheon instead of Vodun, as it is in the Adja tradi-tion. To them, this Yoruba term depicts an appropriate universe of the spirits. While the flesh-and-blood master and slaveowner forced his secular domination and ruled the plantation with an iron fist, the Lwa were the true metaphysical masters of the cosmic forces. Their spiritual dominion overrode all others, since they were omnipresent and omnipotent. It is helpful to know that the Lwa have the same nature as the *ye gaga,* the psychic principle.

Haitians explain that the Lwa come and ride their horses, which are the *hounsi,* the spouses (*asi*) of the Lwa (*hun*). The word *hounsi* comes from the Adja lan-guage (in southeastern Ghana, southern Togo, and southern Benin). However, the seat of the Lwa is the crown of the head. The Lwa takes the place of the *gwo bon anj,* which goes away during the whole period of epiphany, the possession by the Lwa. The *hounsi,* as a person, is absent during the period of possession by the Lwa, leaving her or his body to the Lwa as *ye gaga,* or psychic principle, and coming back at the end of the trance, after the departure of the Lwa. However, the *ti bon anj* remains present, otherwise death would take place, for the body would have lost the vital principle which keeps it alive. The *ti bon anj* does not have the mobility of the *gwo bon anj.* When the former leaves, it cannot come back. However, the *ti bon anj* is not the principle of consciousness. This is why the *hounsi* does not know what happened during the time of his or her absence: the *gwo bon anj* is the one that goes away. There is a semantic continuity from Africa to Haiti: only the lexemes were changed by linguistic acculturation.

These two vital principles also explain the rationality of the sacred meals, *manje Lwa* and *manje lè mò.* The Adja metaphorically call the nutritive substance of the sacrificed meals "*ye.*" It is a metaphor because this nutritive part is as dynamic as the *ye,* yet it is invisible. Thus, when a Vodunist offers a sacrifice, a *manje Lwa* to a Lwa or a *manje lè mò* to an Ancestor (*vosisa* in Adja Fongbe), this Lwa, or the Dead (*mò*), which are also *ye,* eat the *ye* of the sacred meal. The Haitians call this food *nanm manje-a.* The Haitians say that "*Lwa a manje nanm manje-a*" (the Lwa eat the soul of the food). The Haitian Creole lexeme *nanm* is borrowed from the French word *âme* (soul), which lends itself to the metaphor *nanm manje-a,* used to designate the inner principle which lives in the food. In this sense, linguistically, the concept of *nanm* is equivalent to *gwo bon anj,* as explained earlier. Here, again, Vodun metaphysics is consistent with the Adja tradition and is in synchronicity with its tenets (see plate 1).

The Vodun religion, as is the case with any other religion, uses symbolic language to make concrete a non-concrete reality which is invisible otherwise. Consciousness has access to the means to interpret the world. One consciousness is direct; that is, the object itself seems present to the mind, as in a perception or a simple sensation. Another is indirect, because for one reason or another, the object cannot be materially presented to the senses; as for example, the eschatological discourse about life after death. In these cases of indirect consciousness, the missing object is represented to the mind by an image. The Vodun discourse belongs to the second category of knowledge, because the physical stimulus is absent (from the Latin *ab esse,* being away). It is the task of the mythical language to make this reality available to the consciousness through imagery. This act of representation must here be construed in the strict and etymological meaning of the Latin verb *repraesentare* (to make present). The role and nature of this symbolic language is to re-present—that, is make present what is absent or distant in temporal space. The category of myth here must be interpreted as a symbolic story whose character *re-presents* a fundamental reality for a community, providing its members with an explanation which they believe to be basic to their existence, if not to their substance.

The Vodun religion has kept its coherence and consistency through eight centuries because it is a symbolic discourse. As such, it solidifies the quality of symbols which show, join, prescribe, and renew.

1. Symbols *show.* They make abstract values tangible, they are a source of power,

and they stand for particular ideals. Symbols are cultural and have value for the person, for the group, for the community, and for the society. They have the power to bring people together, to create consensus; in other words, symbols are *social*. In this sense, the Vodun religion creates a civilization and cultures because it provides a language which has created and continues to create consensus.

2. Symbols *join*. In this regard, symbols indicate property, belonging, and membership. They indicate membership in a community. They define the group, describe that group, and exclude others from it, because they identify the community which shares in their conceptual content. Belief in the Lwa goes beyond the material and physical manifestations of this religion. It includes metaphysics, and adherence to that metaphysics makes someone truly a *vodunsento,* as the Adja say, a worshiper of Vodun. It is correct to speak of the emblematic function of this symbol. This metaphysical realm also refers to the continuity of a community in time, but it also speaks about its continuity in space. From this point of view, the symbol is meaningful through the intermediary of the social structure and as a part of a whole in which all participate. It is upheld in a pact, by an oath, through taboo, with a tradition, in a bond of spiritual allegiance which makes communication through language possible. Such is the case with the concept of personhood in the Vodun religion and its notion of the *ti bon anj* and *gwo bon anj,* which come from the *ye gli* and *ye gaga* handed down by the Adja.

3. Symbols *enjoin* or *prescribe*. This is a political function. The Lwa, as they are conceptualized through the notion of personhood, together with the *gwo bon anj* of the *mò,* compel respect. The symbol that *represents* also serves as an injunction. From this standpoint, in the Vodun religion as in any other, the symbolic, the psychological, and the technical functions appear to be inextricably bound together. The Lwa and the *mò* inspire awe. They are served (and revered) because, as metaphysical entities conceived in the Adja manner of *ye,* they have power. They are supernatural forces with which we share our space.

4. Symbols *renew*. This is the principle behind periodic ceremonies to renew and rejuvenate a community through the contact with the Lwa and the Dead. The Vodun ceremony is effective because it provides the faithful with a structure for self- and collective expression. However, these practices are symbolic. The humanized or anthropomorphized universe is one that human beings have deciphered and one whose meaning has been fixed by means of symbols. All inhabited places are spaces codified with meaning. It is in this sense that the Vodun religion is a civilizing agent. As with all religions, it has the dynamism that helps organize societies and produce values. Its dogma explains the universe, and it explains human beings within it and their nature. There is a cosmogony in the religion which makes medicine, ritual, and divination work.

The Vodun religion has developed a cosmology which provides believers with a culture and provides the community with a civilization which has structured human life for many centuries and which allows the Haitian nation to live and to survive.[5] This is why wherever the community moves—from West Africa to Haiti and from Haiti to Cuba, the United States, or elsewhere—it does so with its religion, which gives its members fundamental answers. It generates values and meaning. The same can be said about Candomblé in Brazil or La Regla de Ocha (Lukumi) in Cuba. These religions have been doing the work of the *bricoleur* to explain the unseen and the imperceptible. They have transformed a mass of "naked" human beings into coherent social groups, masters of their destiny and their world, organizing and ordering their cosmos in an African manner.

Notes

Guérin Montilus is a senior Haitian scholar who has done original research *sur le terrain* in Haiti, the Republic of Benin (the old Dahomey), Nigeria, and Cuba. He addresses the question of personhood based on his personal experience in these societies in this short essay.—Eds.

1. See the entire opus of Roger Bastide: *African Civilizations in the New World,* trans. Peter Green (New York: Harper & Row, 1971); *The African Religions of Brazil: Toward a Sociology of the Interpenetration of Civilizations,* trans. Helen Sebba (Baltimore: Johns Hopkins University Press, 1978) (originally published as *Les religions africaines au Brésil; vers une sociologie des interpénétrations civilizations* [Paris: Presses Universitaires de France, 1960]); and *Les Amériques noires* (Paris: Petite Bibliothèque Payot, 1967).

2. See George Brandon, *Santería from Africa to the New World: The Dead Sell Memories* (Bloomington: Indiana University Press, 1997); Robert A. Voeks, *Sacred Leaves of Candomblé: African Magic, Medicine, and Religion in Brazil* (Austin: University of Texas Press, 1997); and Karen McCarthy Brown, *Mama Lola: A Vodou Priestess in Brooklyn* (Berkeley: University of California Press, 1991), among others.

3. See Geoffrey Parrinder, *Religion in Africa* (New York: Praeger, 1969); Ifeanyi A. Menkiti, "Person and Community in African Thought," in *African Philosophy: An Introduction,* ed. R. A. Wright (Washington, D.C.: University Press of America, 1979), 171–182; Benjamin C. Ray, *African Religions: Symbol, Ritual, and Community* (Englewood Cliffs, New Jersey: Prentice-Hall, 1976); and Awo Falokun Fatunmbi, *Ibase Orisa: Ifa Proverbs, Folktales, Sacred History and Prayer* (New York: Original Publications, 1994). Fatunmbi has written eloquently about the subject with an emphasis on the neighboring Yoruba religious system.

4. For a discussion of Christianity and slavery, see Roger Bastide, "Color, Racism and Christianity" in *Color and Race,* ed. John Hope Franklin (Boston: Houghton-Mifflin, 1968), 34–49; and Michael Conniff and Thomas Davis, *Africans in the Americas, A History of the Black Diaspora* (New York: St. Martin's Press 1994).

5. See Patrick Bellegarde-Smith, "Peasant Organizations, Structures and Institutions," in Bellegarde-Smith, *Haiti: The Breached Citadel* (Boulder, Colo.: Westview Press, 1990), 161–171; and Claudine Michel, *Aspects éducatifs et moraux du Vodou haïtien* (Port-au-Prince, Haiti: Le Natal, 1995).

2

Shadow-Matter Universes in Haitian and Dagara Ontologies: A Comparative Study

RÉGINALD O. CROSLEY

From the vantage point of the new metaphysics derived from the various fields of modern physics, quantum mechanics, relativity theory, and chaos theory, we view two communities of the Pan-African world, the Haitian and the Dagara. The notion of parallel universes, presented by the physicist Hugh Everett III in the 1950s,[1] has made inroads in the study of the alternate realities of Africans and their descendants in the Americas. According to the tenets of quantum physics, since reality is a matter of choice, the ordinary, everyday dimensions of such peoples, as well as their postmortem abode and the characteristics of their spiritual entities, will reflect the dynamics of their subjectivity in molding the outside world.[2]

From the Neolithic Sahara came the notion of the tripartite nature of man, a notion that was present in the cosmogonies of Egyptians, Dahomeans, Bantu, and others in Africa.[3] In Haiti, the components of man are known as *kò kadav, gro bon anj,* and *ti bon anj,* which correspond to the body, the *semedo,* and the *selido* of the Dahomeans and the body, the *moyo,* and the *mfumu-kutu* of the Bantu or Bakongo.[4] In Dagaraland, Burkina Faso, we have the body, a soul or body double called *siê,* and a third component which is a spirit or a God.[5]

In Haiti as in Burkina Faso, the non-material components of the person—that is, his or her two souls—bear a striking similarity to the invisible matter of the universe recently discovered in the cosmos by astronomers.[6] This invisible matter, also called dark matter or shadow matter, is not made of atoms and molecules like ordinary matter but consists of particles and energy. The particles in the nature of quarks are identified as wimps or axions, very tiny particles that contribute to the formation of nuclear components. These tiny particles are conceived of as coiled energies, strings of space-time, packets of energy-like photons. They are thus physical in nature but immaterial. They belong to the fermion family of invisible particles. In the ontology of invisible or shadow matter, there also exists a counterpart named a boson, which is pure energy, according to the supersymmetric theory.[7]

Furthermore, modern physics has discovered the heresy of the EPR paradox, which claims the existence of psychic properties at the level of particles.[8] In other words, all particles are conscious. They are aware of their position, of themselves, and of their surroundings. This fact was confirmed in experiments conducted by John Clauser and Stuart Freedman at the University of California, Berkeley, in 1972[9] and by Alain Aspect in Paris in 1982.[10]

Dark matter has revealed its presence in the universe, particularly in the galaxies, primarily by its gravity. Shadow matter is the most abundant physical entity in the cosmos; it constitutes 86 percent of its total.[11] One of the most interesting characteristics of the axions or wimps that make up dark matter is the fact that they do not disturb ordinary matter. They coexist with dense, baryonic, ordinary matter in the same location without impediment or interference.[12] This is a true parallel universe endowed with consciousness, like the cosmos described in Paul's Letter to the Romans in Chapter 8 or in David Bohm's concept of unbroken wholeness.[13] This would seem to give credence to the animist vision of Africans and Haitians.

For the metaphysician, the thinker who always tries to see beyond the physical, the large quantity of shadow matter in the universe is not simply an inert mass that allows the stars at the periphery of a galaxy to go at the same speed as the stars near the core, for example. In fact, the properties of shadow matter have drawn our attention to its similarity to what we call our spiritual world. It can be postulated, for instance, that as axions enter into the components of a person, their fermions will produce what Haitians call the *gro bon anj* and their bosons will produce the *ti bon anj,* the equivalent of *sié* and the spirit-god in Burkina Faso.

Acquiring the tenets of these ontologies comes about through ordinary education in which the individual learns the symbolism of things, the hierarchy of beings, the do's and don'ts, and what is taboo and what is sacred. Furthermore, in Haiti, as in Dagaraland, there is an initiation period during which deeper knowledge is acquired. This usually takes place in adolescence. Among the Dagara people there is a community ceremony, during which young males aged thirteen or so are gathered in the forest by their elders and introduced to the parallel universe of the *kontonteg* (spirits).[14] In Haiti, a similar initiation takes place when an individual is between fourteen and eighteen years old or sometime in adulthood. The timing can be a matter of individual choice, the choice of the family, or by decision of the Vodoun himself. In the last case, the individual can accept or refuse the Vodoun's request. Before adolescence, the very young can have a *lave tèt,* a ritual that allows the person to harmoniously experience the approach of a shadow-matter entity, the "brushing" of a Lwa or Vodoun.[15] Thus, in both communities the chance of an initiation is open to any suitable candidate. In both, secret information is imparted that cannot be revealed to outsiders. Severe punishment or death is associated with such caveats.

There are also different levels of initiation. In Haiti, we have the *hounsi kanzo,* the *manbo* or *houngan* level; the underwater initiation; the *pran-zieux* (clairvoyant) level; and the Zandoric, or Zobop, initiation.[16] In the Dahomean tradition, there are initiations in which only old men, and sometimes old women, can participate. The same applies to the Djoto. In general, women predominate in shamanship in Swaziland,[17] while in Cameroon and Burkina Faso, girls and boys are initiated separately. In Haiti, men and women participate together in the *hounsi kanzo* initiation, which takes place in the *djèvo,* a sacred room in the *hounfò* (temple).

In Dagaraland, a full revelation of shadow matter, parallel universes, takes place during the initiation of adolescents, while in Haiti the introduction is a step-by-step, piecemeal affair that takes place over the individual's lifespan. In both places, however, the acquisition of certain powers requires a special apprenticeship.

Ontology is the branch of metaphysics that is concerned with the nature of beings, the different kinds of existence, and existing entities. It offers different theories from those of the Western world and the African diaspora. Western teachings recognize a body and a spirit in a person's makeup, but not as separate entities capable of existing independently of each other. In this tradition, the spiritual part derives from the physico-chemical interaction between the atoms and molecules that compose us. At death, the interaction ceases and we return to the dust from which we first came.

In the twentieth century, however, science has stumbled onto aspects of reality that force us to change this neat, oversimplified version of reality. The supersymmetry theory, among others, postulates that for every particle of matter we know, a "symmetry counterpart" exists which manifests itself as force or energy. In other words, a boson (selectron) exists for every fermion (electron). Thus, for every reality we discover in the solid world around us, we must assume that there exists a symmetric counterpart, or boson, which is invisible but is nevertheless as physical as its visible counterpart. This can be considered a variant of the principle of duality in quantum physics.[18]

In the ontologies of the Afro-Haitian and the people of the Dagara tribe, we find a highly supersymmetric, tripartite person. From the beginning, these peoples have acknowledged the complex structure of the individual. They have maintained that each component, the physical and the spiritual, can lead a separate, independent existence. Through education and initiation they have had the opportunity to experience firsthand the reality of a human's parallel dimensions. For them, the solid body, the *soma*, exists as particle and wave function. The first soul, *siê*, or *gro bon anj*, exists as particle axions, wimps, or neutrinos and has a symmetric or boson counterpart called *ti bon anj,* or spirit—the second soul.

Concerning the origin of the universe, the initial primeval entity that came from Gran-Mèt by fiat or quantum fluctuation is the original master force of modern science. It is a bosonic force that was brought forth together with a fermion counterpart. It is also the primeval pan-psychic field whose fermion can be called a psychion, a particle of consciousness. These have evolved together to produce the four forces of nature: electromagnetic force; gravity; the strong nuclear force, or gluon; and the weak nuclear force, or weakon. These variants all share the basic quality of the master force, which is psychic energy. They are aspects of the unbroken wholeness of the pan-psychic field, the universal soul.

Thus, in the ontologies of Black Africa in general and in Haitian and Dagara versions in particular, the individual as a whole is endowed with supersymmetric doubles, or "souls," that are as real as our ordinary reality of fermions and bosons. This reveals a complexity in our nature that exceeds ordinary understanding. It is as complex as a Lorenz attractor (graphics derived from chaos theory), hence events or avatars can manifest themselves unexpectedly.[19] These supersymmetric doubles constitute the backbone of alternate realities, parallel universes that are displayed in ten dimensions, including our ordinary three-dimensional Cartesian reality.

To come of age in Haitian and Dagaraland, to pass from infancy to adulthood, the individual must obtain the ultimate education. He or she must be initiated into the knowledge of the multiple dimensions of reality, the parallel universes. He and she must acquire *konesans* [knowledge]. When Westerners talk about the Haitian's primitive animism, their imaginal realm and wild fantasies, their visionary rumors, Haitian and Dagaran initiates can only smile at the ignorance of their detractors.

Initiation is "graduation" through a higher education into the fullness of ontology, or knowledge of both the person's own nature and the nature of the universe with all its parallel worlds, including the world of the Voudouns, or Lwa. In Dagaraland, the purpose of initiation is to find the center of self and its composite nature. This initiation is called *baor*. The path to *baor* is full of danger, but not in the sense of the kind of hazing carried out by American fraternities or the U.S. military to test the stamina of neophytes. It is dangerous because a journey into the parallel dimension is associated with disruption of the structure of ordinary matter.

In Haiti, the first full-fledged level of initiation is called *hounsi kanzo*. It does not seem to be as dreadful an experience as the *baor* in Burkina Faso. There are no reports of candidates losing their lives in the process, although it is a very taxing period for the neophytes. In both cultures, when the candidates enter the seclusion of initiation, relatives and friends cry and mourn as if it were a funeral.

In our study we will consider two initiation accounts: first, the account of Claude Planson, a French scholar initiated in Haiti to the grade of *hounsi kanzo,* and second, the account of Malidoma Patrice Somé, a scholar from Burkina Faso with a double Ph.D., who was initiated in his country to the grade of shaman in the Dagara tradition. This grade is the equivalent of *houngan* or *manbo* in Haiti. Planson published his experiences in France in 1987 under the title *Le Vaudou,* while Somé told his story in 1994 in *Of Water and the Spirit.* In these works, the authors offered only what their elders allowed them to reveal. They were bound by an oath of silence not to reveal certain "highly classified" information.

In Haiti, before being accepted for initiation, the individual undergoes a period of probation, during which the individual has to show that he or she is well disposed toward the elders by exhibiting humility and obedience. Once accepted, the candidate is called a *houngno,* or novice. The *hounsi kanzo* initiation lasts six days in Haiti. It is usually undertaken simultaneously by a group of three to five individuals; it is rarely done by one person alone. The novices are isolated in a *djevò,* a designated room of the *ounfò,* where they will undergo an experience of death and rebirth. Planson compared this "born again" experience with similar ones in the secret societies of Demeter, Dionysus, and Mithra in the Mediterranean area. In the Christian religion, this experience reminds one of Jesus' words to the rabbi Nicodemus, when he spoke of being born of water and the spirit, a new birth that allows us to enter the parallel dimension of the Kingdom of Heaven. The Apostle Paul also presented Christian baptism as being symbolic of death and rebirth. In the isolation of the *djevò,* the initiates are subjected to conditions that lead to a state of transcendental meditation, a trance state that opens the avenues of higher consciousness, or the gate of singularities.

"Singularity" is a term derived from modern physics and used by physicists such as Albert Einstein, Roger Penrose, and Stephen Hawking to describe phenomena that are considered impossible in ordinary reality but possible in black holes or wormholes.[20] The trance state of the *houngno* and the Voudouist creates an atmosphere of high energy and high vibration that reproduces inside the person the equivalent of a wormhole vortex in which all particles enter into a frenzied acceleration equal to a supergravity state, an extreme state of space curvature.[21] In this state of supergravity, the equivalence of curvature and mass appears, whereupon the alternation of mass and energy, described by Einstein's E=mc2 equation and Richard Feynman's diagrams, bring about the following singularities:

1) an out-of-body experience, in which the supersymmetric doubles can separate themselves from the body (*soma, nyame,* or *kò kadav*) and materialize themselves into any shape in any branch of the parallel universes

2) a journey into parallel dimensions or the underworld of the spirits (Planson reports entering a universe where the sun shone at midnight)

3) a state of ubiquity in which the individual is everywhere and nowhere at the same time

4) spontaneous propagation, traveling at tachyonic speed (i.e., faster than light, into the past and into the future); in this manner the individual can discover his or her past lives and foresee his future (reincarnation and precognition)

5) discovery of the nature of extrasensory perception such as telepathy, telekinesis, and psychokinesis

6) total revelation of the tripartite nature of self, the discovery of the center of self and its unbroken wholeness with the universal soul

This is the height of ontology and of metaphysical knowledge. This is *konesans.*

Claude Planson speaks mainly about the trance and visions that occurred during his altered state of consciousness. He divided his experiences into two categories, intellectual visions and imaginary visions, but did not make a clear distinction between the two kinds. His account recalls that of the Apostle Paul, who declared that he did not know if his rapturous experience was within or outside of his body. Planson's imaginary vision seems to be associated with physical transmutations, while his dreamlike intellectual vision seems to be the simple out-of-body experience of a supersymmetric double.[22]

Planson says that at the onset of his singular experience, he began to vibrate, thus entering that high-energy vibratory state that is equivalent to supergravity, with its whirling curvature or vortex that leads to singularities. While he was in this state he saw the ineffable. He was in a garden of the parallel universe, comparable to the biblical Eden. The vision did not have the incoherence of a dream for him; he had the impression of penetrating into the ultimate reality. He was in a dense forest containing, in its center, a gigantic tree, which he took to be an archetype of the tree of Jesse of Ezekie, the Oddi-tree of Buddha, or the *potomitan* of the *hounfò* that joins earth and heaven. We are also reminded of the trees in the New Jerusalem of John's Apocalypse.

Planson touched the tree, which was warm and rough like the skin of an elephant or rhinoceros. In his wanderings about the garden, Planson said he reached a clearing in which a little house stood, almost in ruin, with the inscription "Don Juan" on the front. According to priestess Manbo Mathilda Beauvoir, this was a vision of the parallel universe of St. John the Baptist or the Lwa Azaka.[23]

While in seclusion in the *djevò*, Planson had another vision. A beautiful Black woman appeared whom he saw as the archetype of the Great Mother goddess, also known as Venus, Astarté, Cybel, Isis, Artemis, Notre Dame, and Ezili. She was the archetype of all feminine beauties and all loves, platonic, filial, and erotic. She was also the image of Mother Earth.[24] Through her, Planson believed, he had access to the consciousness and knowledge of all the women of the world and all of creation. He also mentions "celestial music," "mystical marriage," and the sensation of being "buried alive in a tomb." He summed up his Haitian initiation as a triple revelation of sacredness, death, and eroticism.[25] The procedure made the initiate a knowledgeable person, a magus with a clear understanding of the deep secrets of nature.

Planson's initiation did not involve introduction to the forbidden zones of nonordinary dimensions. He was aware of them but was not allowed to penetrate into such realms, for they require a higher level of rituals and covenants. He mentions several trials but was allowed to speak about only one of them, the *boulezin,* or manipulation of fire. This involves a superposition or composite state with a Vodoun that enfolds the devotee in a protective field of high energy that isolates his flesh from the ravages of fire.

Planson's spouse, *manbo* Mathilda Beauvoir, has experienced the forbidden zones of singular dimensions. She has experienced out-of-body travel in which the supersymmetric axionic double is separated from the body and ventures into the exploration of other parallel universes. Planson believes that it is the *ti bon anj,* or the Dahomean double called *selido,* that leaves the body. Some adepts, however, believe that it is the *semedo,* or *gro bon anj,* that leaves the body while the *selido* stays behind. At any rate, Beauvoir, in her journey out of the soma, was able to visit Nan Ginen, Vilokan, and Zile (or Ilé-Ilé), places similar to the Magonia of Europeans, all legendary cities of parallel universes located in the air, on earth, under the ground, or under water.[26]

Beauvoir described Cyclopean cities similar to those in the science fiction world of Ray Bradbury. Some were terrestrial, others chthonian, aerian, or subaquatic. Planson recounted a close encounter of the theophanic kind when the Lwa Legba manifested himself in the flesh to a *tambourineur,* a baryonic manifestation of a shadow-matter entity that has passed through a high-energy vibratory state, higher magnetism, and a supergravity state leading to the equivalence of mass and the alternation of the Feynman diagram. Epiphanic manifestations usually do not last very long; they vary in duration from seconds to minutes to hours. They are different from the state of adorcism—also known as channeling or crisis of possession—in that epiphany is associated with visible physical manifestations while in adorcism the shadow-matter entity enters the body of the adept; it is a purely energetic psychionic entity with a devotee or adepts. In the Christian or biblical alternate reality, epiphany would be the theophany of God at Sinai and adorcism would be the outpouring of the Holy Ghost at Pentecost.

One can obtain a deeper knowledge of the ontological realm of the Haitian weltanschauung, or alternate reality, through a Petwo initiation of the Lwa Zandor type. The powerful destructive Lwa of the Zandor family join the devotees in penetrating deeper regions of parallel universes. They facilitate transmutation of mass into energy or matter into psychionic/spiritual energy. Planson and Manbo Beauvoir do not belong to societies that profess the Zandoric initiation (very few Vodouists do); however, after obtaining special permission, they were allowed to attend a *sabbat* of the Zandoric fraternity. There they witnessed, firsthand, singular phenomena that in the Western world belong to the realm of fairy tales or science fiction, including human teletransportation within an orb of light that resembled a shooting star; transmutation of humans into goats, rams, or pigs (for vengeance and consummation); metamorphosis into a bull followed by the animal's instantaneous disappearance; death by strangulation with spontaneous resurrection after rigor mortis had set in; adorcism leading to a dance of fire and the handling of an iron bar heated white-hot in a pyre; and the teleportation of their own automobile. The Zandoric initiation is full of danger. The rituals can lead to a disruption in the structure of ordinary matter, causing death by disintegration or nuclear destruction. It is similar in many respects to the *baor* initiation in Dagaraland.

In the Dagara of Burkina Faso, initiation into the deepest ontological secrets of reality or space-time occurs during an intensive six-week period. It is carried out not in a dark room or *djevò* but naked in the middle of a forest. The neophytes are thus forced to relive the experiences of the first men in a world full of danger. They have to learn how to survive without the tools of an evolved society, to seek food, a place to sleep, companionship, discipline, and protection against wild beasts and the forces of nature. In addition to gaining knowledge of their physical capabilities, they must also acquire deep secrets of their internal, spiritual self to discover the tripartite components of humanity and to penetrate the parallel universe of the spirits, or *kontonteg*.

At the appointed hour, initiates gather at the edge of a forest to bid farewell to family and friends. Most initiates are adolescents between the ages of thirteen and fifteen, but some are older, like the author Malidoma Somé, who was twenty. The farewell is an emotional one, for every year accidents occur and people die during the initiation. Somé records that of the sixty-three candidates who presented themselves for his initiation, four died.

Parents, grandparents, and other knowledgeable relatives have the task of providing spiritual protection for the neophytes, because during their trial they will encounter destructive spiritual forces bent on mayhem. The elders, or *houngan*, responsible for the education of the young people also conduct rituals intended to protect them.

In Somé's group, the first major experience of the neophytes was a psyche-delic type of experience, resembling that of Maya Deren during her adorcistic or epiphanic encounters with a Lwa or Vodoun.[27] Somé reports that during the fire ceremony, an elder, the Great Initiate, already in a state of communion with the underworld, began to speak in tongues. Little by little, using his *ason*, or magic "wand," the elder engulfed the fire itself and the whole assembly around him into the parallel dimension of the invisible world. The color of the fire changed from green to violet, and its roar became louder.[28] The neophyte was in a total trance state, and as the solid, material world became invisible, he found himself in his own center, a whirling tornado, a portal of entry between two parallel universes. He saw himself as a circle of energy with a hyperdynamic center, alternately ex-panding and contracting. It was revealed to him that all humans are circles of the same nature,[29] vortexes of energy and fire that are part of the invisible world. He reported that the fire within us is capable of attracting spiritual forces that are beyond us, thus confirming physicist David Bohm's links of unbroken wholeness.

During his initiation, candidate Somé discovered pan-vitalism and pan-psy-chism, the fundamental ontological realities. Everything around him was life, mo-tion, and consciousness. Everything came to life—a strange life—and was "pul-sating, down to the smallest piece of dirt on the ground."[30] The trees in the forest revealed their hidden reality to him. They were not immobile, as in ordinary re-ality, but shared an inner center of energy and fire that could move from place to place and become ubiquitous.

During his psychedelic experience, Somé also discovered certain principles of equivalence that are similar to those found in the *Correspondances* of the nine-teenth-century French symbolist poet Baudelaire. "Sounds were blue or green and colors were loud." Somé also saw spiritual entities in alternate reality as in-candescent visions that were "breathing colors" in a state of "persistent immo-bility" and ubiquity.

For Somé, everything was alive with consciousness and meaning; there was no difference between meaning and being. "Things had become their meaning," he said.[31] Somé was face to face with pure universal pan-psychic energy. He also discovered his multidimensional nature. Like Maya Deren in Haiti, he felt for a while as if he were out of his body, standing in front of himself, watching.[32]

The candidates' next step in their ontological journey was the discovery of the Great Mother goddess through self-hypnosis or transcendental meditation, achieved through hours of persistent staring. Somé found this technique very tax-ing, for he was obliged to sit immobile in plain daylight in the middle of a forest and stare at a tree. Sudden illuminations occurred when he finally mastered the technique. We are reminded in this case of the spiritual adventures of Arthur Rim-baud, the nineteenth-century adolescent French poet who used the same technique of staring to develop extrasensory perception, which probably led him to write his book of poetry entitled *Illuminations*.[33]

The elders instructed Somé to keep staring until his mind was blank. When he succeeded, there was a sudden flash of lightning in his spirit and a cool sensation ran down his spine into the ground. His entire body then became cool, though he was sitting in the hot sun. He was catapulted into a realm of singularities. Staring had induced a state of high vibration, high energy, and high magnetism that overrode the normal physical sensations of a body under the hot sun. Somé's shadow-matter components, his supersymmetric doubles, or souls, took over the existential realm. They were no longer constrained by the boundaries of the baryonic or dense physical body. They were able to open the gate of invisibility to the neophyte. He could see the wave function, the shadow-matter component of the trees in the forest as they glowed like fire, breathing light.[34] The permanent alternation of the Feynman diagram, which depicts the continuous passage of visibility to invisibility, from mass particle to energy or wave function, produced the perception of "breathing lights."[35] He felt weightless and boundless as he became ubiquitous at the center of the universe. For him, the experience was a revelation of the nature of death, a rejoining of the universal soul, the pan-vitalist and pan-psychic space-time continuum.

Next came the appearance of the Great Mother goddess, whom Planson called Mother Earth. "Out of nowhere, in the place where a yila tree had stood, appeared a tall, green woman dressed in black from head to foot."[36] In this vision of the "eternal feminine," Somé, like Planson, experienced a feeling of overwhelming love.

This kind of vision has led other initiates, such as chemist Max Beauvoir,[37] to state that God is a woman. Planson's black lady and Somé's green beauty seem to be avatars of the Eternal One. In the Judeo-Christian tradition, God has revealed himself to be a man. He wrestled with Jacob in Genesis. Before that he visited Abraham, accompanied by two men. At Sinai, Moses saw the back of a man. Jesus of Nazareth always addressed him as Father. However, it is not necessary to start a third world war over God's gender. The first chapter of Genesis reveals that God created mankind in his image and his image is male and female. Some cultures have been blessed with a feminine avatar of God and others have received a masculine manifestation. So be it!

From an ontological point of view, the woman of the visions shares the nature of the universal self. The neophytes discovered the unbroken wholeness between them and the woman; therefore she better corresponds to a Mother Earth image than to the biblical Yahweh. By revelation, Yahweh is "total otherness" with a nature completely different from space-time and the universal soul. The universal self had a beginning and will have an end, but Yahweh has no beginning and no end. Thus, the woman/Mother Earth received a command from Yahweh at the beginning of time to "bring forth all kinds of living beings."[38] We can assume that Mother Earth did just that with great love. The lovestruck Somé declared, "The sensation of embracing her body blew my body into countless pieces, which became millions of conscious cells, all longing to reunite with the whole that was her. . . . We exploded into each other in a cosmic contact that sent us floating adrift in the ether in countless intertwined forms. . . . I felt as if I were moving backward in time and forward in space."[39]

The next great ontological revelation came to the initiate as transmutation of matter into spirit, or total wave function through penetration into a wormhole by forcing the ambiguous barrier that separates ordinary reality from the dimension of the spirits. This wormhole is called a light hole by the Dagara medicine man. A light hole is the equivalent of the intragalactic black hole. It is a site of singularities where a cascade of equations leads to the equivalence of mass and energy and the initiates' body is translated into a total spiritual entity capable of journeying through other dimensions in the space-time continuum. This is the point on the Feynman diagram when permanent alternation between visibility and invisibility shifts completely toward invisibility (psychionic energy) and shadow-matter fermion (or boson). Inside this tunnel, the neophytes discovered the nonrotating black hole equivalent that leads to permanent imprisonment in the world of shadow entities, or the bottomless pit of the Apocalypse.

This analysis is not the product of a runaway imagination, because three of Somé's companions died while journeying through the light hole. Two never returned to the world of visible reality, the third came back too late, having passed too close to the nonrotating Einstein-Rosen bridge. His body when returned resembled the body of a person who had been burned by nuclear radiation.

From this brief overview of ontological discoveries in Haitian and Dagara metaphysics, we recognize that reality is a many-splendored thing, stranger than we can imagine. The Western world has much to learn from the African masters. When it comes to the supernatural world, Western scholars will eventually discover, as did Malidoma Somé, that "the supernatural is natural."[40] The supernatural is an alternate expression of the universal space-time continuum, which has branched into multiple parallel universes, some visible, dense, and baryonic, others invisible, light, and leptonic. It is a way of expressing the nature of energy through the weakly interacting massive particle, called an axiom in modern physics, and endowing it with a psychic dimension. The supernatural is physical without being material: familiar matter is composed of dense particles that form atoms and molecules, while the supernatural is an invisible, physical expression of space-time manifested as pure energy that is commonly described as "immaterial."

The invisible parallel universe that makes up the "supernatural" realm should not be confused with the truly spiritual, nonphysical, and nonmaterial dimension of Yahweh, because he is not of the nature of space-time or the universal self. The Yahweh dimension is "total otherness," a dimension that has no beginning and no end, no entropy, no change. It is called Eternity.

This brief overview of the ontological data of two Black African diasporic communities is only a beginning. We can expect many more studies of an interdisciplinary nature to shed additional light on the richness of Black African metaphysics.

Notes

1. B. DeWitt and N. Graham, eds., *The Many-Worlds Interpretation of Quantum Mechanics* (Princeton, N.J.: Princeton University Press, 1973), 3.

2. Fred Alan Wolf, *Taking the Quantum Leap: The New Physics for Nonscientists* (New York: Harper & Row, 1989), 215–218.

3. Cheick Anta Diop, *Civilization or Barbarism: An Authentic Anthropology* (New York: Laurence Hill Brooks, 1991), 309–326.

4. Lilas Desquiron, *Racines du Vodou* (Port-au-Prince: Editions H. Deschamps, 1990), 105–109.

5. Malidoma Patrice Somé, *Of Water and the Spirit: Ritual, Magic, and Initiation in the Life of an African Shaman* (New York: Penguin, 1994), 186.

6. Joel R. Primack, "The Case of Dark Matter," *Science Year* (1990): 114–127.

7. Ibid., 127.

8. A. Einstein, B. Podolsky, and N. Rosen, "Can Quantum-Mechanical Description of Physical Reality Be Considered Complete?" *Physical Review* 47 (1935): 777–780.

9. S. Freedman and J. Clauser, "Experimental Test of Local Hidden-Variable Theories," *Physical Review Letters* 28, no. 14 (1972): 938–941.

10. Alain Aspect, J. Dalibard, and G. Roger, "Experimental Test of Bell's Inequalities Using Time-Varying Analyzers," *Physical Review Letters* 49, no. 25 (December 1982): 1804–1807.

11. Michael S. Turner, "The Universe," *Science Year* (1994): 174–199.

12. Primack, "The Case of the Dark Matter."

13. David Bohm, *Quantum Theory* (New York: Prentice-Hall, 1951), 48.

14. Somé, *Of Water and the Spirit*, 191–201.

15. Alfred Métraux, *Le Vaudou Haitien* (Paris: Gallimard, 1959), 107.

16. Claude Planson, *Le Vaudou* (Paris: MA Editions, 1987), 76.

17. James Hall, *Sangoma: My Odyssey into the Spirit World of Africa* (New York: Putman, 1994), 252–258.

18. Wolf, *Taking the Quantum Leap*, 133–141.

19. James Gleick, *Chaos: Making a New Science* (New York: Viking Press, 1987), 28.

20. Peter Coveney and Roger Highfield, *The Arrow of Time: A Voyage through Science to Solve Time's Greatest Mystery* (London: W. H. Allen, 1990), 99–102.

21. Fritjof Capra, *The Tao of Physics: An Exploration of the Parallels Between Modern Physics and Eastern Mysticism* (Boston: Shambhala, 1991), 314.

22. Planson, *Le Vaudou*, 138.

23. Ibid.

24. Ibid., 140.

25. Ibid., 141.

26. Ibid., 143.

27. Maya Deren, *Divine Horsemen: The Voodoo Gods of Haiti* (New York: Thames and Hudson, 1953), 259–260.

28. Somé, *Of Water and the Spirit*, 197.

29. Ibid., 199.

30. Ibid., 201.

31. Ibid.

32. Ibid., 204.

33. Arthur Rimbaud, *Illuminations* (Neuchatel: La Baconnière, 1986).

34. Somé, *Of Water and the Spirit*, 219–220.

35. Kenneth Ford, *The World of Elementary Particles* (New York: Blaisdell, 1965), 208.

36. Planson, *Le Vaudou,* 152.

37. Max G. Beauvoir, "Foreword" to *The Vodou Quantum Leap: Alternate Realities, Power and Mysticism,* by Reginald Crosley (St. Paul, Minn.: Llewellyn Publications, 2000), xv–xvi.

38. Genesis 1:24.

39. Somé, *Of Water and the Spirit,* 221.

40. Ibid., 226.

3

Broken Mirrors: Mythos, Memories, and National History

PATRICK BELLEGARDE-SMITH

The river that doesn't know its source soon dries up.

—Yoruba proverb

Rock in riverbed knows not how stone in sun suffers.

—Haitian proverb

The Western world typically holds the view that there are two sides to a story. If this is true, this chapter might be the other side, as told by the Other. Stories by outsiders are seldom told and rarely heard. One side mutes the other. The recent discovery of multiculturalism in the United States, a country that has always been multicultural, augurs well for the future. Fortunately, the world is immensely more complex than acknowledged in these "two sides"; it reveals a richness in which the devil is in the details, in historical continuities and breaks, in false starts and dissimulation, in cultural continua in which bleedthroughs, *bavures,* occur. Though this chapter is written in English, some of the ideas expressed fit uneasily in that language. Each language develops out of a specific way of thinking about the world or "thinking a world." It sets parameters for thought and the social construction of reality. I speak here of a sort of metalanguage, of cultural codes that are both transcendent and limiting. Thus, the world is many.

Events, as moments in their re-telling (and retailing), constitute a flexible discourse. Events and their (re)interpretations are part of phenomena that, at once, create and are shaped by so-called objective reality(ies).

In English, the concept "people" seems deeply unsatisfactory, as the word does double duty for two disparate constructs: people = both persons qua individuals and the collective, as in "the American people." Better suited for this essay are the Haitian terms *pèp* (in French, *le peuple*) and *moun* (in French, *la personne*). *La personne charrie des histoires qui la ramènent (et se ramènent) à l'histoire de son peuple* (People carry, in a stream, stories that draw them into the history of their people). (Of necessity, translations are approximate.) People are the raw material inscribed by experience as they suffer the impact of the collective while they create that collectivity. The creator/creature merges, an important concept in Haitian religion. The Vodou religion and those who *sèvi Lwa,* those who serve the Spirits and the Ancestors, are synchronous elements in the dance of life. But as streams meander to the ocean, oftentimes through a harsh landscape, they loop. The epigraphs that introduce this chapter hint at waters whose shimmering surface resembles the shards of a broken mirror The watery abyss and the mirror are major pictographic symbols in Haitian Vodou. Forms marry substance; they are a part of the same message. The stories of Haiti commence.

The tension in which opposites subsist in *each* entity is fundamental to many West African religious and philosophical systems. Haitians are a part of that world. They are, nevertheless, the end product of the most negative historical processes, born of the rape of one continent and the enslavement of another. The Haitian national identity, as it evolved, was born on the plantation, where options were severely circumscribed by the power differential between the emerging identity and a dominant and Manichean Western world. That identity was also born in the Maroon communities that had some success in preserving what might have been lost, in the *fusion*—not a syncretic synthesis, more of a synergetic whole and a symbiosis—of these African worlds. Both the plantation and the Maroon encampment defined and delineated the realities of an enslaved population captive to an emergent European capitalism.

Haiti's economic history had subtexts of "race," color, and class. All are social constructs. In that inherited world, one is given versions of events interpreted by those well-read enough to write and those well-heeled enough to publish. Competing versions can easily be disparaged or simply ignored, relegated to safe oblivion from recorded history. This is what one would expect from dominant classes that seek to maintain their hegemony. A totalitarian impulse flows from necessity. "Recall" becomes mythology or folklore. Time and space collapse, particularly as memory recedes.

The subaltern Other, a dominant culture in the making, recognizes within its ontological domain the necessity of the validity (and the validation) of multiple stories. This vision is important in Vodou. Vodou's easy acceptance of difference seems anchored in the dualism embedded in all/each object/subject as part of innate existence. This philosophical construct is rendered even more acute by (neo)colonial conditions in which survival forced individuals to absorb something of the dominant West. That situation is reminiscent of the (re)creation of extended family patterns in the African diaspora from the twin impact of original cultures and slavery, both of which contain matrilineal and matrifocal elements.[1] Seldom told in their proper contexts, the narratives of majoritarian but subaltern cultures are often revealed in the creative tension, the dynamic interaction, and the one-sided dialogue they maintain with the dominant culture. Often, the thought expressed by persons from disparaged cultures, *les cultures meprisées,* is camouflaged, reinforcing an ideological framework in which Deities select persons and secret initiations are the rule. People are not divorced from culture, though they can be divorced from reality; they are neither totally enslaved nor entirely free.

Memories are retrievable. Although they have not relied on indigenous or traditional paradigms, Haitian historians have utilized oral history. In the early nineteenth century, the country's first historian, Thomas Madiou, wrote partly from reminiscences. Contemporary historian Roger Gaillard used oral sources to chronicle the watershed period illustrated by the U.S. occupation of Haiti, 1915–1934.[2] Most Haitian literature, predictably, since the country is about 80 percent non-literate, is steeped in *oralitude,* an oral tradition, and not in the tens of thousands of books and pamphlets of poetry, plays, novels, and philosophical treatises written by the small and prolific Franco-Haitian elite.[3]

Mirrors in Which We Reflect . . .

Kaka kankou chen pa anyen; se tranble janm nan ki tout. (Defecating like a dog is no big thing; it is the trembling of the dog's leg that makes it real.)

—Haitian proverb

Haiti's national religion played a primordial role in the history and the evolution of the Haitian psyche, as did Shinto in Japan and Judaism in Israel.[4] But all manner of categories remained essentially fluid in the ostensibly mercurial religion. It is both conservative and progressive. It preserves African traditions by transforming and transcending them. It emanates from a "creole" culture, yet Haiti remains the most africanized society in the Caribbean. And the very essence of the religion—qua an intellectual and spiritual discipline—combines polar opposites in the form of metaphysical dialectics. One is reminded that at the time of the Haitian Revolution and the wars of Independence, when two movements conflated into one, between two-thirds and three-quarters of enslaved Africans and erstwhile Haitians had been born in West and Central Africa, not in French Saint Domingue. These *bosal,* in contrast to the locally born creoles, had not been fully domesticated, "*apprivoisés,*" in the way intended by the French colonists. Indeed they were seen as less civilized, though no African could ever truly be defined as civilized at the time. The *bosal* were nonetheless the repository of traditions thousands of years old. And though time, space, and materiality force us to recreate and relocate ourselves ad nauseam, it bears remembering that transgenerational memories in the collective unconscious are neither tamperproof nor foolproof. Here is a news item that discusses Vodou as defined by others. It ran in the *Peoria Journal Star* on October 11, 1985, with the title "Seven Seek Treatment for 'Voodoo Beans' Rash."

> "Voodoo beans," used in some tropical countries to menace people, were maliciously placed in an apartment here, causing severe rashes that led seven people to seek hospital treatment, authorities said Thursday. . . . The pods, from a vine called *Mucuna Pruriens,* are called "voodoo" beans in some Caribbean cultures, where they are used as part of a botanical arsenal. Voodoo is a religion based on a belief in sorcery and in the power of charms and fetishes. It is still practiced in the West Indies.

The subconscious predispositions, beliefs, and wording of this news item are the result of centuries of ahistorical arrogance and racial and cultural supremacy. I forwarded a response to the newspaper which it chose not to publish. I identified myself as a university professor (a good thing) and as a Haitian (a bad thing). Obviously, I could not be "objective." My response read in part:

Cap Haitien Haiti (AFP).

"Crosses" used in some temperate climate countries to frighten people about the afterlife, were maliciously placed in a house here, causing severe stress that led seven people to seek psychiatric treatment, authorities said Thursday.

Police were trying to determine who stashed the hand-sized crosses in a bed and couch in the home of Cetoute and Asefi Dorleans, said police sub-lieutenant, Joseph Tranquilus.

The crosses are called "crucifixes" in some Western cultures, where they are used as part of an arsenal of religious paraphernalia. Christianity is a religion based on a belief in superstition, and in the power of charms and fetishes. It is still practiced in the United States.

The newspaper, I am told by an acquaintance who worked there, was not amused. It did not seem to get the point or the sarcasm.

Haitians now know that almost any religion outside Christianity, especially when attached to "race," is considered a public relations nightmare.

Much earlier, Haiti's foremost mainstream philosopher of the first part of the twentieth century, Dantès Bellegarde, concluded that Vodou was hopelessly primitive and that Christianity represented a higher stage in the evolution of religious thought and practices. He admitted the difficulty of imposing Christianity on Haitians, writing candidly that "the ethnic element is of fundamental importance in determining the quality of a religion."[5] Bellegarde's willing acceptance of his own cultural inferiority (but not racial inferiority, since French racism, contrary to Anglo-Saxon forms of racism, allowed for the *perfectionnement* of Negroes), based on European international norms, was heartfelt. Bellegarde continued:

Last year [1947] a most detailed description of Haitian Vaudou ceremonies was published in an American publication. This American publication is titled *The Primitive Man*. I urge my Haitian readers to consider that the expressions "primitive religion" and "primitive man" are applied to peoples [*peuples*] declared by sociologists to be non-civilized. I remind my compatriots who might not know it that peoples with the reputation of being uncivilized or simply retarded [*sic*] are placed under the mandate or trusteeship of more civilized nations.[6]

The clearly stated objective was the acceptance of the Haitian state by "civilized nations," through the "rehabilitation of the Negro." One notes that neither "Negro" nor "Black" exist in the state of nature but are social constructs emanating from Western Europe and the Americas. That persons, members of Westernized or of Westernizing middle classes, born quite literally of the sexual interaction between (white male) slaveowner and (African female) slave and from the clash of cultures, had internalized their inferiority, is never surprising. That they would heartily implement the assimilationist cultural policies of a militarily

Houngan at ceremony.
Individual in photo: Patrick
Bellegarde-Smith. Photo-
graph by Claudine Michel.

vanquished France was more complicated. The survival of the fittest and the survival of the fledging Haitian state hung in the balance, international conditions not being propitious to independent policies of renegade nations. Dantès Bellegarde was my grandfather, a man I continue to adore. Born of two prestigious families which had lost their fortune, the Fresnels and the Bellegardes, his mother, because of this "*revers de fortune,*" was poor, illiterate, and creolophone. Her niece and his cousin, Luce Boisson, assumed a primary role in the religion, so that Vodou rituals, particularly concerning the cult of the Ancestors, were satisfied. Two of Bellegarde's grandchildren, myself included, are Vodou priests. This was/is common in upper-class and middle-class extended families that decry Vodou and the Haitian (Creole) language publicly but practice them in private.[7]

The state policies enshrined in the Haitian political discourse over the last two centuries would appear to lead to a dichotomous and Manichean bifurcation of all major cultural systems, as illustrated by the "chasm" between French- and Haitian-speakers, Vodou and Christian practitioners, shades of brown skin, "good"

hair and facial features close to European standards of beauty, relative wealth and
abject poverty. The majoritarian religion was and is persecuted, often by presi-
dents who practiced it in secret, and the national language is disparaged and de-
spised by creolophones themselves. Fortunately for Haiti, reality is always more
complex and immensely more complicated than appears. As members of a small-
ish society of 8 million souls, Haitians locate themselves along a cultural continuum that busily interferes with the neatness of ideological arguments and an
official stance that subscribes to the "two sides" view of reality.[8] *Le besoin de paraître,*
one's positioning in the international stage, has obfuscated *le besoin d'être,* remaining true to one's cultural "core," however defined.

At Molière's tercentenary celebrations in Paris in 1922, Dantès Bellegarde, who
had just completed an extraordinary speech (where the French intellectuals declared him "articulate"), responded to the query of a French reporter in the following manner:

(Q) What is the language spoken in Haiti?

(A) French.

(Q) What do Haitians read?

(A) A bit of everything, from Pierre Benoît to Marcel Proust. We receive the *Revue
des deux mondes* and *La vie parisienne.* "What an astonishing little people,"
someone said, buttoning his coat, "I never would have thought it possible that
La Bruyère was being commented upon in Port-au-Prince."[9]

Light-skinned and increasingly darker elites would adopt their fathers' voca-
tions—an early form of multiculturalism. It was to their social, economic, and
political advantage to do so. After all, the inherently unequal relationship between
worldwide dominant culture(s) and subaltern cultures could last for many more
centuries. Europeans and their descendents would go on merrily defining culture, civilization, language, religion, social class, and "good taste" and their opposites and who could be legally "Black." If one could escape the opprobrium of
one's station, one simply did. Mother would (just have to) understand.

Constantin Mayard (1882–1940), a Haitian poet laureate, wrote early in the
twentieth century:

*Tant que sous notre ciel plein de
fleurs adamantines
Notre île, comme un corps de femme
frémira,
Soyez sur que ce sol seulement
nourrira
Dans l'humus africain des semences
latines.*

As long as in our heaven
diamond-hard glittering flowers bloom full
Our isle, trembling like the body of a woman.

Be sure, our soil will only grow
n the African mold, a Latin seed.
(trans. P. Bellegarde-Smith)

Psychologically, anyone understands that position. The West is the norm, whiteness the standard. Haitians could not provide the world any of its definitions, not even those applied to Haiti.[10]

Oralitude: Monuments and Markers

Nou fèt pou n mouri (We are born [in order] to die).

—Haitian proverb

In a book describing the horrors wrought by an international embargo against Haiti under which the poor suffered inordinately after the government of Jean-Bertrand Aristide was overthrown in 1991, a Haitian writer juxtaposed the punishment then meted out to Haiti with the circumstances of the early nineteenth century, when Haiti was severely punished for having wrecked the prevailing colonial order and abolished slavery. She wrote: "The citizens of the country realized suddenly that their fabulous history—illustrated by a past underlined by bursts of splendid achievements and a particular culture, perhaps too different from neighboring states—was not entirely innocent. [That history] was a defiant challenge, a provocation, [seen] almost [as] an imposture."[11] This was a challenge and a provocation for which Haiti would have to suffer again and again. The wounds inflicted on the West by the Haitian Revolution of 1791 cut deeply. It remains the least studied of the great world revolutions in U.S. academic institutions.[12]

The evidence surrounding the role of Vodou in the Haitian Revolution and in the history of the nation's early years is incontrovertible. The elites preferred to view it as folklore in an attempt to render it relatively harmless as a curiosity that might continue to inspire music and dance. My mother told me on numerous occasions when I was a child that the Haitian ethos had refused to die to become true folklore. After all, she argued, Christian clergy had displaced the Druids, heralding a higher European "civilization." Vodou, our *"malchance,"* our misfortune, continued to infuse all fields and all systems.[13]

In April 1997, thirteen Haitian scholars meeting at the University of California in Santa Barbara proposed the creation of an academic and scholarly association with strong roots in Haitian popular culture. The Congress of Santa Barbara, better known by its Haitian (Creole) acronym, KOSANBA, declared as part of its mission statement that:

the presence, role and importance of Vodou in Haitian history, society, and culture are unarguable, and recognizably a part of the national ethos. The impact of the religion qua spiritual and intellectual disciplines on popular national institutions, human and gender relations, the family, the plastic arts, philosophy and ethics, oral and written literature, language, popular and sacred music, science and technology and the healing arts, is indisputable. Development, when real and successful, always comes from the modernization of ancestral traditions, anchored in the rich cultural expressions of a people.[14]

This is what happened in Asia (Hinduism, Shinto, Buddhism) and Europe (Christianity), but not in Africa and the Americas, where colonialism and its modern variants and racism were most severe and the attempts to submerge indigenous civilizations were more complete.

The saying *"nou fèt pou n mouri* [we are born to die]," as with most facets of the Haitian (Creole) language, is multilayered and pregnant with meanings. While it expresses fatalism and pessimism, the saying carries elements of scientific truth expressed nonchalantly. The precise meaning depends on the context. This meaning reminds us of the meaning of African American gospel music that, in its religio-philosophic dimensions, also gave "body" to rebelliousness and hope and rebellion. Learning the language is deceptively simple; knowing it, more arduous. Each language carries a world on its broad shoulders. In contrast with Spanish and Portuguese within La Regla de Ocha (Lukumi) and Candomble in Cuba and Brazil, the Haitian language *becomes* the liturgical language, thus merging two purposeful cultural megastructures: idiom and the religio-philosophic, ethical, and ideological structures that are necessary in all autonomous and autochthonous social systems. This consortium of language and religion provides the core that is jettisoned only under duress. They make Vodou a "creole" religion, perhaps more so than Santería and Candomblé (these are clearly more syncretic), without, however, needing to question its theological foundations erected from a number of African polities that contributed to the enslaved Haitian colonial population. The physical link to Africa was broken after Independence; this was not so elsewhere in the Americas, where "salt-water" Africans continued to arrive in bondage. And though the structures established by elites in power were almost always considered "modern," about 80 percent of the population of Haiti lived lives of virtual *marronage,* willfully oblivious to the half-hearted attempts to "civilize them."[15]

It is perhaps useful to juxtapose a poor, fledgling, and embattled Haiti with an article published in the *New York Times,* "There Will Always Be an England," and the subsequent letter written in response by an anglophile: "It is not vain jingoism to say that 'there will always be an England,' as long as its institutions, core culture and language *spread with ever-greater influence around the globe.* British influence may be expressed less visibly than by display of the Union Jack, but it could be more powerful for being less ostentatious."[16] God save us all! Against this stark declaration, I offer the statement by the Guatemalan leader Juan José Arévalo that small countries are sardines and powerful ones, the sharks among which they swim.[17]

That Vodou survived the Middle Passage was due to its capabilities and capacity to adapt. It was also due largely to the *logic* and the *reasoning* of these particular African-derived religions such as Vodou that are, in essence, more spiritual than religious. The argument goes that all spiritual disciplines (as distinct from religions) have similarities and validity. Newly transplanted Africans found such solace in their spiritual beliefs that colonial authorities became anxious to convert them to Christianity.[18] *Bosal* slaves, those born in Africa, seemed to have been far more rebellious than creole slaves, who had had time to adapt to the demands of slaveowners.

To revisit the title of this chapter, mythos is a good term to use to categorize the memories that shaped Haiti's national identity during the colonial and post-colonial periods. Mythos is the compendium of national myths that help define Haiti. I propose to the reflection of my readers that the term "broken mirrors" is reflexive of the shards of flesh, the pools of blood, the broken hopes of Haiti's interaction with the world and the way that Haiti was in turn viewed by the world. Early Independence (after merely 200 years of French colonialism, rather than nearly 400 years, as in the case of Jamaica or Barbados) ensured the survival of many African-derived features, despite that physical break with Africa at the end of the colonization. Though somewhat mangled by the realities it endured, Haitian Vodou is far more complete than New Orleans "voodoo" (or hoodoo), which has become a shell of its former self. Style is as important as substance, which Vodou reflects.[19] Haiti's 51 kinds of love, the 201 Haitians at the ceremony of Bois-Caïman, the 401 Lwa add to a complex reasoning that allowed disaggregated slaves from 101 African nations to (re)create an organization and a well-tempered military force that led them (albeit momentarily) to a modicum of freedom.[20]

Secrecy was a part of the process. The fear of colonial authorities and the slave-owning class and then of Haitian elites after Independence was justified. Belle-garde wrote that Vodou had

> maintained the confidence of the slaves who had found in [it] a particularly strong ferment capable of exalting their energies, because Vodou, created from a variety of cults imported from Africa, had become less a religion than a political association— a kind of Black "*carbonarisme*" whose *mot d'ordre* was the extermination of the whites and the deliverance of the Blacks. The ceremonies of the cult were surrounded with the most profound secrecy. Each initiate took the solemn oath to undergo the worst tortures rather than to reveal the secrets entrusted to him.[21]

Using the logic of the foregoing analysis, one would have to question the ability of Christianity to inspire the slaves. The Black church in the United States remained/remains a monument to ambivalence toward whites and Europe. It never occurred to Bellegarde, or to any members of his class, that Haiti could build its own structures, models, and paradigms for national development. J. G. A. Pocock argued that "since so large a part of men's consciousness of environment and time is gained through consciousness of the frame of social relationships which they inhabit, the conceptualization of tradition is an important source of their images of society, time and history. The importance of these visibly transcend the political; we are looking at one of the origins of a distinctly human awareness."[22]

Anthropologist Roger Bastide made the observation that "[religions] . . . had to seek out, in the social structures imposed on them, 'niches' where they could establish themselves and develop. . . . This [often] called for radical transformations of religious life itself. The superstructures that had formally connected family, village and tribe had to be linked with new substructures."[23]

In his fable "Le chêne et le roseau" [The Oak Tree and the Reed], Jean de la Fontaine described the resilience of the reed as a pragmatic characteristic that the oak tree does not possess. Janheinz Jahn declared that "Philosophy, theology, politics, social theory, land law, medicine, psychology, birth and burial, all find themselves logically concentrated in a system so tight that to *subtract* one item from the whole is to *paralyze* the structure of the whole."[24] Jahn's statement may perhaps be an exaggeration, but he makes the point that despite cultural borrowings freely undertaken or forced imposition from a dominant culture, change and adaptation do occur, propelled by both internal and external conditions. The questions that remain are these: What is the rate of change? In what directions does this change take place? Under whose agency?

At the first colloquium of the Congress of Santa Barbara (which uses the acronym KOSANBA) held in April 1997, I addressed the ramifications of subject matter as illustrated by the papers presented. These looked at an educational *process* in which Haitian children of all classes would not be disconcerted by their own culture or be divorced from it but might embrace it instead. The pioneering work of Claudine Michel, both in French and in English, stands out in this area. Rural life and social organization needs to be studied more diligently from within the premises and assumptions of a social science anchored in indigenous paradigms. Rénald Clérismé explored such themes in his work. The human complexity mirrored in the psychological archetypes of the Lwa is the domain of expertise of *manbo* and *houngan*. Significant research is now taking place in Haiti and abroad by some psychologists who are Vodou priests who are coming out from the shadows of secrecy and from under the veil of fear deployed by anti-Vodou religious persecution. The lifework of Viviane Nicolas and the late Thérèse Roumer comes to mind. Careers could be at stake for challenging the hegemony of Western social science.[25]

On the ground, as it were, things were changing. *Rasin* (roots) music groups such as Boukman Eksperyans and Boukan Ginen have given Haiti recognition never previously granted it in "world" music. Haitian "naïve" (outsider) painting, divorced from Western conventions of academic art, has been praised by non-Haitians for the past fifty years. Both artistic genres erupted from a working-class ethos and are deeply inspired by Vodou. More playwrights and poets are using the national language, whose orthography is now set by governmental statute. The Constitution of 1987 called for the establishment of an Academy of Letters, on the model of the Académie Française Richelieu created in 1634.

The rise of the middle classes to governmental power in 1946 and 1957 expanded various cultural options. Neither the Vodou religion nor the Haitian language is a priori "bad" or shameful for members of these middle classes. The growing political maturity of the urban and rural working classes, an *éclatement des cadres,* has been vigorously resisted by Haiti's power structure. After the overthrow of President Jean-Bertrand Aristide's government in 1991, a government that had embodied the hope of the majority of Haitians perhaps for the first time since Jean-Jacques Dessalines in 1804, the Haitian army and semiprivate militias killed as many as 5,000 men and women of the popular movement. Aristide, a young Roman Catholic priest from the southern village of Port-Salut, advocated Roman Catholic liberation theology but never disparaged Vodou. His successor, René Préval, declared the significance of Bois-Caïman and the Vodou ceremony that took place there as the signal moment that initiated the Haitian Revolution and the subsequent wars of Independence in a formal decree. The Haitian Constitution grants the power to make such decrees to the president.

Historians are slowly recognizing the ideological significance of Vodou in the war of liberation at the end of the eighteenth century, in the guerrilla warfare against the United States Marine Corps during the years of the American occupation of Haiti in the 1920s, and in the overthrow of the Duvalier dynastic dictatorship in the mid-1980s. Oral history states unequivocally that most, if not all, Haitian chiefs of state knew the religion well, most for its magical powers rather than as a spiritual force or as an intellectual discipline. Patterns are emerging to the observant scholar, in broad brush strokes. Smaller areas of the canvas will need to be shaded and nuanced so that the picture can be more fully revealed. Will school textbooks teach a complementary vision of the national flag's symbolism, in which the blue represents the cosmic powers and the Lwa Ezili Dantò, the archetype of (Black) motherhood, and the red is the color of Ogou Feray, the Fon and Yoruba deity of war? One version does not obliterate the official state-sponsored version, in which the blue represents the "pure" Africans and the red, the *mulâtres* in color- and class-conscious Haiti and in colonial Saint Domingue.

Only those who control the state apparatus erect monuments; the rest of the country must erect such markers of important nodes of history and culture in their psyches and in powerful memories cloaked in myth. In anti-democratic (*bourgeois*) democracies, "*le peuple*" do not rule. They neither write books nor enact laws. Yet national heroes, as Ancestors, find themselves enshrined in the Vodou pantheon. The existence of a cultural continuum between Brown and Black Haitians, francophones who are creolophones (and their fundamental ambivalence about what constitutes Haitian culture), is seen in ostensibly insignificant items—January 2nd is "Ancestors' Day"; November 2nd, the "Day of the Dead." The whole month of November is dedicated to the Lwa of the cemeteries, the Gédé, who cherish life and adore children. The national anthem, "La Dessalinienne," speaks of the Ancestors. Those without formal power are not necessarily powerless. The survival of a culture and of truncated cultural elements over the span of five centuries indicates that compromises and adaptations are the sine qua non of a living and dynamic culture and that Vodou is a "living religion," to quote the anthropologist Michel Laguerre.[26]

A *manbo* who has a graduate degree in psychology from the London School of Economics told me, "*Les couleurs changent; les Lwa eux-mêmes changent*" (The [sacred] colors change; the Deities, too, also change). She went on to describe the series of initiations one submits to, and surrenders to, as an "*ouverture sur la conscience collective*" (an opening on the collective subconscious).[27] Perhaps the mother of all battles for the soul of Haiti is more apparent than real, as Haitian culture seems to want to survive. On *paper,* Haitian history remains fragmentary and segmented, expressed in a binary opposition—perhaps the price it pays for acceptance in Western academic circles. The link between all Haitians, however, is a Black mother, albeit with different fathers. We may, indeed, be stepsisters and stepbrothers, but we need not access the reality of *pitit an deyò,* the canard of illegitimacy. The sum is greater than the total of its parts.[28]

Notes

1. There are competing views about what remains of African cultures in the Americas and what evolved from slavery and its aftermath, and where. See Roger Bastide, *Les Amériques Noires* (Paris: Petite Bibliothèque Payot, 1967). See also Osei-Mensah Aborampah, "Family Structure in African Fertility Studies: Some Conceptual and Methodological Issues," *A Current Bibliography on African Affairs* 18, no. 4 (1985–1986).

2. Thomas Madiou, *Histoire d'Haiti,* 4 vols. (Port-au-Prince: Imprimerie J. Courtois, 1847–1848). Madiou lived many years in Paris as a youth and returned to Haiti after Independence. See Roger Gaillard, *Les Blancs Débarquent,* 7 vols. (Port-au-Prince: Le Natal, 1974–1984).

3. Until the 1950s, Haiti was apparently the most prolific nation in Latin America in terms of published materials per capita, according to American literary critic Edmund Wilson. See his *Red, Black, Blond, and Olive; Studies in Four Civilizations: Zuni, Haiti, Soviet Russia, Israel* (New York: Oxford University Press, 1956), 110.

4. See Patrick Bellegarde-Smith, *Haiti: The Breached Citadel* (Boulder, Colo.: Westview Press, 1990), which indexes thirteen different categories and many dozens of entries on Vodou.

5. Dantès Bellegarde, *La Nation Haitienne* (Paris: Editions J. de Gigord, 1938), 312.

6. Dantès Bellegarde, *Dessalines a parlé* (Port-au-Prince: Société d'Editions et de Librarie, 1948), 176.

7. Among others, see Hannibal Price, *De la réhabilitation de la race noire par la République d'Haiti* (Port-au-Prince: Verolot, 1900), and the argument made by Roger Bastide in *Les Ameriques Noires* on the distinctions between *sociétés Africaines* and *sociétés nègres* in the African diaspora (29–50). As concerns alienation, see Frantz Fanon, *Peau noire, masques blancs* (1952; reprint, Paris: Editions du Seuil, 1995).

8. Patrick Bellegarde-Smith, *In the Shadow of Powers: Dantès Bellegarde in Haitian Social Thought* (Atlantic Highlands, New Jersey: Humanities Press International, 1985).

9. See Patrick Bellegarde-Smith, "Rum as Cognac: Fluidity of an Etho-Cultural Crisis—Haiti," *Kaleidoscope II* (Spring 1994): 13–18.

10. Bellegarde-Smith, *In the Shadow of Powers,* 170.

11. Edith Lataillade, *Le Dernier fil: ou les sanctions au quotidien* (Port-au-Prince: Le Natal, 1998), 5.

12. See Frantz Fanon, *Peau noire,* and Albert Memmi, *Portrait du colonisé précédé du portrait du colonisateur* (Paris: Editions Buchet/Chastel, Correa, 1957).

13. Various conversations between the mid-1950s and 1979, the year Simone Bellegarde died.

14. By-Laws, Congress of Santa Barbara (KOSANBA), adopted in 1997.

15. Latin American states with an indigenous "base" and a European or quasi-European upper and middle class, find themselves in a precarious situation soon after Independence in the area of cultural allegiances. The objective of the elites was to europeanize the masses and whiten the population. This objective was met with varying success, depending on the country.

16. Lawrence Cranberg to editor of *New York Times,* in "Letters to the Editor," *New York Times Magazine* (February 7, 1999).

17. Juan José Arévalo, *Fábula del triburón y las sardinas, América Latina estrangulada* [The fable of the shark and the sardines] (Buenos Aires: Ediciones Meridión, 1956).

18. Michael Conniff and Thomas Davis, *Africans in the Americas: A History of the Black Diaspora* (New York: St. Martin's Press, 1994), 81–82.

19. Thomas Kochman, *Black and White: Styles in Conflict* (Chicago: University of Chicago Press, 1984). Kochman argues that despite a common language, white Americans and African Americans conceptualize their worlds in very different ways.

20. This formulation, 11 or 21, indicates an infinite number within the bounds of realism/reality. Freedom and liberation are juxtaposed as distinct concepts: the first relates to bourgeois political and civil rights within the bounds of individualism; the second represents mid- to late-twentieth-century efforts by Brown and Black populations that transcended politics to include cultural elements, such as language and religion, within a collective ethos.

21. Dantès Bellegarde, *Histoire du peuple haïtien* (Port-au-Prince: Collection du Tricinquantenaire, 1953), 59. *Carbonarisme* refers to the movement for the unification of Italy led by Guiseppe Garibaldi (1807–1882) that met in secrecy in the woods.

22. J. G. A. Pocock, *Politics, Language and the Time: Essays on Political Thought and History* (New York: Atheneum, 1971), 235, cited in Brenda Gayle Plummer, *Haiti and the Great Powers* (Baton Rouge: Louisiana State University Press, 1988), 15.

23. Roger Bastide, *The African Religions of Brazil: Toward a Sociology of the Interpenetration of Civilizations* (Baltimore: Johns Hopkins University Press, 1978), 58.

24. Janheinz Jahn, *Muntu: The New African Culture* (New York: Grove Press, 1961), 14.

25. For instance, see Claudine Michel, *Aspects éducatifs et moraux du Vodou haïtien* (Port-au-Prince: Le Natal, 1995), and Laënnec Hurbon, *Le Barbare imaginaire* (Port-au-Prince: Editions Henri Deschamps, 1987), among others. In the same vein, recent books have been published on principles of Islamic and Buddhist psychology. See, for instance, David J. Kalupahana, *The Principles of Buddhist Psychology* (Albany: State University of New York Press, 1987).

26. Michel S. Laguerre, *Voodoo Heritage* (Beverly Hills, Calif.: Sage Publications, 1980), citing Roger Bastide.

27. Conversations with the late Thérèse Roumer, Port-au-Prince, August 8, 1998.

28. Three represents "twin-ness," the two whose powers are increased by the birth of the next child, *marasa dosou/dosa*. The sacred number three can represent the collectivity as a whole. Philosophically, the concept represents symbiosis and power.

4

Of Worlds Seen and Unseen:
The Educational Character of Haitian Vodou

CLAUDINE MICHEL

World events continue to place religion—in particular, teaching religion and teaching about religion—in contemporary education discourse. Ernest Boyer, though not supporting religious indoctrination in schools, posits that quality education will not exist until comparative religion is part of the regular curriculum and students understand that "the sense of the sacred is inextricably interwoven with the most basic human impulses, the most primal experiences of birth and growth and death." He recommends that students "should understand that the search for meaning is universal and that religion has profoundly shaped the human experiences on this planet."[1] Whether or not one accepts religious education in the curriculum, the effect of religious forces on world history, social systems, and politics must be examined.

It is also evident that religious forces can no longer be interpreted within the rigid boundaries of old paradigms meant to study the exotica of myths and ritualizing. New models are emerging to explain the complexities of religious phenomena as well as tensions between religious experience and such materialities as colonialism, race, culture, gender, class, economics, and politics. New religious realities should be seen less as areas of continuity or discontinuity than as "conjunction." Indeed, religion is no longer the instrument the West has used for centuries to marginalize and dominate other people; in some forms it has become a point of contact and conjunction for marginalized cultures. Vodou is such a form, adapting traditional African practices to New World realities.[2] This chapter illustrates the rehabilitation of religion in the lives of people with a long history of subjugation, people whose beliefs have frequently been dismissed by outsiders as primitive if not inherently evil. In particular, I examine the worldview of Vodou and the use of education to transmit it from one generation to the next in Haiti.

Origins and Sociopolitical Background of the Vodou Tradition

After being forcibly removed from their land, culture, and families, Africans in the New World, having come from different ethnic and linguistic groups, could not recreate their old order. To restitch their past, they developed a new definition of family based no longer on blood or tribal appurtenance but on a new religion, Vodou, and on their common aspiration for freedom. The imposition of European values, including Catholicism, which accompanied slavery forced the Africans to hide allegiance to their ancestral religions and stimulated them to develop innovative forms of worshiping African deities. Repressive measures and the resulting clandestine nature of Vodou ceremonies led to the revalorization of the very African cultural values that Europeans tried to suppress.[3] Thus, Vodou became not only the means for revitalization through ancestral traditions but also the channel par excellence to organization and to resistance.

Haiti's history of persecuting Vodou practitioners, marked by a number of anti-superstitious campaigns spearheaded by the clergy and the state, is concomitant with forced assimilation and acculturation. Despite their resistance, sociopolitical realities impelled Haitians to integrate such Catholic elements as prayers, hymns, and the Gregorian calendar into Vodou cosmology. Originally used by Haitians as stratagems to mask their religious beliefs, these Catholic practices have become an integral part of Vodou worship and exemplify syncretic fusion of heterogeneous cultural and religious elements.

Vodou as Theology

"Animism," "fetishism," "paganism," "heathenism," and "black magic" are some of the terms that have been used improperly in the West to describe a religion that is presented as one of blood and sacrifice and of sexual orgies and malevolence. There is a widely shared perception that "Vodou" means sorcery and witchcraft.[4] Nothing could be further from the truth. Vodou is portrayed in the West in opposition to "true" religion: Christianity. Yet it does not contrast with Western religions as much as the media would like us to believe. Vodou differs from the official church (whether Catholic or Protestant) mostly in dogma, phenomenology, hierarchy, and monumental architecture. It is not a system imposed from above; it is a democratic and functional religion, embedded in its followers' daily existence and in the struggle to make their life whole. As in African and many other non-Western traditions, there is complete unity of religion and life; every aspect of a person's existence is "sacred."

Vodou shapes experience in the search for purpose. Like other religions, it is a place where the human and the divine meet to create interpretations and meanings. In fact, no human experience is beyond the influence of the *loa,* or Vodou spirit. Patrick Bellegarde Smith explains that:

> Vodun is a coherent and comprehensive system and worldview in which every person and everything is sacred and must be treated accordingly. . . . This unity of all things translates into an overarching belief in the sanctity of life, not so much for the *thing* as for the *spirit* of the thing. The cosmological unity of Vodun further translates into a vaunted African humanism in which social institutions are elaborated and in which the living, the dead, and the unborn play equally significant roles in an unbroken historical chain. Thus all action, speech, and behavior achieve paramount significance for the individual and the community of which the individual is part.[5]

Vodou is more than rituals of the cult, temple, and family. As a comprehensive religious system, it ties together the visible and invisible, material and spiritual, secular and sacred. It is a philosophy, a way of life for the majority in Haiti that permeates and sustains their entire being and brings coherence where there might otherwise be chaos.

The monotheistic religions of Christianity, Islam, and Judaism are prescriptive and use a sacred text from which followers derive doctrines and basic laws. In contrast, Haitian Vodou offers few absolutes and generalities and does not have a prescriptive code of ethics. Followers define moral principles for themselves and are guided by life's lessons, the wisdom of ancestors, and communication with spirits. Vodou, central to Haitian culture, is based on a conception of reality that includes life's goals, forces that determine the fate of living things, proper social organization, balanced interpersonal relations, and practices that promote the welfare of the community. Its devotees ask of it what people have always asked of religions: a basis for daily living, remedy for ills, help in times of hardships, satisfaction of needs, and hope. Karen McCarthy Brown explains that Vodou is a "repository for wisdom accumulated by a people who have lived through slavery, hunger, disease, repression, corruption, and violence all in excess."[6] People turn to the spirits and their ancestors to assure the survival in this lifetime of the self and the group. Vodou does not have a concept of Eden or Heaven; the afterlife may turn out to be as harsh as the present. Therefore, survival in this lifetime and healing for immediate well-being become an ongoing process that engages Vodou adepts throughout their life. Despite the absence of a formal church and clergy, written dogma, and formal listing of members, Vodou is omnipresent in Haiti's social life and by providing moral coherence through cosmological understandings represents a key element of Haitian consciousness.

Vodou Followers: Servitors of the Spirits

Vodou is the national religion, practiced across class boundaries by more than 6 million Haitians. Said to be 85 percent Catholic, 15 percent Protestant, and 100 percent Vodouist, perhaps 95 percent of Haitians believe in the *spirits*. Nevertheless, all are not active participants all the time and under all circumstances, though they likely turn to the *loas* during periods of need and crisis.

Partly because of the stigma imposed on Vodou and its African cultural tradition, most Haitians have always publicly participated in Catholicism, the country's sole official religion until 1987, while practicing Vodou in private. This is especially true of the upper classes and upwardly mobile who customarily reject overt association with their African heritage. Vodou adepts perceive themselves as good Christians and see no conflict with practicing both Catholicism and serving the spirits;[7] the same saints who ornament Catholic churches watch over Vodou altars. Catholicism becomes then an extension of the quest for protection from the saints/spirits and the omnipotent God, Bondye.[8]

Whereas few Haitians of all social classes are not exclusively Catholics or Vodou adepts, the same cannot be said of those who profess Protestantism, a religion that remains problematic in Haiti because it requires abandoning Vodou beliefs and practices. Few are raised in Protestant families; people typically convert to Protestantism if they decide that their religion no longer works for them. According to Glenn Smucker, Protestant conversion "is a legitimate means of escaping ritual indebtedness to spirits when they turn a deaf ear or withhold pity in hard times. The threat of conversion is a serious threat to the spirits, for a saint without followers loses prestige and is forgotten."[9] However, I maintain that few Haitians stop believing in the spirits, and it is not unusual to see people go back to Vodou if Protestantism fails for them.[10]

Family and Temple Vodou

Haiti is a rural society where the cult of ancestors guards peasant traditional values and is largely linked to family life and the land. Haitian peasants serve the spirits daily and gather with their extended family on special occasions for ceremonies, which may celebrate the birthday of a spirit or a particular event. In remote areas, people sometimes walk for days to partake in ceremonies that take place as often as several times a month or as rarely as once or twice a year. Vodou is closely tied to the division and administration of land as well as to the residential economy.[11] Concerned with conflict resolution, family or domestic Vodou, especially among the Haitian diaspora, uses African spirituality to help assure the family's collective survival in hostile physical and social environments.

The absence of a formal place of worship is noticeable; all places are sites of worship. The *hounfò* (Vodou temple) is a place where followers gather to communicate with the spirits and, except if owned by a rich family or government officials, is so informal it may not be readily identified as a place of worship, even during a ceremony.[12] The cemetery as well as many crossroads are meaningful places of worship—the cemetery as repository of spirits and crossroads as points of access to the world of the invisible. Other places of religious importance include oceans, rivers, sites of pilgrimage, the parish church, fields, markets, compounds, and households.[13] Often, in a Vodou home the only recognizable religious items are images of saints and candles with a rosary. In other homes, where people may more openly show their devotion to the spirits, noticeable items could include an altar with Catholic saints and iconographies, rosaries, bottles, jars, rattles, perfumes, oils, dolls, and rags. This systematic absence of readily identifiable religious objects in designated sacred locations is understandable for two reasons: Vodou's continuous presence in all aspects of Haitian life and the fact that for so long Haitians had to practice their religion clandestinely. The lack of formal settings of worship reflects the persistence and adaptability of the religion (see plate 2).

Vodou in densely populated urban areas is called "temple" Vodou, where communal life revolves around the *hounfò, manbo* (priestesses), and *houngan* (priests). Though in most cases few characteristics distinguish these sites of worship, they remain the center of urban life where devotees recreate family left behind by migration and continue their quest for religious and moral values. Vodou temples are often located near churches, and it is not unusual for people to leave a Vodou ceremony in the morning and later attend a 4 o'clock Catholic mass in the afternoon. Traditionally, to be seen in church was protection against persecution and was perceived as a sign of being a "good" Christian, someone who honors both God and the saints, a practice that does not reduce respect within the Vodou community.

Although myths and rituals may differ from one *hounfò* to another as well as from one family to another, depending on the region, types of spirits served and invoked, style of worship, and issues specific to a given community, they also have much in common. Places of worship are not mutually exclusive, compartmentalized, and categorized. In a context where teaching takes place everywhere and where everything represents an opportunity for learning, written dogma and specific instructional materials are not necessary.[14] more simply, Haitians have not developed texts and doctrinal curricula for the same reason they have not built recognizable and elaborate temples: they do not need them because they have no use for them.

Teaching Methods and Instructional Strategies

What methods and strategies are used to transmit religious values, moral principles, and the Vodou worldview in Haitian communities? Educators no longer question the notion that teaching and learning extend beyond schools. However, the traditional conceptualization of education as occurring either in school or in the home fails, as Thomas La Belle says, to "recognize a middle ground of systematic teaching and learning."[15]

In Africa and among people of African descent, the transmission of values is part of traditional education inseparable from religious beliefs and practices, and a distinction between different forms of education has never existed as it has in the West. Indigenous African education encompasses the globality of human experience.[16] In Haiti, religious values and moral principles are not taught as separate subjects; they are still transmitted in an African style. Vodou is lived; life consists of religious experiences that become educational opportunities. Learning occurs through being involved with the Haitian religion and through living as a Vodou adept.

Education specialists might argue that this type of lifelong education is not specific to Haiti. However, in the West, learning is more compartmentalized; to learn about religion, children attend church Sunday school and discuss it at home or in school. Teaching about Haitian Vodou is not a type of instruction that simply supplements formal or nonformal education: it is *the* way of life. Propagation of the Vodou worldview occurs during ceremonies while interacting with the spirits or with other Vodou participants; in homes while fulfilling daily activities around family members; and in the larger community at work or while shopping. More than moral principles, the *Vodou* ethos is formed and informed by African cosmological understandings and American and Creole realities. Its soul is taught and learned by the sophisticated convergence of spoken language with action and aesthetics.

Teachers and Learners

In Vodou society, everyone takes the roles of teacher and learner in a process of exchanges and dialogues with family members, the community, and the spirits. Elders, parents, members of the extended family, neighbors, and priests and priestesses most often are teachers for the younger generations, though they can act as learners among their peers and the spirits. Senior members of the community may become learners, for example, when a young child carries a message from an elder or a spirit. Both teacher and learner must respect Vodou's nonhierarchization as well as its functionality. Having similar agendas, they achieve goals differently. Vodou's flexibility and limited directiveness "is not a system imposed from above, but one which pushes out from below. It is a thing of the family; a rich and complex inheritance from a man's own ancestors. It is not the priests of Vodoun who control and direct its course. They, like the lowest peasant, simply move about within it and make use of its resources."[17]

Vodou life is *movement* between people and between the living and departed; teaching and learning entail balancing commonalities and differences to create global harmony and peace.[18] These concepts dictate that teachers and learners play equally active roles in learning and teaching about the fluidity of the Vodou world and its ever-evolving cosmology. In that respect, Vodou's teaching approach is, in many ways, "learner centered," with "teachers" serving primarily as guides and facilitators. This democratic foundation makes Vodou quite a progressive system compared to other doctrinal world religions.

THE TEACHERS: THOSE WHO HAVE "KONESANS"

One who has *konesans* is typically a *teacher;* that is, a person who continuously participates in the propagation of the Vodou worldview and assists in clarifying choices for less-experienced individuals.[19] However, effective teachers perform more complicated tasks; have seniority, and their *konesans* is always coupled with "style." They are skilled at helping others balance their lives within the web of community relationships and restore equilibrium after disturbances in nature's harmony. All Vodou adepts can be teachers, but *houngan* and *mambo* hold specially designated teaching roles that involve sophisticated ministration and healing.

Though they do not wear recognizable garb and do not receive theological training, priests and priestesses are well respected and powerful members of society. Having undergone the highest level of initiation, *houngan* and *mambo* have leverage in the world of the spirits, a status that allows them to lead their community.[20] In Vodou, however, good leaders follow; good teachers listen, help participants choose wisely among different paths, and perform functions essential to the communal well-being. They keep balance through various rituals in which the skilled ritualizer is a powerful technician of the sacred who orchestrates the arrival of the spirits and solicits their intervention in human affairs. *Houngan* and *mambo* are teachers par excellence, not necessarily as moral exemplars but because, with assistance of the spirits, they help the community find cohesion and teach Vodou adepts how to avoid the source of moral decay: imbalance.[21]

Most Vodou teachers officiate exclusively in their own community, although a few have extended their ministrations outside Haiti.[22] They and other cosmopolitan Vodou practitioners believe that race and nationality should never be factors in deciding whether to include a person in ritualizing or in a Vodou family. In addition, many Haitian artists are important teachers, both locally and in the international community. Through paintings or iron-cast work, they teach about Black aesthetics and the Haitian world; the Vodou soul and the Haitian spirit are powerfully expressed in artwork where signs and shapes become a message.

Also influential teachers, *loas* harmonize specific aspects of life and serve as intermediaries between humans and the Supreme Being, *Bondye*. Although there is a distinct monotheism in Vodou, despite its henotheism and pantheon of divinities and ancestral spirits, God is not the focus of worship in a service; people typically pray to Bondye through the spirits. In turn, *Bondye* is not involved directly in devotees' daily existence or in their personal relations with the spirits. To create harmony and maintain equilibrium, female and male spirits are invoked and served with equal deference, each one presiding over a specific, often "gendered" realm of human affairs. The power of female *loas* represents an important lesson; in Vodou, women are priestesses, revered spirits, and fully participating members of their religious communities.

The spirits most often served, and consequently some of Vodou's most prominent teachers, include: Dambala, supreme, oldest, most respected, represented by a snake; Aida Wedo, his wife; Legba, the spirit of the crossroads who must be invoked to "open the gate" for the other *loas;* Ogu, who does not tolerate injustice and who controls *power;* Erzilie, representing sexuality, lesbianism, and motherhood; Azaka, the peasant, the worker, and the one who controls money; Baron Samedi and Gran Brigit, guardians of the cemeteries; and Gédé, the spirit of death and sexuality. Most of these divinities exhibit various personalities and characteristics depending on the names that they rake. For example, Ogu Badagri behaves quite differently from Ogu Ferraille, Erzilie Freda from Erzilie Jèrouge, and Gédé Nimbo from Gédé Loraille, although the family relationship remains.

Each *loa* is an archetype of a moral principle that he or she represents. Like humans, they are whole, with strengths and weaknesses. McCarthy Brown says it well: "Vodou spirits are larger than life but not other than life . . . The spirits talk with the faithful. They hug them, hold them, feed them, but also chastise them . . . The Vodou spirits are not models of the well-lived life; rather, they mirror the full range of possibilities inherent in the particular slice of life over which they preside. Failure to understand this had led observers to portray the Vodou spirits as demonic or even to conclude that Vodou is a religion without morality, a serious misconception."[23] From Vodou's holistic perspective derives the idea that spirits are not saints because they are good but because they are all-encompassing, mirroring human life. Though conflicts are manifestations of existing contradictions and disturbances in the web of human relations, "the point is not to make conflict go away, but to make it work for, rather than against life."[24] Vodou spirits are teachers of distinction not because they guide by rigid examples or indoctrination but because they heighten worshipers' vision of the world. Usually *loas* do not preach; rather, they show devotees how to see clearly. Through possession performances that highlight destructive and constructive aspects of particular situations, *loas* help participants explore choices. At times, spirits may appear disorganized or unfocused because they find it necessary to throw people off balance to help them find balance. Rarely off target, they always know the issues (sometimes before the parties involved).

THE LEARNERS: THE ENTIRE HAITIAN COMMUNITY

From its youngest members to its most acclaimed technicians of the sacred, all are lifelong learners in the Vodou faith. Adepts continuously struggle to balance their lives to follow a moral path. A good learner makes efforts appropriate to age and status to incorporate the spirit and worldview of Vodou in a harmonized existence during which interconnected and responsible relationships are maintained for the benefit of the group. Additionally, a good learner is receptive to the spirits, elders, or peers; is attentive to the aesthetic guiding every endeavor and encounter; and while mindful of content as well as style, always strives to stay in touch with both the inner self and the outside world.

Children learn informally by imitating adults and elders until behavior and rituals have become habitual, and young adults have incorporated traditional values into all their activities. Participation in Vodou family life creates opportunities for nonformal education outside the Haitian school system. Servitors of the spirits, in particular those who have *konesans,* use informal settings to teach preplanned curricular items to those coming of age. With age come increased privileges and additional responsibilities. Young people participate rather frequently in Vodou rituals, guide younger children, show increased respect for elders, develop their sense of humanism, and learn to emphasize the common good over individual satisfactions. They are expected to incorporate Haitian secular and religious beliefs in a sustained effort to live a relevant and moral existence and to maintain equilibrium within their community.

The four levels of Vodou initiation (the specific steps taken to confer "ascending degrees of control" to humans in their relationship with the spirits), with the highest of these levels being the actual rising to the status of priesthood, fit into this category of nonformal education. Specific training is also undergone by other functionaries of a *hounfò,* such as the *laplace* and the *hounsi* who go through long and formal apprenticeship with the head of the temples. Sustained and organized efforts are made during each stage of initiation to teach about particular rituals and reinforce character. Initiation is a complex, sophisticated, highly ritualistic and sometimes costly process.[25] Katherine Dunham made these revelations:

> We began the ritual of the crossed and recrossed handclasp, the bow with the knees flexed, turn under arm [those] of highest protocol guiding the other. Then, the turn to all four directions of the compass, hand gripped tightly in hand, with sacred words spoken in each direction, the approach to the altar, the recognition of each grade of protocol by obeisance and work . . . It was up to my instructors to decide what to do, and I followed them, asking no questions . . . We danced, not as people in the houngfor, with the stress of possession or escapism of hypnosis or for catharsis, but as I imagine dance when it must have been executed when body and being were more united, when form and flow and personal ecstasy became an exaltation of a superior state of things, not necessarily a ritual to any one superior being.[26]

Vodou cosmology emphasizes uniformity, conformity, group cohesion, and support for one another. Initiation ceremonies are a primary conveyor of this worldview, and initiates are rid of their will and desire to impose their ego on others. They are taught to liberate themselves from obstacles that may hinder spiritual development, representing the death of the old self. During days of seclusion, they become one with all other living creatures as well as with the four forces of nature (air, fire, water, and earth). One is forced to regress into infancy and childhood, to be brought back through rituals designed to overcome fear, pain, and selfishness to a new maturity that originates from a nonindividualistic collective consciousness. An initiate explains some of the feelings accompanying the initiation process: "It was hard to become a child again, to let go of being in charge of myself, to give the care of myself over to another. Most difficult was letting go of words, of the appearance of control . . . I bit my tongue to stop the *How?* and *When?* and *Why?* . . . Entering the chamber was like dying . . . The drums were pounding, as they had been for hours . . . Seven times I raised my hand, and then darkness . . . I was thrown off balance in order to learn to find balance . . . Ever so briefly, I died."[27] The forces of life and death are reckoned with, the limits of knowledge and power are challenged, and truth and faith are revalorized through the initiation process.

Curriculum Content and "Style"

Assessing learners' mastery of Vodou cosmology and corresponding moral path is not accomplished through a formal evaluation model. Instead, such techniques as observation, verbal exchange, reports from elders, communication from the spirits, and performance measure the learning experiences of Vodou participants as well as evaluate individual proficiency regarding style and curriculum content. Teachers do not compare students to each other, rank them, or decide who will continue their "course of studies." In Vodou all are welcome to learn, though some may take longer than others in their journey to become balanced Vodou adepts. Each student is provided with suitable activities in the home and in the larger Vodou family where a collective self is developed through elision of the individual self.

A nonwritten criterion-referenced measure is used to assess competence in a particular content area; each student is evaluated by personal progress, not against others. The knowledge and skills of each member of the Vodou family are continuously assessed to maximize the availability of daily learning experiences, arrange for consequential encounters between humans and deities, identify and strengthen patterns of relationships, stress the significance of particular events and behavior, impose the right course of sanction when necessary, and, at all times, suggest choices of greatest benefit for each learner in accordance and harmony with spirit volition. Vodou teachers evaluate how much each learner has assimilated Vodou's cosmology and philosophy and become proficient at rituals and ritualizing. Adequate performance is viewed in terms of acquiring the understanding and abilities necessary to live a relevant and "equilibrated" existence, and competence is evaluated on the basis of style and *konesans* of the Vodou worldview as shaped by the African ethos.

STYLE

Style refers to the general expressions used by each participant in rituals, oral/social performances, and daily life. Though the essence of Vodou does not change, servitors of the *loas* base individual religious expressions on the customs of each family and use variants reflecting personal aesthetics. These styles become an adept's own voice through which is revealed the beauty of the social and spiritual message as lived by each person who "dances" with the spirits. Everyone dances in an individual, everlasting quest to find a rhythm and balance deeply rooted in the inner self and which is the only means to live a moral and ethical life. The mastery of various styles in rituals and ritualizing and an artistically balanced life, combining interdependent and interconnected words and actions, lead to increasingly paramount roles in the Vodou family. Confidence, liveliness, relevancy, flexibility, endurance, musicality, and rhythm are appraised for their usefulness as parameters enhancing religious beliefs, rituals, experiences, and healing.

"KONESANS" OF THE VODOU WORLDVIEW

Konesans is both a means and an end; it signifies knowledge and wisdom but also implies their appreciation, assimilation, and application in daily life. By striving to live according to Vodou principles, adepts develop their own *konesans* which represents a code of ethics—though not a rigid or written one. Assessing *konesans* is appraising participants' mastery of Vodou's substance, content, meaning, purpose, and practices in an aesthetically engaging manner as well as evaluating whether members of the Vodou family are sufficiently immersed in the values emanating from the African ethos. One's holistic conception of life, humanism, centrality of communality; respect for elders; beneficence; forbearance; forgiveness; and sense of justice guide adepts' morals and values in daily life and in interactions with others.[28] Monitoring learners' progress is important. However, evaluation is always goal oriented: one assesses in order to intervene, to foster the development of both ritual knowledge and spiritual insight among all Vodou congregants, and always in an artistically balanced manner. But very little reappraisal of the belief system itself is ever conducted. Vodou's teachings are never questioned or challenged in a world where the Haitian national religion represents the only source of unity, strength, and hope.

Conclusion

Vodou's comprehensive and diffuse influence on Haitian society is key to understanding how this religion's worldview is passed from one generation to the next. To understand history, politics, literature, art, institutions, social systems, and racial and cultural conflicts, one must grasp how religion has shaped the course of the human story over time in almost every culture and country. For instance, how can one understand the conflicts in the Middle East, in Bosnia, or in the Sudan without studying the culture and religion of the people? In the case of Haiti, democracy will not prevail until both the Haitian elite and international forces learn to respect the Haitian mass culture with its traditional African values and modes of expressions fashioned within its indigenous Caribbean mold. No positive identification with the real demands of the people's economic and political existence will be possible as long as their cultural identity is still in question.[29] A critical study of the Vodou religion might well raise the consciousness of an oppressed people who have been subjugated by a dominant Western culture with an antithetic individualistic ethos that continues to be valued and reinforced by the formal school system. Clearly, Vodou, with its powerful communal message and its effective teaching methods, could have a lot to offer that system. In its affirmation of an African ethos and its efforts to sustain humanism and communality among its practitioners, Vodou is an expression of national consciousness and one of the few authentic manifestations and cultural forces plausibly capable of mending the loose seams of Haitian history, contemporary politics, and the educational system. In this respect, Vodou's teachings have the potential not only to modify attitudes and behaviors, values, and lifestyles but also to create a more egalitarian society.[30]

I appeal for a nonindoctrinating study, on a global scale, of comparative religion along with a rigorous examination of secular thinking in schools, not only because of the political and historical importance of religions but also because these living traditions enhance our understanding of the meaning of diversity in an increasingly complex world.[31] Vodou—its worlds seen and unseen—offers a wealth of lessons that serve as both mirror which reflects and clarifies the present and map tracing humanistic and educational directions for the future.

Notes

I gratefully acknowledge the inspiration of Charles H. Long, Karen McCarthy Brown, and Patrick Bellegarde-Smith whose works have shaped my vision of Haitian Vodou. I also wish to thank Mathew Zachariah, R. Murray Thomas, and Richard Turner for their useful comments. This chapter was originally published in *Comparative and International Society,* vol. 40 (August 1996), pp. 194–280. © 1996 by the Comparative and International Education Society. All rights reserved.

1. Ernest Boyer, "Teaching Religion in the Public Schools and Elsewhere," *Journal of the Academy of Religion* 60, no. 3 (Fall 1992): 515, 524.

2. *Vodou,* of Dahomean origin and derived from the Fon word for "God" or "Spirit" is the term most commonly used by Haitian scholars to refer to the Haitian religion. *Vaudou, Vodun,* or *Vodoun* are other accepted spellings. The Euro-American creation, "Voodoo," along with its *associated* misrepresentations, is *inappropriate* and is not used here.

3. This regrouping around a common past and ideal has consistently played a key role in Haitian political life and has fueled a number of mass movements culminating eventually in the war for independence and, much later, in the overthrow of the Duvalier dictatorship in 1986.

4. These views are presented not only in the tabloid press and Hollywood movies but also in magazines and scholarly publications. For example, William B. Seabrook's notoriously distasteful book *L'ile magique: Les mystéres du Vaudou* (Paris: J'ai Lu, 1971), translated from his 1929 *The Magic Island* (New York: Harcourt Brace & Co.), continues to be widely influential. Another such book is *The Serpent and the Rainbow* (New York: Warner, 1985) by Harvard ethnobiologist Wade Davis. Even supposedly neutral sources are plagued by enthnocentrism and racism, as is the case with the 1993 *Webster's* derogatory definition of Vodou: "A primitive religion of West African origin, found among Haitian and West Indian Negroes and the Negroes of the southern United States, characterized by belief in sorcery and the use of charms, fetishes, witchcraft" (*New Illustrated Webster's Dictionary of the English Language* [1993]).

5. Patrick Bellegarde-Smith, *Haiti: The Breached Citadel* (Boulder, Colo.: Westview Press, 1990), 12.

6. Karen McCarthy Brown, *Mama Lola: A Vodou Priestess in Brooklyn* (Berkeley: University of California Press, 1991), 98.

7. Practitioners of Vodou do not say they are followers or adepts of the religion; they instead say that they "serve the spirits"—which is a revealing statement about the nature of the religion, the importance of withdrawing the self and serving others, and about the spiritual connections existing between human beings, their ancestors, and their Gods. Similarly, a Vodou ceremony is called a "service" because one of the goals of the gatherings is to serve the living, the ancestral spirits and God, the ultimate master. The services represent an opportunity for the *loas* to partake in the life of the Vodou family.

8. For example, all Haitians, unless they are Protestant, receive in the course of their lives a number of Catholic sacraments although they may not regularly attend church. All are typically baptized, many receive the first communion, some get married in the church, and all go through some type of Catholic funeral rites—these being particularly important for Vodou adepts who engage in frequent interactions with the spirits and the departed.

9. Glenn R. Smucker, "The Social Character of Religion in Rural Haiti," in *Haiti, Today and Tomorrow: An Interdisciplinary Study* (Washington, D.C.: University Press of America, 1984), 43.

10. In particular, Leslie G. Desmangles, in *The Faces of the Gods: Vodou and Catholicism in Haiti* (Chapel Hill: University of North Carolina Press, 1992), and other authors before him have documented Haitians' joint involvement with Vodou and Catholicism. Similar research is needed on Protestantism, especially to determine the extent to which the "converted" truly abandon their ancestral religion.

11. A residential area, *Lakou,* means "yard," evoking the idea of many large extended families sharing a common compound and yard and representing a residual structure of the African village.

12. The *hounfò* is made of very simple material. not completely enclosed, sometimes with a dirt floor. and sparse furnishings—except a few chairs, drums, flags, and pictures.

13. Haitians believe that some people spend time "under water," down in Ginen (a Haitian appellation for Africa) as part of their initiation as priests and priestesses. This "inexpensive" type of initiation, unlike the more formal ones that may be somewhat costly, is considered a special gift. Mathilda Beauvoir, who officiates primarily in Paris, may well be the most renowned *an ba dlo* (underwater) initiate. See Harold Courlander, *The Drum and the Hoe: Life and Lore of the Haitian People* (Berkeley: University of California Press, 1973), 19.

14. Other reasons include, by order of importance: 1) the essence of the Vodou worldview itself; 2) the orality that characterizes Haitian culture; 3) until recently, the lack of standardized Creole spelling; 4) the unavailability of writers to produce such documents; and 5) a clear lack of funding and resources to engage in such an activity.

15. Thomas La Belle, "An Introduction to the Nonformal Education of Children and Youth," *Comparative Education Review* 25, no. 3 (1981): 313–329.

16. Elleni Telda, "Indigenous African Education as a Means for Understanding the Fullness of Life: Amara Traditional Education," *Journal of Black Studies* 23, no. 1 (Fall 1992): 7; John S. Mbiti, *African Religions and Philosophy* (New York: Praeger, 1969).

17. Harold Courlander, *Haiti Singing* (New York: Cooper Square Publishers, 1973), 7.

18. *Movement* refers to complex interactions among people and with the spirits reflecting various roles and functions. In Haitian Creole, balance (*balanse*) means to bring about equilibrium, to harmonize; it implies metaphysical elements not rendered by the English word "balance."

19. *Konesans* means knowledge, but the Creole word is stronger than its English counterpart in that it encompasses the notions of experience mixed with wisdom, usually acquired with age. Typically, elders, *houngan* and *mambo,* the departed, and ancestors have much *konesans.*

20. Especially during the Duvalier era, many such religious "leaders" were also members of the government.

21. Karen McCarthy Brown, "Alourdes: A Case Study of Moral Leadership in Haitian Vodou," in *Saints and Virtues,* ed. John Stratton Hawley (Berkeley: University of California Press, 1987), 167.

22. Two examples are Mathilda Beauvoir, who officiates in Paris, and Mama Lola in Brooklyn. Mama Lola's reputation goes further than the boundaries of the Haitian community. Though many other technicians of the Vodou religion share her worldly approach, the international effect of her ministrations remains unusual. See Brown, *Mama Lola.*

23. Brown, *Mama Lola,* 6.

24. Brown, "Alourdes: A Case Study," 166.

25. For more details on Vodou Initiation, see Karen McCarthy Brown, "Plenty Confidence in Myself: The Initiation of a White Woman Scholar into Haitian Vodou," *Journal of Femi-*

nist Studies in Religion 3, no. 1 (Spring 1987): 67–76; and Katherine Dunham, *Island Possessed* (Garden City, N.Y.: Doubleday, 1969; reprint, Chicago: University of Chicago Press, 1994).

26. Dunham, *Island Possessed,* 108–109 (page citations are to the reprint edition).

27. Brown, "Plenty Confidence," 73–75. Brown wrote that although one is not allowed to reveal the secrets of Vodou initiation, she was permitted to write about her reactions to the process. She cautioned, however, not to "overinterpret" her "metaphoric speech" (72).

28. See Peter J. Paris's model of "virtue theory" in *The Spirituality of African Peoples: The Search for a Common Moral Discourse* (Minneapolis: Fortress, 1995).

29. See the important work of Bellegarde-Smith (n. 5 above), where this argument is fully developed.

30. For a study of culture as political weapon, see the work of Cynthia Hamilton: "A Way of Seeing: Culture as Political Expression," *Journal of Black Studies* 22, no. 3 (March 1992): 429–443.

31. See Warren A. Nord, "Public Schools Should Teach Religious Studies," in *Education in America: Opposing Viewpoints,* ed. Charles Cozic (San Diego, Calif.: Greenhaven, 1992), 189–196.

5

Vodun, Music, and Society in Haiti: Affirmation and Identity

GERDÈS FLEURANT

The World Council of Churches officially "recognized" Vodun in 1983. Vodun is perhaps the least understood of all non-Western forms of worship. In the United States, terms such as "voodoo economics," "voodoo politics," or "voodoo methodology" are commonly used to denote any schemes that are "devilish" and deemed nonsensical. Because Vodun, a sociocultural religious phenomenon that is intimately linked to the life and the fate of the Haitian people, a people which has affirmed itself and maintained its identity over the past two centuries in the face of the greatest odds, has been so maligned, it seemed important as well as significant that Haitian scholars undertake a series of studies grounded in the social, political, cultural, and economic realities of the country to shed some light on this obscured aspect of Haitian culture.

Since the publication of Moreau de Saint-Méry's *Description Topographique de L'Isle de Saint-Domingue* in 1797, Vodun has been the object of studies ranging from the journalistic and popular to the scientific.[1] The recent proliferation of such publications prompted VèVè A. Clark and this author to devise the *"bosal, kanzo, pridèzye"* model, which emerged from the nomenclature of Vodun, to help evaluate the published literature.[2] Our model stems from Dunham's observation of Vodun degrees of initiation.[3] We found that the majority of works on Vodun falls in the *bosal* category, which corresponds to the least-informed degree of knowledge about the religion. Only a few works fall into the more-informed categories of *kanzo* and *pridèzye*. It is encouraging, however, that academe has recognized the value of the reflexive approach, which attempts to study a culture from an insider's view and on its own terms.[4] Consequently, because of their initiation into Vodun (moving from the *bosal* to *kanzo* or *pridèzye*), researchers who are practitioners now have access to more-accurate data and are beginning to report more sensibly on that cultural practice. This development has made it possible to reach a higher level of understanding of Vodun's belief structure and its artistic dimensions, particularly the music that concerns us in this chapter. This essay links Vodun music to issues of self-affirmation and collective identity in the context of Haitian culture.[5]

The primary unit of Vodun social organization is the *lakou* (compound), an extended family and socioeconomic system whose center is the *ounfò* (temple), to which is attached the *peristyle* (the public dancing space). Vodun, a danced religion, acknowledges the unity of the universe in the continuity of Bondye, or God; the Lwa, or mediating spiritual entities; humans; animals; plants; and minerals. Vodun is also a family religion in the sense that its teachings, belief system, and rituals are transmitted mainly through the structure of the family. It has a sacerdotal hierarchy comprised of the *oungan* (male) and the *manbo* (female) and their assistants, the *laplas* (sword bearer), *ounsi kanzo* (spouses of the spirits), *oungenikon* (chorus leader), and *ountò* (drummers). In the absence of priests, the head of the family, much like a traditional paterfamilias, conducts the service. Most ceremonies take place in the *peristyle*, whose *potomitan* (center post) is believed to incarnate ancestral and spiritual forces of family and community. The people dance around the *potomitan,* which is the point of genesis of essential segments of the ritual process. The religion consists of many rites or styles of worship such as Rada, Kongo, Nago, Petwo, Ibo, and Makanda, or Bizango. But in actual practice, Haitian Vodun is divided into two major rites: the Rada, whose music and structure are retained quite faithfully from the Fon/Ewe and Yoruba of Dahomey and Nigeria, and the Petwo, which might be called Kongo-Petwo, for it retains syncretic elements from the Kongo/Angola region that were redefined in the crucible of the colonial plantation system of Saint Domingue, presently Haiti. Contrary to what was believed in the past, the division between Rada and Kongo-Petwo is not so rigid, for Vodun results from the fusion of cultural practices of what the Haitians call the 21 (or 101) nations/African ethnic groups. Many Lwa, known as "*an de zo,*" or "in two substances," are worshipped in both the Rada and Kongo-Petwo cults.[6]

According to Vodun beliefs, Bondye (called Mawu-Lisa among the Fon or Olorun among the Yoruba) created the universe, the Lwa, human beings, and the animal, vegetal, and mineral worlds. After creating the world, Bondye retired far into the sky and left the management of all earthly matters to the Lwa, who have dominion over natural elements such as fire, water, wind, trees, and plants, including the secrets of the medicinal properties of these elements and illnesses and their cures—in sum, all actions, sentiments, and virtues.[7] In the Vodun belief system, one finds a series of spiritual entities, who are often synchronized with Roman Catholic saints in their varied specializations that enhance human existence. For example, Legba, the opener of the cosmic gate, must be invoked at the beginning of all undertakings; Azaka rules over agriculture; Erzuli's domain is love; and Ogou, the entity of defense, stands on guard. This knowledge and its teachings are preserved in songs and dances that are also reminders of the attributes of the Lwa. The following songs to Legba, Kouzen Zaka, Erzuli, and Ogoun introduce some of the characteristics of those Lwa:

Legba lan baryè a	Legba at the cosmic gate
Se ou ki pote drapo	You are the flag bearer
Se ou ka pare solèy	You will prepare the way
Pou Lwa yo	For the Lwa
Bonjou Kouzen (Zaka)	Good morning Cousin
Bonjou Kouzin-o	Hello my (female) Cousin

O kou yo wem' nan	I may be humble and poor
Konsa mwen danjere	But I am still a proud man
Ala yon bel fanm	What a beautiful woman
Se Erzuli	That Erzuli is
Erzuli map' fè w oun kado	I will give you a present
Avan ou ale, Abobo	Before you leave
Ogoun-o, nèg gè	Ogoun-o, man of war
Kanno tire	They fired the cannon at us
Nou pa pran yo	We didn't get hurt

As shown here, Vodun is a "practical" religion where relations between humans and spirits are maintained through exchanges and the mutual reinforcement of energies and where solutions to concrete problems are devised according to means established long ago through an ancestral tradition passed down orally. The Vodunist serves the Lwa, who come to their aid in difficult times, and the Lwa rely on the *sèvitè* to help them meet their need to partake in human actions, such as dancing and feasting (see plate 3). Music and dance are therefore central elements in Vodun.[8] Through these media, the community calls the Lwa, who come to participate in the feast offered in their honor; the religious service consists of preparing the Lwa's favorite ritual foods in exchange for their guidance. In this regard, the *oungenikon* (chorus leader) and the *ountò* (drummers) fulfill important functions; they are chosen for their knowledge of ritual matters as well as for their artistry.

The Music of Vodun

The pioneering works of Harold Courlander made sophisticated analyses that opened the way for today's scholarship. He inspired ethnomusicologist M. Kolinski, who in 1980 contributed an article on the music of Haiti for the *Grove Dictionary of Music.* Subsequently Claude Dauphin, Gerdès Fleurant, Lois Wilcken, David Yih, and Elizabeth McAlister followed in his footsteps by contributing important studies which advanced our understanding of the music of Haitian Vodun.[9]

Drumming, singing, and dancing are the main components of the music of Vodun. Haitian scholars Lamartinière Honorat and Jean Fouchard have penned works on the ritual dance and on *méringue,* Haiti's national popular dance music.[10] Katherine Dunham and Lavinia Williams-Yarborough have also published useful works on dance. The works of Africanist musicologists who studied the organizing principles of African music must also be mentioned. The turning point occurred with a shift in the discipline of ethnomusicology from "armchair" scholarship to fieldwork and with the rise of the concept of "bi-musicality."[11] Ethnomusicologists became convinced of the need for fluency in two musical cultures and the need perhaps to learn to perform the music one was studying. The leaders in these new developments were A. M. Jones, J. H. Kwabena Nketia, Hewitt

Pantaleoni, David Lawrence Locke, and John Miller Chernoff. Their work allowed us to decode the principles of African music such as the guiding role of the bell, the two-against-three rhythmic structure, cyclicality, call and response, and functionality. All this helped open the way for an understanding of the logic of Haitian Vodun music.

The music, which follows the logic of African music, not only accompanies the ritual but is essential to most phases of the ceremony. There are songs and special rhythms for each group of Lwa; songs for the human participants in the service such as *oungan, manbo, oungenikon, laplas, ounsi kanzo,* and *ountò*; and songs for sacred objects such as the *drapo* (flag), *govi* (earthen jar), *zen* (fire pot), *dife* (fire), *kolye* (necklaces), *tanbou* (drum), and *vèvè* (ritual drawing). Here is one example of a song for *oungan* and *ounsi.*

Ounsi la yo	My dear Ounsi
Kouman nou ye?	How are we doing?
Kote oungan nou	Here is your *oungan*
Kap' simen farin atè	Drawing the *vèvè*
Ounsi la yo	My dear Ounsi
Kouman nou ye?	How are we doing?

The music played for the Rada Lwa is the *yanvalou, mayi,* and *zepòl,* or *yanvalou debout.* Among the Lwa, the Marasa are saluted with the beat "*twa rigol*" and not the "*pas rigole,*" as it has been called in some of the literature. Kouzen Zaka takes the *dyouba/matinik* and Ogoun takes the *nago grankou, nago cho* (or *yanvalou debout*), and *mazoun.* The Lwa of the Gédé family, entities of life and death, are found in both rites. This is true for several other Lwas that dance to the music of *banda* or *mazoun.*

In Bòpo, for example, a village located some ten miles north of Port-au-Prince, five major Kongo-Petwo Lwa are worshipped. They dance to the rhythms of *boumba, kita sèch,* and *kita mouye.* However, the late Philoclès Rosenbère, a.k.a. Coyote, one of the last authentic *ountò,* or master drummers, contended that there is no such thing as the two rhythms *kita sèch* or *kita mouye.* There is only one *kita* rhythm, he insisted, which is played to salute all the Lwa in the Kongo-Petwo category. For him the music of Kongo-Petwo consisted of *boumba* and *kita.* In the Artibonite Valley, in the *lakou* of Nan Soukri, near the city of Gonaïves, where Haitian Independence was proclaimed in 1804—and where the Vodun tradition has been maintained faithfully—only the Kongo rite is observed. Its music is in many respects identical to that of Petwo, a fact which led me—after a conversation with Aboudja,[12] a Vodun leader and a promoter of the "root music" (*rasin*) movement—to conclude that Petwo should be called Kongo-Petwo.

In both Rada and Kongo-Petwo drumming ensembles, a special off-beat phrasing occurs at certain moments during the performance. This is the *kase* (break), whose main function is not only to add *élégance* to the music but also to facilitate trance or possession or a better epiphany—the coming of the Lwa. Epiphany is considered the climax of the ceremony, for "immanence"—God in us and with us—

is central to Vodun. Thus, the *kase* enhances the structure of the musical performance by breaking the fluidity of the cyclical development characteristic of a Vodun piece, a movement that is aesthetically generated as well as spiritually grounded.

Meaning of the Songs

Vodun songs are interpreted at two levels, the manifest and latent, or the surface and deep levels.[13] Songs of the Lwa, or songs uttered by a person in trance and songs which reveal the attributes of the Lwa, can be interpreted at even deeper levels, depending on the interpreter's degree of *konesans,* or esoteric knowledge about ritual matters. Some songs are in ancient Dahomean languages, like Fon, Mahi, or Yoruba, generically called *langaj.* They may contain words from other African tongues as well. Others are partly in *langaj* and partly in Haitian (Kreyòl). Songs sung entirely in Haitian may have a hidden meaning, known as *pwen,* or the "point,"[14] where the reference may be to sacred/ritual matters, sociohistorical issues, community sanctions, or downright plain gossip. For example, the song

Oungan pa manke	*Oungan* are numerous
An efè, se bon ki ra-e	The good ones are few
O Legwa-e	O Legwa-e

refers to an *oungan's* ability and willingness to serve the community and maintain the dignity of the faith. This song also signals that the presence of a particular *oungan* who may have violated the code of ethics may be unwelcome at a ceremony.

Songs about the *drapo* (flag), *vèvè* (ritual symbols drawn on the ground with flour, corn powder, ground coffee, or cinder ash), the *govi* (an earthen jar containing ritual ingredients), *kolye* (necklaces), *zen* (pots made of either ceramic or iron used for boiling herbs and other ritual objects), and *bwapen* (pine wicker) are usually straightforward and mean just what is being sung. I call them songs of action/direction, for they indicate an impending action or an action in progress. For example:

Aleksina wa antre la ounfò-a	Aleksina, go in the *ounfò,*
Ou a wè yon kolye vèvè	You'll see a ritual necklace
Ou a pran potel ban mwen	Take it, bring it to me
Aleksina ankò mwen malere	Aleksina, is it because I'm poor?

This song refers to both the action indicated and the *pwen* (the "point") about the status of the person making the request. The emphasis here is on communication, learning by doing, the power of observation, and the ability to grasp figurative language and maximize the use of one's senses. The apprehension of the person's total environment—material and spiritual—seems to be the aim expressed in this song here. The point, "because I am poor," speaks specifically to the socioeconomic and historical conditions of Haiti's peasant class and subproletariat.

Some rhythms and dances symbolize action, either action that is impending or action that is in progress. The *yanvalou* is a prayer, an invitation, a dance of body purification in keeping with the African holistic principle of body and soul as one. The African conception of time (past, present, and future) as one is symbolized in the music/dance *twa rigol* (which is danced for the Lwa Marasa, or the Twins entity), whose beats appear in groups of three. The reference here is to the three healing leaves, three healing roots, three lines of descent, three moments of time/existence, and the enduring nature of the family (mother, father, child) as the guarantor of the human race. The music reflects and symbolizes the drama of human existence as it unfolds on the African continent and its diaspora. Despite the great depth of the symbolic meaning of the music and dance, care is taken to keep the ritual songs and dances simple in order to facilitate collective participation, for an overriding principle in African life, as in Haitian life, is inclusion. The restorative function of participation has always been recognized in Haitian traditional circles. A patient who is brought to the *peristyle,* the public space of the Vodun temple, for treatment is invited to participate in his/her own cure by learning the songs and dances when he or she is well enough to do so. Traditional African society, the Vodun community, and the *lakou* are in essence democratic. Simplicity of action and word is highly prized in an effort to be inclusive. Everyone participates; everyone is healed. In this sense, the conception of the universe in Vodun circles is communalistic and what I call *humanocentric,* for the person, regardless of ethnicity or gender, is welcomed to participate fully in the spiritual and community encounter with the Lwa.[15]

The songs and dances contain the wisdom of a community facing severe stress both internally and externally, domestically and abroad. A Haitian saying goes as follows, "*fò w konn viv, pou viv lan lakou malviv,*" meaning that one has to be diplomatic to get along in a community under stress. This is particularly true of the Haitian situation today. The Lwa taught the people how to navigate their way through the turbulent waters of national and international politics from the time of the revolutionary war (1791–1803) to the New World Order of the 1990s; people do not hesitate to take to the high seas in search of a new day, new opportunities for survival, away from repressive conditions at home. Some of that wisdom and determination to survive is summarized in the following song:

Si se pate bon Ginen sa-a	If it weren't for the Lwa
Nou tout ta peri deja-e	We would have all perished
M'di gras papa Ginen	Have mercy, Papa Ginen
M'di gras manman Ginen	Have mercy, Manman Ginen
Si se pate bon Ginen sa-a	If it weren't for the Lwa
Nou tout ta peri deja-e	We would have all perished.

The Vodun orchestra, as in most West African orchestras, consists of an ensemble of bells, rattles, and three conic drums that accompanies a chorus of singers and dancers. There is some variation in the instruments used in the Rada and Petwo rites; they are made of different materials and are played differently.

The Rada drums are named according to their size and function. The smallest, called *boula,* is played with two sticks in a continuous and regular pattern that produces a high pitch. The middle-sized drum, the *segon,* also played with two sticks, one straight and the other curved like a half-moon, provides the cyclical patterns to which the participants in a ceremony dance. The largest drum, the *manman,* played with one bare hand and a hammer-shaped stick, punctuates and choreographs the dance movements. Rada drums are made with hard wood such as mahogany or oak and are covered with cowhide attached to the drumhead by means of pegs inserted on the side of the instrument. Cowhide is strong enough to withstand the heavy blows of the stick players. In the Kongo-Petwo rite, three conic drums are used equally. They are about the same size as the Rada instruments and are made of soft wood such as pine. Because these drums are played with bare hands rather than sticks, it is possible to use softer wood and a softer skin to cover the head. Goatskin is used to cover them, and they are attached to the drumhead by means of laces. They are often used in procession-like rituals, such as Mardi Gras and a parallel rural festival held in the spring, the *rara,* which involves carrying the drums around. Technically, two drums form the core of the Kongo-Petwo ensemble, but a third, and the smallest, is often added to lend color to the music. The pattern played with two sticks on this drum is called *kata* or *katabou,* an onomatopoeia which refers to the sound that it produces—a regular, continuous sound in the high register. The middle-sized drum, the *ti baka,* or *gwonde,* a name which also refers to the low roar it produces when played, sounds in the middle register. The patterns played on the largest drum, the *gwo baka,* are variations that punctuate the general choreography. In both the Rada and the Kongo-Petwo rites, bells and rattles are used. The *ogan* (bells) provide the steady beat that guides the music, and the *ason* (sacred rattle used by priests) for Rada and *tcha-tcha* (rattles) for Kongo-Petwo are played in counterrhythms with the other instruments.

The Kongo-Petwo rite, whose origin is African, evolved in the crucible of the plantation slavery system in Saint Domingue. In the literature on Vodun, the Kongo-Petwo rite, simply referred to as Petwo, is often seen as the negative or even the evil side of Rada. To many, Petwo is considered an aggressive practice, a set of powerful "recipes" that Haitians use against their enemies. Some say that if such practices exist, they are a result of the brutality of Haitian history. From the colonial period to the time of contemporary dictatorships, Haitians had to devise ways, they contend, to deal with the abject conditions the people had been enduring for the past three centuries. This is why, it seems, that the music of Petwo reflects the rage of the oppressed. While there is an element of truth in such an assertion, the record needs to be rectified.

First, the rite should be called Kongo-Petwo, as I have called it here, for it evolved over the years, like its counterparts Nago, Ibo, or Rada, absorbing a variety of minor rites in the passage from Central Africa to the Americas. As mentioned earlier, Vodun, the generic term used for all the traditional religious practices retained from all Africa, encompasses the rituals of "101 *nanchon*" (nations), or ethnic groups. Thus, none of the rites alone could be a typical product of the new milieux without transformation. They are grounded in African practices that have been reconstituted to meet the people's needs to survive. The division of Vo-dun rituals into categories such as Rada, Nago, Kongo, Ibo, and Petwo is more a matter of conceptual convenience than one of rigid distinction. Second, as Milo Rigaud, one of the most perceptive practitioners and analysts of Haitian Vodun, observed, "It is useless to try to separate the Kongo rite from the Anmine, the Anmine rite from the Petro, the Petro rite from the Rada or the Nago. Between these 'rites' or 'nations of Lwa,' there is rather some practical difference in the manner in which the magical science is applied, for nothing scientific could be subtracted from those great fundamental Lwa."[16] Finally, the fact the Petwo rite was reconstituted from the major elements of a variety of Kongo practices, which has already been well documented, justifies joining the two terms in expressing the ritual and musical realities of this aspect of Haitian Vodun.[17]

The songs of the Kongo-Petwo rite are among some of the most assertive of the Vodun repertoire. Some writers (Courlander, Deren, Dunham, and Métraux, for example) use terms such as "aggressive" and "evil magic" to characterize the tenor of this rite; these characterizations are accepted as "fact" in much of the lit-erature on Haitian Vodun. I offer an alternative explanation, which emerges from my research and practice of Vodun. The songs of Kongo-Petwo refer to the many trials and tribulations of the African in exile. They speak of the mistrust which existed among the captive workers on the plantations of Saint Domingue. They also mention the need for secrecy and swift action as the core of the liberation process. The divide-and-conquer tactic of the plantation owners that drove a wedge between different ethnic/linguistic groups by favoring some rather than others was a factor in the behavior of the Africans in captivity. Yet people forged bonds of solidarity as Maroons in establishing underground trails that led into the mountains, where they reproduced their social and political organization, at the center of which was the religious practice of Vodun. The plantation workers must have realized that their salvation resided in a strategic unity, a feat achieved in the face of brutal oppression. Hence, the songs of the Kongo-Petwo rite, to an extent, reflect the historical complexities of the plantation system and the im-peratives of the struggle for liberation from slavery. The songs of the Kongo-Petwo rite have their roots in the social organization of the Maroon societies, the pre-cursors of the *bizango*, the secret societies of present-day Haiti. Their roots also lie in the Bwa Kayiman (Bois-Caïman) ceremony of August 14, 1791, a starting point in the struggle which led to the Independence of Haiti in 1804.

Independence brought relief from slavery but did not translate into liberation from class oppression, for the Westernized literate minority, consisting of both blacks and mulattos, arrogated for themselves the spoils of the war for Indepen-dence. The songs of Kongo-Petwo reflect this class and status differentiation of post-Independence Haiti. To describe this rite solely in terms of aggression or a pro-pensity toward evil, as is done to this day in most writings on Vodun, is to miss an important dimension of the sociohistorical context of Haitian life. Let us consider some songs of Kongo-Petwo taken from fieldwork done in Bòpo and Arcahaie:

Legwa o, Legwa e	Legwa o, Legwa e
Legwa lan baryè e	Legwa at the gate
Papa Legwa Papa	Papa Legwa Papa
Na veye zo nou	You watch out for us
Legwa Kalfou Legwa	Legwa of the Crossroads
Lan baryè e	You stand at the gate

Legwa of the Crossroads not only opens the cosmic gate but also stands guard at the gate to protect the servants of the Lwa. The crucial point here is "*na veye zo nou*," a Haitian Creole idiom which means that a person should look after his/her welfare, both physical and spiritual. A more literal translation of this expression reads "we will watch over our bones/body." The "we" refers to the dialectical conception of the body and soul (the person and the Lwa) as one. The next two songs refer to the socioeconomic context of Haiti and show the little guy, the poor, the peasant in his/her everyday struggle with an oppressive structure:

Mwen di de o	I say two
Mwen di de o jiska twa e	I say two, even three
Yo fè conplo pou yo touye m'	They are plotting to kill me
Lè yo rive	When they arrived at
Gangan yo mande non m'	Gangans who asked my name
Yodi yo pa konnen m'	They could not remember it
Se wè yo wè mwen	For they only see me and
Yo pa konnen mwen	Have no idea how strong I am

This song clearly uses the structure of Vodun (with the possibility that one can be hurt through magic) to express one of the concerns of the community. The point here is that some are plotting to kill the poor, but with the help of the guardianship of the Kongo-Petwo spirits, the oppressed can survive. The oppressors cannot even remember the victim's name, for they know little of the strength and ability of the poor to overcome a legacy of misery. Vodun songs, which are grounded in the African circumlocutions, are often judiciously ambiguous. Only a deep-level interpretation can begin to unravel the extent of the coded message lodged in them. The next song seems opaque even in its use of Vodun beliefs to express a collective claim:

Legwa fèm' sa anye	It is Legwa that did it to me
Legwa fèm' sa anye	It is Legwa that did it to me
Legwa Petro a	It is Legwa Petro
Kap fèm' mande charite	That caused me to beg

It is easier, indeed safer, to put the blame on Legwa Petwo than to confront the sociopolitical system, known historically for brutally repressing the attempts of the masses to reclaim their rights. It is clear that Legwa Petwo, whose function is to protect the worshipper, cannot cause the *sèvitè* to go out and beg—in other words. It is the government that has reduced its people to a state of abject poverty, and in this song "Legwa Petro" is also a figurative appellation for the government. The songs of the Kongo-Petwo rite, using figurative language, contain the essence of a side of Haitian life that few researchers associate with Vodun consciousness. The democratic aspirations of Vodun communities, as expressed in many song lyrics, need further scholarly attention. The events of the last ten years show that almost all of the Vodun *lakou* responded enthusiastically to the dialectic of the liberation theology preached by Jean-Bertrand Aristide and others. Aristide was referring to the revolutionary dimension of the Kongo-Petwo rite when he confessed that before he became a Roman Catholic priest he was Haitian and that therefore he needed to connect with Vodun.

Conclusion

In this essay, I have presented the music of Haitian Vodun in a new light. This analysis could not have been possible without the work of pioneers such as Courlander, Comhaire-Sylvain, Dunham, and Kolinski, on the one hand, and the contributions of informants/consultants/teachers such as Coyote and Ti Be on the other hand. The concept of "bi-musicality," which favors apprenticeship and the reflexive approach that suggests initiation as a way to acquire much richer data made it possible for me to study the music of Vodun from an insider's perspective. It has been possible to establish that this music, which is grounded in the functional and structural principles of African art and life, is the foundation of the ritual process. The music is the central element in the Vodun ceremony, and as such, drummers and song leaders are indispensable individuals who are chosen as much for their artistic talents as for their liturgical knowledge. Vodun as a comprehensive system of universal knowledge requires very moral conduct from its priests, participants, and practitioners, precisely because information is power. But that power must be used for the benefit of the community. Much of this information is passed down to the generations through songs and dances. Thus, not only does the music of Vodun have great aesthetic value but it is also a means of teaching the moral values of the community. The songs are an instrument of socialization. In the *lakou,* the extended family compound, people sing all day long, even outside the context of ritual, for music forms the matrix of community living, where the Lwa are always present, whether or not they are manifest.

It is no exaggeration to say that the music of Vodun constitutes the foundation of Haiti's musical life, secular or sacred. Vodun has contributed to Haitian music in a number of ways. The folk and popular music of the past two centuries have emerged from the beat of Kongo-Petwo rhythms. In the past fifty years, on of Haiti's major dance bands, the Jazz des Jeunes, which was founded in 1943, has extensively and successfully used both Rada and Kongo-Petwo beats in their compositions. Artists and singers such as the late Lumane Casimir, Haiti's "Billie Holiday," who performed in the 1950s; Martha Jean-Claude, the grande dame of politically committed music, who has resided in Cuba since the late 1950s; and Emerante de Pradines, one of the first women of the elite to sing Vodun music used Rada and Kongo-Petwo rhythms as the basis for their performances and recordings. Vodun music was the constitutive element of the freedom culture movement of the 1970s, a movement of affirmation that preceded the popular "*rasin*" (roots) music of today. Vodun and its multiple manifestations are being studied, some would say overstudied, but what has been missing is a sophisticated analytical framework, a praxis, that links such studies to Haiti's development, understands the practice as a quest to transform the people's material conditions, and is grounded in socioeconomic and spiritual understandings. An emphasis on the role of music as an active ingredient in building a positive identity and maintaining a people's integrity is one of the directions that Haitian scholarship must take in the twenty-first century. The music of Vodun has indeed been the common denominator of all Haitian musical life.

Notes

1. Moreau de Saint-Méry, *Description Topographique de L'Isle de Saint-Domingue, physique, civile, politique et historique de la partie française de l'île de S. Domingue,* ed. Blanche Maurel et Etienne Taillemite (Paris: Société de l'histoire de la Colonie Française, 1958) is the first known work to address religion on the island of Saint Domingue. It was originally published in 1979. Many works tainted with racist ideologies of the nineteenth and early twentieth centuries have followed. In the popular category, William B. Seabrook's *The Magic Island* (New York: Harcourt Brace, 1929) is particularly racist, as is anthropologist Melville Herskovits's *Life in a Haitian Valley* (1937; reprint Garden City, N.Y.: Doubleday and Co., 1971). Recent scholarship on Haitian Vodou includes works by Laënnec Hurbon, Leslie Desmangles, Patrick Bellegarde-Smith, Karen McCarthy Brown, Elizabeth McAlister, LeGrace Benson, Michel Laguerre, Claudine Michel, and others.

2. See the work of Gerdès Fleurant, *Dancing Spirits: Rhythms and Rituals of Haitian Vodun, the Rada Rite* (Westport, Conn.: Greenwood Press, 1996); and Vèvè A. Clark, lecture at the Arts Connection, New York, 1982.

3. Katherine Dunham, *Island Possessed* (Garden City, N.Y.: Doubleday, 1969). Dunham is a pioneer African American dancer who became a Vodou initiate.

4. It is significant that the "*bosal,*" or most rudimentary approach, prevails, since it is more accessible to the uninitiated. See Victor Turner, *The Ritual Process: Structure and Anti-Structure* (Ithaca: Cornell University Press, 1969) for an argument about a more-reflexive approach.

5. Other chapters in this book address the place of painting in Haitian life and culture and the place of issues of personal and communal identity in the Haitian universe.

6. A most sophisticated rendition of these thoughts occurs in Lilas Desquiron, *Racines du Vodou* (Port-au-Prince: Editions Henri Deschamps, 1990). See especially 17–34.

7. Desquiron, *Racines du Vodou,* 45 and passim. See also Falokun Fatunmbi, *Ibasé Orisa: Ifa Proverbs, Folktales, Sacred History and Prayer* (New York: Original Publications, 1994) for the related Yoruba *panthéon.*

8. Katherine Dunham, *Dances of Haiti* (1947; Los Angeles: Center for Afro-American Studies, UCLA, 1983). Another treatment of popular dance that deals with Vodou is Gage Averill, *A Day for the Hunter, A Day for the Prey: Popular Music and Power in Haiti* (Chicago: University of Chicago Press, 1997), especially 131–140, where the new Vodou culture in dance/music is presented.

9. Courlander's books, *Haiti Singing* (Chapel Hill: University of North Carolina Press, 1939) and *The Drum and the Hoe: Life and Lore of the Haitian People* (Berkeley: University of California Press, 1960), are well known as pioneering efforts by an American. See also Mieczyslaw Kolinski, "Haiti," in *The New Grove Dictionary of Music and Musicians,* ed. Stanley Sadie (New York: Macmillan, 1980), 33–37; David Y. M. Yih, "Music and Dance of Haitian Vodou: Diversity and Unity in Regional Repertoires" (Ph.D. diss., Wesleyan University, 1995); and Claude Dauphin, *La Musique du Vaudou: Fonctions, structures et styles* (Québec: Editions Naaman, 1986).

10. Lamartinière Honorat, *Les Danses folkloriques Haïtiennes* (Port-au-Prince: Imprimerie de l'Etat, 1955); and Jean Fouchard, *La Méringue: Danse Nationale d'Haïti* (Québec: Lémeac, 1973). Both books are key works by important Haitian scholars.

11. Mantle Hood, "The Challenge of Bi-Musicology," *Ethnomusiciology* 4: 55–59. See also J. H. Kwabena Nketia, *African Music in Ghana* (Evanston, Ill.: Northwestern University, 1959), and Hewitt Pantaleoni, "The Rhythm of Atsia Dance Drumming among the Anlo (Ewe) of Anyako" (Ph.D. diss., Wesleyan University, 1972), for other examples of "bi-musicality."

12. Personal communication with author in summer 1997. "Aboudja" is Donald Derenoncourt, a *houngan* and artist in his own right.

13. Michel S. Laguerre discussed "songs" in selected *hounfò* in Haiti in *Voodoo Heritage* (Los Angeles: Sage Publications, 1980).

14. Karen McCarthy Brown, "The VéVé of Haitian Vodou: A Structural Analysis of Visual Imagery" (Ph.D. diss., Temple University, 1976), discusses *voye pwent*. For an African American version, see Henry Louis Gates, Jr., *The Signifying Monkey: A Theory of Afro-American Literary Criticism* (New York: Oxford University Press, 1988).

15. In contrast with other "isms," I have coined the concept "humanocentric," which allows all a full encounter with the Haitian spirits.

16. Milo Rigaud, *La Tradition Voudoo et le Voudoo Haitien* (Paris: Editions Niclaus, 1953), 159. Translation is mine.

17. Robert Farris Thompson, *Flash of the Spirit: African and Afro-American Art and Philosophy* (New York: Vintage Books, 1984).

6

Vodoun, Peasant Songs, and Political Organizing

RÉNALD CLÉRISMÉ

Anthropologists, novelists, and historians have written much about how Vodoun "functions" and how it affects the Haitian collective imaginary. They portray Vodoun as a religion which includes a pantheon of spirits, Lwa, who take possession of their worshipers. Increasingly, scholars are recognizing the complexities inherent in the beliefs and practices associated with the religion. Vodoun incorporates elements of African ancestor veneration, and practitioners believe that death is the portal for return to a mythical Africa by means of the *potomitan,* the center post which links Haiti to Nan Ginen across the sea. Vodoun's principal objective is to capture all divine energetic forces in favor of its adepts. This religion has become a point of contact for a marginalized Haitian culture which adapts traditional African practices—kept alive through songs and proverbs—to those of the New World.

The strength of Vodoun is best explained when placed in its historical and symbolic contexts. Vodoun, like any other complex system, is a living body of ideas carried through time by practitioners and characterized by an ability to adapt to change and be transformed.[1] It is a language. In order to grasp its meaning, one needs to understand its code in order to decode it and learn a vocabulary created through a long historical process.[2]

Vodoun affected political organizing and economic changes that were at the base of a thirteen-year revolution which led to Haiti's independence. The 1791 slave uprising started with a Vodoun ceremony in which the sacrificial blood of a pig was distributed to all those present and committed to wage war against inhuman conditions. Haitian philosopher Jean Price-Mars once wrote, "*1804 est issue du Vaudou,*" meaning that Haitian Independence owed its success to Vodoun beliefs. And even the Haitian guerrillas who waged the valiant but doomed struggle against the U.S. intervention 130 years later (1915–1934) seemed to have worn Vodoun amulets. Charlemagne Péralte and Benoît Batraville, two leaders of the resistance to American occupation, had very close links with Vodoun practitioners and their religious system.

In the preface to Alfred Métraux's *Le Vaudou Haïtien,* Sidney Mintz wrote:

> The Haitian Revolution was in no sense a 'religious war,' but a revolution against an inhuman system. . . . *Vaudou* surely played a critical role in the creation of viable armed resistance by the slaves against the master classes. . . . *Vaudou* cannot be interpreted apart from its significance for the Haitian people, and for Haitian history. . . . Haiti cannot be understood if . . . one chooses to ignore *vaudou.*[3]

Vodoun has shaped and continues to shape the culture of Haiti to such an extent that some equate Vodoun with Haitian culture. Nonetheless, it is important to recognize the impact of Vodoun beliefs and practices in all aspects of everyday life: water, coffee, and alcohol libations to venerate the Lwa *rasin,* or deities connected with family practices; consultation with *manbo, divinò, oungan,* or *bòkò* to decipher the meaning of dreams, causes of illnesses, future life prospects, and success in commercial ventures; and explicit Vodoun rites of passage at births, weddings, or deaths. It is difficult to underestimate the influence of Vodoun on Haitian culture in the countryside and in the cities, in the lower strata as well as in the dominant classes, among Roman Catholics and Protestants. Vodoun plays an important role in the cultural politics of Haiti. This chapter focuses on grassroots peasant songs as a way of sustaining cultural traditions and as a way of political empowerment.

Jean Price-Mars described a Haitian's life as a life of songs. He wrote:

> From birth to death, song is associated with the Haitian's whole life. He sings when he has joy in his heart or tears in his eyes. He sings in the furor of combat, under the hail of machine gunfire, or in the fray of bayonets. He sings in the apotheosis of victories and the horror of defeats. He sings of the muscular effort and of the rest after the task. He sings about a deeply rooted optimism and of humble intuition in that, neither injustice nor suffering are eternal and that, moreover, nothing is hopeless since *Bondye bon,* God is good. . . . He sings always, he sings ceaselessly.[4]

Price-Mars argued further that artistic and emotional expression is an essential part of Haitian identity. He stated, "In this respect, I really think that one could justly define the Haitian people as a people who sing and who suffer, who grieve and who laugh, who dance and are determined." Jean Price-Mars referred to the Haitian people as *"un peuple qui se résigne."*[5]

Here we are faced with a semantic problem. In the French language, *"se résigner"* means accepting one's fate passively. In the Haitian language, Creole, *"reziyen"* means both accepting one's fate passively and one's determination to fight.[6] Considering that the history of the Haitian people is a life of struggle, it would be unfair to describe such a people as accepting their fate passively. Thus, my reading of Jean Price-Mars's statement is that he favors the Creole meaning that the Haitian people are determined to transform their destiny. Haitians suffer and sing, grieve and laugh and dance, but they are determined to transform their destiny. Various songs of organized peasant groups are a perfect expression of such a combative state of mind: *c'est le ton qui fait la chanson* (the feelings and tone transcend the oral text). Because Haitian Creole is mostly oral, it implies meanings that written sentences in French may not adequately convey.

This chapter details the central role of Vodoun in organized peasant resistance through songs. It emphasizes the political message of these songs for these rural organizations. I shall use evidence gleaned from songs to focus on the importance of Vodoun in the peasantry's imaginative world and to suggest that all Haiti could learn lessons from the interweaving of religion and political experience.

Most scholars have limited their works to the magico-religious aspects of the aesthetic dimension of Vodoun without analyzing its social and political impact. From Jean Price-Mars, Maya Deren, Alfred Métraux, and Katherine Dunham to

Guérin Montilus, westerners as well as Haitians have emphasized the phenomena of possession, trance, and dance. Rémy Bastien touched on religion and politics, but it was only in the late 1980s that Laënnec Hurbon (in *Culture et Dictature*) and Michel Laguerre (in *Voodoo and Politics in Haiti*) began to address the political dimension of the Haitian religion in any depth. Despite its notoriety in North America as an account of the zombie phenomenon, Canadian Wade Davis's *The Ethnobiology of the Haitian Zombie* touches on political economy and politics.[7]

What might be surprising to some is that Vodoun succeeded in bringing together enslaved Africans from numerous ethnic groups in the fight for Haitian national independence. This aspect of history is crucial to the understanding of Vodoun's potential to transform Haitian society. Though enslaved Africans had come from diverse regions of West and West-Central Africa, they nonetheless organized effectively to win the wars of independence, the war against Spain and England, and the war against the powerful Napoleonic forces. The ethnonational groups that came from those regions of Africa to the island of Hispaniola are classified as follows: from the western Sudan region, Wolof, Poulah, Bambara, Kimba, Sousou, Manding, Malinke, and Hausa; from the Dahomean region, Fon, Arada, Mahi, Mine, and Ewe; from Yorubaland, Nago, Igbo, and Caplaou; from the Congo region, Kongo, Fang, Mondong, Mayombe, Bafiote, and Mazinga.

Some songs suggest that other individuals could have come from Angola, Senegal, or the Fulbe region. Though the core of Haitian Vodoun originated from what is today the Republic of Benin, most of the ancestors of present-day Haitians came from the Guinea Coast. They refer to Guinea as the paradise where they expect to escape after death: "*Si nan ginen pa te lwen, mwen ta va ale chimen mwen*" (If Guinea was not so far away I would go there), the refrain says, implying that this mythical land can be reached only upon death.

In Vodoun, "magic" and religion go together; hence their impact on Haitian politics. Usually Vodoun's religious aspect is attributed to the Rada and Nago cults and its magical dimension to the Kongo and Petwo cults. But these are not clear-cut classifications. Politicians fear Vodoun but use it to strengthen their power. Some chiefs of state, such as Toussaint Louverture, Rivière Hérard, or Fabre-Nicolas Geffrard, persecuted the practitioners of the national religion while using it themselves; others, without persecuting practitioners openly, attempted to use it to oppress the populace, as François Duvalier did. In these instances, the image of the religion was tarnished.

The knowledge of botany and pharmacology of Vodoun practitioners brings to the fore a medical dimension to the religion which can be used for ill and good. The chapter on healing sciences by my colleague Max-G. Beauvoir addresses these issues in great detail. This knowledge is the main reason why the Vodoun system is built not only around the *ounfò,* the temple under the leadership of the *oungan* or the *manbo* but also around the *gangan/doktè fey* (herbalist), the *bòkò/divinò* (diviner), the secret societies, the *rara* festival, and the *malongo* bands, among other elements.

Though this religious system brought from West Africa by hundreds of thousands of slaves contributed handsomely to the Haitian Revolution (1791–1803) and to the resistance against the U.S. occupation (1915–1934), it came under severe attack in 1896, 1942, and, more recently, in 1986, when it again suffered religious persecution in the aftermath of the fall of the Duvalier regime. Nevertheless, Vodoun has recovered lost ground since the 1987 Constitution vowed to protect the practice of all religions on Haitian territory.[8]

In Vodoun there is no dogma that is written, no unified code, no national "church." It is not a proselytizing body. Yet beneath the apparent absence of formalized structures, there is a body of fundamental beliefs and widespread practices that characterize Vodoun throughout the country. The Cult of the Twins (Marasa), the phenomenon of possession, the link between the *ounfò* and the secret societies, the cult of the ancestors, respect for authority, the sense of solidarity and community, and a relationship between deities and the land all provide a core of beliefs, a series of philosophical postulates about Haitian reality. Some of these attributes, somewhat unfortunately, have been used by politicians to strengthen their powers.

In the late 1980s, grassroots national organizations were built to counterbalance these political manipulations. However, ZANTRAY (Children of Haitian Traditions, under the leadership of *oungan* Hérard Simon) and BORDE National (under *oungan* Max Beauvoir) have had some difficulties in their efforts to institutionalize Vodoun communities in order to work for political change. There were attempts to deflect their purpose when they brought together a large number of Vodoun priests. But while its practitioners have been persecuted, which occurred most recently in 1986 at the hands of some Christian church members with government complicity, Vodoun has never led persecutions of its own. Within a well-balanced society, with proper political leadership, Vodoun can be a powerful instrument in Haiti's development. Each one of its temples and each association is a center of power where priests have hundreds of followers in both urban and rural areas.

During a survey I conducted in 1979 in a *section rurale* called Beauchamp, a subdivision of the northwest region, I discovered 96 *ounfò*. There are 564 such subdivisions in Haiti. It is not an exaggeration to suggest that in the countryside alone there are around 40,000 *oungan, manbo,* and *bòkò*. With an average of perhaps 100 worshipers per *ounfò,* we easily reach 4,000,000 souls in the rural areas alone. Even if fewer persons adhere to the religion in the towns and cities, we still find significant numbers of Vodouists in the nation. One can guess the social and political importance of such religious institutions, especially if they have close connections with secret societies and other groups, including traditional work associations. Remembering that Vodouists are simultaneously Christians (Catholics or Protestants), it is important to undertake a scientific survey to elicit accurate statistics. I have often come across this phenomenon of practitioners with one foot in two religions in my field research.[9]

Throughout Haitian history, peasants have organized around their Afro-Haitian and Vodoun heritage and have formed armed groups to press for their own self-interest. Peasant organizations gave no rest to deceitful politicians and played a role in the overthrow of a number of governments. For instance, during the first three years of the American occupation, the Cacos fought back defiantly under the leadership of Charlemagne Péralte and Benoît Batraville, two fervent Vodouists. They used songs inspired by Vodoun to energize the combatants. Presently the strength and durability of small peasant organizations, rooted in the structure of Haitian rural society, continue to be interwoven with the religion. The peasantry, which represents 70 percent of the population, pays a high price for its determination to stay organized.

The tradition of using Vodoun discourse, symbols, and rhythm in peasant song has been present in various geographical areas of the country throughout Haitian history. The peasantry's tradition of composing songs based on Vodoun rhythm and using them to ridicule, to *voye pwent*, is traceable to the days of slavery, when slaves put words to existing Vodoun melodies to laugh at their masters and voice their pain. After slavery, the practice continued with regard to people in positions of power and those who were guilty of misconduct.

The use of songs within peasant associations, agricultural collectives generically labeled as *konbit*, and entertainment bands became the milieu for keeping such practices alive. Traditional forms of working the land include loosely knit groups as well as better organized units that carry different names according to regions: *eskwad, sosyete,* or *konvre* in the south; *mazinga* in the northwest; *ranpono* in the north and in the central plateau; and *kounabe* in the Petit-Goâve region and *paloya* in the region of Anse-à-Veaux, both of which are in southern Haiti. These work groups that sustain the peasant economy receive moral support from the temples and are oftentimes linked to secret societies such as Chanpwèl and Bizango. Some are linked also to seasonal festivities such as the *rara* at Easter and *malongo,* but they all have common characteristics.

Songs are composed out of a general Vodoun repertoire to which are added aspects of Vodoun rituals and liturgy. Some groups draw their rhythm and melodies from specific religious affiliations, such as *sosyete Kongo* or Nago. Many peasant songs come from Zaka's repertoire, such as *juba* and *banda*.[10] One recalls the traditional song:

Yo bare Sovè, Sovè vole o	Sovè got caught, Sovè flew (like a werewolf)
Yo bare Sovè sèt fwa devan	Sovè got caught seven times
Lakay	in front of the house
Ewa ewa yo bare Sovè woy	*Ewa, ewa* Sovè got caught, *woy*

This song recounts how a peasant who has turned into a *lougarou,* a werewolf, is caught seven times. Note the number seven, a magical number in Vodoun. Three, seven, and twenty-one are believed to have specific significance. Outside the political realm, some songs are composed to denounce misconduct and the infidelity of spouses. The purpose of such songs is always to redress incorrect behavior and reestablish moral order.

However, in the mid-1970s, leftist and liberation theology activism, in which Father Jean-Marie Vincent was a prominent figure, began to suggest that liberating words replace gossip. Vincent and I, along with others, founded Tèt Kole (Heads Together) in an effort to empower the Haitian peasantry. This became our priority in assisting peasant organizations. We encouraged the spread of song narratives in which they recounted their ordeals and claimed their rights. Vodoun-influenced songs became an educational and conscientizing device.

In recent years, three organizations have played especially vital roles in the attempt to infuse progressive and liberating lyrics in songs—Tèt Kole in 1986, which has a national audience; Peasant Movement of Papay (MPP), founded in the 1970s in the Plateau Central (it became MPNKP in 1987); and Solèy Leve (The Sun Is Rising), founded in 1990 in the south. All three came directly out of a long historical tradition of peasant organization with added political dimensions.

These three movements continued the tradition of composing songs around peasants' experiences of daily life while interjecting a liberating political message. Tèt Kole is a case in point. In May 1987, Tèt Kole members in the town of Jean-Rabel sang about their suffering, the horror of their defeats, and their determination to continue to struggle for change and for justice. Their collective songs were labeled *fòk sa chanje* (things must change). While these songs, which were also played on the radio, pleased peasants and their advocates, they enraged the dominant classes and their conservative allies. In July 1987, two months after making political demands in their songs, 139 people were murdered. They were killed because they had organized to protest the terror of the section chiefs and rural police officers and because they had wanted to gain access to state land, receive social services in return for their taxes, and get compensation for their *kochon kreyòl*, locally bred pigs, which were destroyed because of an epidemic. Their battle was also against U.S.-sponsored "Food for Work" programs which had undercut the price of locally grown food.

In 1989, two years after the massacre, members of the movement sang with sorrow but also with courage "Premye So Pa So" ("The First Time One Falls, One Bounces Back"). In that song, they used the expression *"tonnè"* (thunder) to express discontent and anger which come directly from the Vodoun context. *"Hey fout tonnè"* (gash by thunder) is sometimes uttered by a Lwa *mèt tèt* to express joy but also to disconnect after the first time it visits or connects with the Vodouist.

Women in Tèt Kole generally play a significant role in cultural institutions and in performing songs. They support Jean Price-Mars's assertion that "woman has a preponderant role in the gatherings where people tell and sing tales. If she is not always the leader of the chorus, she is at least a pre-eminent figure whom the populace call queen of the song [*reine chanterelle*], queen forever[,] so to speak, given the considerable importance that the chant in all its forms holds in the life of our people."[11] Tèt Kole's best *sanba*, composer-singer and queen of song, Marceline Fidélien, was a woman in her mid-thirties who was non-literate, as are most of her fellow Tèt Kole members. As do many peasant composer-singers, she sang her songs to a literate person who put them in writing (the national literacy program in which we urged Tèt Kole members to enroll was far from successful). The majority of the singers are women, while the musicians are men. They sing

by heart, no matter how many verses. Their songs are structured around political, economic, and social preoccupations.

Their music is chosen directly from folklore traditions influenced by Vodoun
rhythms, such as Yanvalou, Nago, Kongo, Djoumba, Igbo; from the working-
group music of traditions such as Konbit; from secret society and festival band
music such as *rabòday* and *banda*. In Haitian peasants' song performance, their
whole bodies move with the rhythm of the drums and the *vaksen* (musical instrument made of bamboo). Movement that accompanies the singing starts with
the head, then the shoulders, then the rhythm fills the whole body (see plate 4).

The songs under study are an expression of the impact of progressive activists
in the Tèt Kole movement. The movement is structured in a bottom-up pattern
in which women and men have the same opportunities for self-development and
the practice of democracy in everyday life. The foundation of the Tèt Kole structure is the *gwoupman*, a working group. It encompasses seven to fifteen families
with small landholdings or none at all. Three to five *gwoupman* constitute a Tèt
Kole *bitasyon*, a small neighborhood group led by an elected committee in charge
of finance, education, legal issues, and health care. Five to ten Tèt Kole *bitasyon*
constitute an *inyon* (union) led by an elected committee. Three to five unions are
an *asosyasyon* (association). Five to ten associations constitute a regional *federasyon*
(federation). The National Konfederasyon (National Confederation), which is led
by an elected committee of peasants, is comprised of all the regional federations.
In 1997, the movement encompassed eight federations which included over
50,000 members. Most federations have their *samba*, individuals who express the
political stands of the movement in song.

Three songs in the remaining sections of this chapter, "Sonde," "Peye san," and
"Tè ak Dlo," illustrate conscientization through their political content. The first
Tèt Kole song, "Sonde," was composed in the midst of very risky political situations in the mid-1980s. I first heard and learned it from Joseph Seraphin (Zo), a
prominent leader of Tèt Kole. He and I were delegates representing Tèt Kole from
the northwest region. He taught me this song a few weeks before he was decap-
itated, put on a pole, and circulated triumphantly amid Tèt Kole's enemies in La-
montay on the day the massacre started on July 23, 1987. We were coming back
from a Tèt Kole national gathering held at Jackzil in the northeast. Having left
the town of Plaisance, seven of us were crowded in a Land Rover. To shorten the
journey, Zo started singing "Sonde" when we reached the Pilboro mountain. I
found the song meaningful and learned it by heart.

Sonde o sonde gwoupman peyizan	Put to the test, put
yo sonde	peasant groups to the test
Se wè yo wè mwen, yo pa konnen	They see me on the
sa mwen peze o	surface, they don't know our
	strength
Moun yo kap pale gwoupman mal la	Those who gossip about our groups
Vin wè pou n al pale.	May come to see and gossip

The rhythm is borrowed from Vodoun's symbology. "*Sonde*" means testing, probing one's strength and weaknesses. As one gauges the depth of a river, one challenges an opponent to come and measure and be measured. "*Moun yo kap pale gwoupman ma vin wè pou nou al pale*": Those who are gossiping about members of the *gwoupman* are challenged to come and to respond. Often when something goes wrong in a ritual, there is a *chante voye pwen* challenging those who are hindering a positive ceremonial outcome. "*Yo vini gade pou yale pale tripotay*": they talk without understanding the power of the one they have gossiped about. The only way to understand is to come and measure oneself against the others. This is *sonde*. This approach of reconciling and recentering antagonistic forces is typical of Vodoun.

The influence of Vodoun imagery, symbolism, and rhythm is detectable in the following song, "Peye San an" ("Pay the Blood"). The criminals must pay by being brought to justice and punished for the blood they have spilled. Taking lives, human or otherwise, never goes unpunished or unpaid for. The song goes:

Nikol Poitvien	Nicol Poitvien
Peye san an wo	Pay for the blood [of the peasants]
Remy Lucas	Remy Lucas
Peye san an wo	Pay for the blood [of the peasants]
Patrick Lucas	Patrick Lucas
Peye san ti peyizan yo	Pay for the blood of the peasants
Kapten Saint Julien	Captain Saint Julien
Peye san an wo	Pay for the blood [of the peasants]
Peye san an wo	Pay for the blood [of the peasants]
Loudy	Loudy
Peye san 23 Jiyè a	Pay for the blood spread July 23
Erilien Delien	Erilien Delien
Peye san an wo	Pay for the blood [of the peasants]
Peye san an wo	Pay for the blood [of the peasants]
Prosper Gentilhomme	Prosper Gentilhomme
Peye san peyizan	Pay for the blood of the peasants
Janrabel yo	of Jean-Rabel
Leonard Lucas	Leonard Lucas
Peye san an wo	Pay for the blood [of the peasants]
Peye san an wo	Pay for the blood [of the peasants]
Anovil Saint Vil	Anovil Saint Vil
Peye san 23 Jiyè a	Pay for the blood spread July 23
Joel Jean-Baptiste	Joel Jean-Baptiste
Peye san wo	Pay for the blood [of the peasants]
Peye san an wo	Pay for the blood [of the peasant]
Joel Jean–Baptiste	Joel Jean-Baptiste
Peye san Peyizan	Pay for the blood of the peasants
Mawotyè yo	From Marrotière

Henri Namphy	Henri Namphy
Peye san an	Pay for the blood [of the peasants]
Peye san an wo	Pay for the blood [of the peasants]
Williams Regala	Williams Regala
Peye san	Pay for the blood
27 Novanm nan	Spread November 27
Franck Romain	Franck Romain
Peye san an wo	Pay for the blood [of the peasants]
Peye san an wo	Pay for the blood [of the peasants]
Henry Namphy peye san	Henri Namphy pay for the blood
Saint Jean Bosco yo	Spread at St. Jean Bosco church
Olivier Nadal	Olivier Nadal
Peye san an wo	Pay for the blood [of the peasants]
Peye san an wo	Pay for the blood [of the peasants]
Olivier Nadal peye san	Olivier Nadal pay for the blood
Peyizan Pyat yo	Of Pyat peasants.

Tèt Kole members openly denounced the killers associated with mass murder at both the local and national levels. Their testimony was accurate; they had first-hand information. They took the risk of going public with the names of power-ful individuals who knew them and could attack them. In a *banda* rhythm they wove together the Vodoun ritual of sacrifice and a cry for political justice. They used the metaphor *peye san an* to ask that those who had participated in one way or another in the killing of thousands of Haitians be brought to trial. In the song, the culprits included military officers such as Henri Namphy, Williams Regala, and Saint Julien; rural policemen such as Anovil Sainvil, Erilien Délien, and Joel Jean-Baptiste; landlords such as Olivier Nadal, Nicol Poitvien, and Remy and Patrick Lucas; politicians such as Franck Romain; and other accomplices such as Prosper Gentilhomme. Sadly, the Haitian system of criminal justice is not strong enough to respond to the peasants' demands for justice. Through their testimony via those songs, the peasants put themselves in grave danger because the killers remained at large and, in some places, continued to hold positions of power.

In that song, none of the accused were women; but some of the victims were women who were murdered because of their progressive democratic stance. The song is like a judicial file that will be preserved in the Haitian collective memory. It evolves according to the litany format characteristic of a Vodoun ritual called *adore,* which consists of calling worshipers to come in a procession, dancing, bal-ancing their bodies, kneeling down, and making an offering of money. They pay their share so that the blood of the sacrificed animal may benefit them; otherwise they could face punishment.

In another song, "Premye So pa So," peasant activists use the same litany for-mat, *noble,* to remember the names of the 139 murdered in 1987. The Vodoun

PLATE 1. Offerings for the Marasa. Individual in photo: Paulette Denis. Photograph by Claudine Michel.

PLATE 2. Ceremony. Individuals in photo (left to right): Delanie (Mamoune) Placide, Patrick Bellegarde-Smith, Myrtha St. Louis, and Nostalie (Minou) Placide. Photograph by Claudine Michel.

PLATE 3. Dancing for Ogou.
Individual in photo: Nostalie
(Minou) Placide. Photograph by
Claudine Michel.

PLATE 4. Dance for Azaka/*po-tomitan*. Individual in photo:
Myrtha St. Louis. Photograph
by Claudine Michel.

PLATE 5. Jacqueline Epingle in front of a table for Gédé. Photograph by Claudine Michel.

PLATE 6. Saint Marc, *The Pleasure Ship of Agwé Taroyo*. Courtesy Marc A. Christophe.

PLATE 7. Serge Legagneur, *Secrets Désirs (Secret Desires)*. Reprinted from Mari-Jose Nardo Gardère and Gérard Bloncourt, *Le Peinture haitienne* (Éditions Nathan, 1986), p. 144.

PLATE 8. Roosevelt Sanon, *Le "manger-Loas," offrande aux dieux* (The manger-Loas, food offerings to the gods). Reprinted from Mari-Jose Nardo Gardère and Gérard Bloncourt, *Le Peinture haitienne* (Éditions Nathan, 1986), p. 172.

PLATE 9. Haitian *Pakèt Kongo*. Photograph by Don Cole. Courtesy UCLA Fowler Museum of Cultural History.

PLATE 10. Vodou altar. Photograph by Don Cole. Courtesy UCLA Fowler Museum of Cultural History.

PLATE 11. Salnave Philippe Auguste, *Paradis Terrestre* (*Earthly Paradise*). Reprinted from Mari-Jose Nardo Gardère and Gérard Bloncourt, *Le Peinture haitienne* (Éditions Nathan, 1986), p. 103.

PLATE 12. Fernand Pierre, *Jungle imaginaire* (*Imaginary Jungle*). Reprinted from Mari-Jose Nardo Gardère and Gérard Bloncourt, *Le Peinture haitienne* (Éditions Nathan, 1986), p. 105.

PLATE 13. Rémy Paillan, *Région de Jacmel (Around Jacmel)*. Reprinted from Mari-Jose Nardo Gardère and Gérard Bloncourt, *Le Peinture haitienne* (Éditions Nathan, 1986), p. 175.

PLATE 14. Camille Torchon, *Paysage utopique (Utopian Landscape)*. Reprinted from Mari-Jose Nardo Gardère and Gérard Bloncourt, *Le Peinture haitienne* (Éditions Nathan, 1986), p. 176.

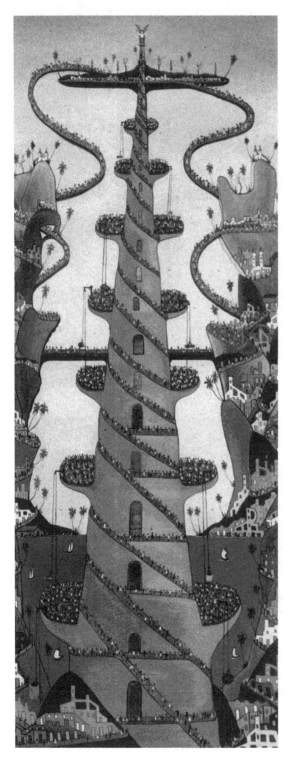

PLATE 15. Préfète Duffaut, *Vierge au sommet de la montagne* (*Virgin on the Mountain Summit*). Reprinted from Mari-Jose Nardo Gardère and Gérard Bloncourt, *Le Peinture haitienne* (Éditions Nathan, 1986), p. 111.

noble ritual consists of naming in chronological order ancestors in whose honor a ceremony is held.

Privatization of government services was a major focus in the 1990s. Peasants expressed their opposition and contributed to the political dialogue by means of songs drawn from the Vodoun repertoire. They offered other models for grass-roots rural economic development. Peasant demands contained elements of both private investment and continued state control over essential resources and projects. They wanted a mixed economy. They hoped to meet basic needs in ways that did not harm the physical environment and the social ecology of peasant life. They asked for irrigation systems, land reform, and the return of their creole pigs instead of imported food. They were concerned about privatization because they thought it would harm Haiti. In their song "Sele Pa Monte" ("Saddle but Don't Ride [the Haitian People]"), they communicate directly with urban politicians and foreign military forces in Port-au-Prince:

Pèp nan Nodwès	We people from the Northwest
Pi gwo bezwen nou genyen	Land and water are
Se tè ak dlo	Our greatest needs
Nape mande	We are asking where are
Kot mesye responsab yo	Those in charge
Nape mande kot	We are asking where are
Senatè ak depite yo	Our senators and deputies
Pou ban nou Twa Rivyè	To give us Trois-Rivière's water
Pou nou rouze wo.	To irrigate our lands.
Nan Nodwès gen sechrès	Drought is common in the
Mezanmi	Northwest
Kon Pèp Nodwès rele anmwe	As soon as we cry out for help
Se sinistre yo voye	They send unwanted imported food
Ban nou Twa Rivyè	Give us Trois-Rivière's water
Pou nou rouze tè n yo.	To irrigate our lands.
Senatè ak depite mezanmi	Senators and deputies
Ape mande manje sinistre	Are asking for unwanted food
Se pa sinistre k solisyon	This is not the solution
Ban nou Twa Rivyè	Give us Trois-Rivière's water
Pou nou rouze tè n yo!	To irrigate our lands!

In this song yet another aspect of religious influence on the imaginative world of the peasant emerges. The composers refer to water and earth, two core elements in Vodoun beliefs. They call upon the political sector responsible for their destiny, urging it to act responsibly.

Considering the many threats that still hang over the Haitian peasantry, it may amaze some that members of the Haitian masses who are organized are so resolute and steadfast in their struggle for participatory democracy. But those peasants who belong to an organized movement are very determined. When attacked, they react in self-defense. For them it is a life-or-death issue; they cannot live a real life without organizing. A widow who lost her husband in the 1987 Jean-Rabel massacre put it this way: "We have begun to organize. Organization, for us, is our lives. I have lost my husband in this very struggle to organize. If now I should abandon that struggle, it's all over for me. I must continue to organize. We lost a man, now we must keep fighting for change in this country. It's such a good cause!" This widow inherited her wisdom and her determination from Vodoun philosophy. *Toutotan tèt pa ko koupe nou pa dezespere pote chapo* (As long as our heads have not been cut, we do not despair of wearing a hat; put another way, as long as we are alive there is hope for a better future).

Despite the assertion by novelists Jean-Baptiste Cinéas and Jacques Stéphen Alexis that Vodoun would die as technology and literacy developed, I argue to the contrary that Vodoun will survive. With songs that draw upon Vodoun and carrying conscientizing messages, peasant movements are now better organized and have become stronger politically. The national religion has played a major role in Haitian history and will continue to determine the future of the country in significant ways. Vodoun might help the peasantry realize its dream of participation in the decision-making process; it could become the foundation for democracy and justice. The decentralization mandated by the Constitution of 1987 suggests that Vodoun be taken seriously both in terms of its organizational structures and with reference to its ideologies.

Notes

Dr. Rénald Clerismé is an anthropologist, activist, and grassroots organizer who writes firsthand of many events described his chapter.—Eds.

1. Michel S. Laguerre, citing Roger Bastide, has argued that Vodoun is a "living" rather than a "preserved" religion, as Christianity is, since its revelations continue to unfold across time. See Michel S. Laguerre, *Voodoo Heritage* (Beverly Hills, Calif.: Sage Publications, 1980).

2. The issue of language is complex. *Langaj* contains words and sentences that came directly from different African languages. The meanings of *langaj* are known only by priests and initiates and are learned through a long process.

3. Alfred Métraux, *Voodoo in Haiti,* trans. Hugo Charteris (New York: Schocken Books, 1972), 10.

4. Jean Price-Mars, *So Spoke the Uncle,* trans. Magdaline Shannon (Washington, D.C.: Three Continents Press, 1983), 26.

5. Jean Price-Mars, *Ainsi Parla l'Oncle. Essais d'ethnographie* (Paris: Imprimerie de Compiègne, 1928), 18.

6. This also conveys the metaphysical notion that in Vodoun, opposites can at times be part of the same dimension.

7. Price-Mars, *Ainsi Parla l'Oncle*; Maya Deren, *Divine Horsemen: The Voodoo Gods of Haiti* (1953; reprint, New Paltz, N.Y.: McPherson and Co., 1983); Métraux, *Voodoo in Haiti*; Guérin Montilus, *Dompin: The Spirituality of African Peoples* (Nashville, Tenn.: Winston-Derek Publishers, 1991); Rémy Bastien, *Religion and Politics in Haiti* (Washington, D.C.: Institute for

Cross-Cultural Research, 1966); Katherine Dunham, *Island Possessed* (1969; reprint, Chicago: University of Chicago Press, 1994); Wade Davis, *Passage of Darkness: The Ethnobiography of the Haitian Zombie* (Chapel Hill: University of North Carolina Press, 1988).

8. However, a resurgence of fundamentalist Protestant groups at the beginning of the new millennium may prove to be another challenge for Haitian Vodoun.

9. Vodoun is not exclusive; its adepts are expected to be Christian. It does not work the other way around.

10. This may partly be due to the fact that Zaka, according to *manbo* Jacqueline Epingle, is perhaps the only true Creole Lwa of the Vodoun pantheon. Conversation with Jacqueline Epingle, Santa Barbara, California, April 1997.

11. Price-Mars, *So Spoke the Uncle,* 26.

7

From the Horses' Mouths:
Women's Words/Women's Worlds

CLAUDINE MICHEL, PATRICK BELLEGARDE-SMITH,
AND MARLÈNE RACINE-TOUSSAINT

Noye n ape noye
Noye n ape noye
Ezili si ou wè m tombe an dlo pran m non
Ezili si ou wè m tombe an dlo pran m non
Sove la vi pitit ou
Ou pa wè n ape noye

We are drowning
We are drowning
Erzili [Dantò] if you see me fall in the waters, take me
Save the life of your child [children]
You see that we are drowning

Ezili Dantò is a deity whose divine principle represents maternal love. She is the mother of several children and takes care of those of her sister Ezili Freda, who pretends not to have any. With Ogou Feray—the deity of warfare and iron—she participated in the Haitian war of independence. For her troubles, her tongue was cut off by the French colonial authorities. She cannot speak, but she is heard clearly. She is also, in the words of Audre Lorde and other Black feminists, a "woman-identified-woman," a lesbian. She is Black.

This well-known song sung in ceremonies in honor of Dantò reveals a free flow between "me" and "us," between the singular and the collective. One seldom notices the change, if one ever did. "If you see *me* fall in the waters, [it means that *we* are drowning]."

Though our chapter is not grandiose in its scope, we urge our readers to ponder the broad issues of what religions have done to and for women. We want to raise issues of interconnections that might exist between two unrelated concepts, ethos and ethics. If we succeed in our quest, one may be able to perceive content in context and vice versa. Vodun's myths, sacred stories, rituals, and symbolism—topics outside the purview of this work—allow us to speculate that in that religion, women are not Other.

Haitian Vodun has always operated as a *"foyer de résistance,"* meaning that its evolutionary path, as distinct from its theology, has made it countercultural. Vodun is opposed to a dominant, non-indigenous religious ethos that is, by defini-

Visit by Erzuli Dantò.
Individual in photo:
Nirva Chérasard.
Photograph by Claudine
Michel.

tion and the logic of the situation, assimilationist, reductionist, and totalitarian. The roles, position, and concerns of women in most social systems place them in similar subaltern conditions to those in which Vodun itself is found. The Haitian religion thus becomes an ideal fit: a social category (women) finding its realization in a religious system (Vodun) that is itself categorized as inferior, one that speaks to the issue of women's equality and inequality.

It is at the juncture between Franco-Haitian and the Afro-Haitian variants of the cultural continuum, between a colonized universe and a neocolonial society, in the blend of power and powerlessness of worlds neither free nor enslaved that Haitian women who are involved with Vodun find maneuverability and the spaces in which to negotiate.

Ten *manbo* (female priests) were interviewed for this project between November 1997 and January 2000. They come from diverse class backgrounds and origins and were various ages. Nine spoke on the record, while the tenth chose to remain anonymous. These *manbo* are Margaret Armand, Carole Desmesmin, Jacqueline Epingle, Carole Lalanne De Lynch, Anastasia De Lynch, Georgette Roger, Nicole Thomas Miller, Elisabeth Beauvoir, Marthe Bauzile Charles, and A (Anonymous).[1] All are Haitian-born except for Elisabeth Beauvoir, who is French but who is a *manbo* who has lived in Haiti for the past forty years or so.[2]

Though fully integrated within their spirituality, *à l'aise* (comfortable in their skins), some of these women were apprehensive that their status as *bourgeoises* would lead the social class to which they belong to discriminate against them or to ostracize them. Others wanted to be interviewed but were not for a variety of reasons, including the time factor. All were graceful in sharing their experiences, thoughts, and emotions, in expressing their truths on issues large and small affecting their ministries, their sacerdotal functions, and their country. The interviews were conducted in Haitian (Creole), French, and English, sometimes in all three languages, with the participants going back and forth from one language to another, as many Haitians typically do.

Why did we interview women? Most cultural traditions in the world have made it difficult for women to function as the equals of men. Their inferior status has been enshrined in science, philosophy, and religion in most cultures. Haitian Vodun has not necessarily escaped these unequal relations of power and history of dominance. Despite the many recent advances in feminist scholarship in the area of spirituality, too often the introduction of women's experiences has meant importing Western, white, and middle-class perspectives that exclude women of color, who remain marginalized. Though Haitian women have always been at the center and core of their religion, academic writing has barely started to give credit to the leadership of women in Vodun. Let us note the work of pioneers Odette Mennesson-Rigaud and Katherine Dunham, the recent contributions made by Karen McCarthy Brown in her work with the Haitian *manbo* Mama Lola, and the writings of Déita, Rose-Marie Desruisseau, Joan Dayan, and Elizabeth McAlister, among other feminist scholars. One of our goals in this research project is to challenge marginalization and problematization of women in the Haitian religion and to expand the Vodun feminist discourse by incorporating the voices of the *manbo* we interviewed, all women whose crucial leadership has not been recognized outside their immediate communities. We believe that the work of these women leaders as *potomitan* deserves attention in scholarly circles in Haiti and abroad. They are sisters, mothers, lovers, workers, community organizers, and spiritual leaders in their own right.

The words Toni Morrison uttered in the lecture she gave upon receiving the Nobel Prize for literature in 1993 underscored the exploratory nature of a project such as ours and gave us hope. Her words are a recipe and, in their poetics, a key to African aesthetics and metaphysics: "Narrative is radical, creating us at the very moment it is being created. We will not blame you if your reach exceeds your grasp; if love so ignites your words they go down in flames and nothing is left but their scald. Or if, with the reticence of a surgeon's hands, your words suture

only the places where blood might flow. We know you can never do it properly—
once and for all. Passion is never enough; neither is skill. But try."[3]

This is what we have attempted to do. As Morrison suggested, we try and try
harder. The *manbo* interviewed shared their thoughts and visions and expressed
complex and conflicted emotions about their religion and their *sacerdoce,* their
priesthood. As researchers, we tried to understand those commentaries in the
spirit in which they were offered. We tried to avoid monolithic categorizations
and an overemphasis on commonalities or differences. What was important to
us was the specificity as well as the particularities of their experiences. As Judith
Plaskow and Carol Christ wrote in *Weaving Visions: Patterns in Feminist Spirituality:* "The notion of women's experience must be taken as an invitation to explore
particularities rather than to homogenize significant differences. . . . The inclusion of personal experience in feminist work is also a way of addressing the cri-
tique of false universalism. . . . This diversity presents a formal challenge to the
canons of scholarly objectivity."[4] This is particularly true when dealing with persons and peoples who are female and Black.

Although we have completed only a preliminary analysis of the interviews with
the Haitian *manbo,* it is already evident that their testimonies challenge Western
canons and add to the complexity of our understanding of the feminine experience in Vodun. Themes which will serve as an organizing framework are family
and national heritage, gender, class, the communal self, relationship with the sacred, and social change and transformation.

Defining Religious Heritage

"Se pou nou femin sèk la" (We must close the circle), intoned Georgette Roger, al-
luding to the need to birth *"de nouveaux indigènes,"* a new indigenous population
with a culture to match, the need to preserve a worldview that is deeply rooted
in traditional African systems but is also authentically Haitian.

Haiti grew in a transitional culture zone, neither indigenous nor traditional
nor modern (in the popular understanding of this term), a fact that social scientists who seek a genuine or pure culture have perceived as calamitous.[5] But because Haiti falls in that transitional zone that is neither African nor Amerindian,
and certainly not European, it enables both movement and improvisation based
upon many cultural influences and varied modes and forms of resistance. The
country stayed in rhythm in a symbiotic relationship between an old (African)
cosmological universe and a new (American) place and historical circumstances,
as mediated by European and American power brokers. Georgette Roger's plea
"Se pou nou femin sèk la" asks these outside forces to stay at bay; she sees Haitians
and Haitian women in particular as agents of their own transformations. "Women/
Haitians ought to take things in their own hands," she says.

"Bon ak move mache ansanm" (Positive and negative [must] work together, never
in isolation or apart), declared Jacqueline Epingle, defining one of the most ba-

sic tenets of Haitian spirituality. Everything is on a continuum—nothing is ever totally good or bad. Things, people, situations, and events are interconnected, interdependent, always complex and grounded in the idea of a cosmic whole. Good (*bon*) indeed walks hand in hand with bad (*move*), but Haitians/women have a say in what direction the course of things will follow. Out of "bad," valuable lessons, when learned, turn into "good," while after all the road to hell is paved with good intentions. *Zafè nèg pa janm piti* (The Black person's thing is never small [is complex]), states the proverb. Epingle's comments can also be appropriated to understand the birth of all things Haitian as described in the previous paragraph. She completed her thought with a saying: *"Si kreyol tronpe ginen, se ginen ki vle"* (If [creole] people fool the [African] Spirits, it's because these Spirits have allowed it). Children do not fool mothers. The ancestral spirits have allowed us to think that they were fooled, that they have allowed machinations from both *sevitè* (servants of the gods) and non-*sevitè* (non-believers) alike. Some resulting changes may have been good; others not—indeed, *bon ak move mache ansanm* (Good walks hand in hand with bad). We survive though we transgress; we survive because we transgress. Mothers always understand (see plate 5).

Vodun functions as a place of comfort and belonging—perhaps as do many or most religions. Nicole Thomas Miller finds strength in her morning ritual: "I get up, I pour water on the ground, salute the four directions, light my candle, and do my things. . . . I ask for courage, peace, poise, and direction (routing). I ask for those things for me, my son, my family, and even my enemies." Vodun is a down-to-earth religion which assists with everyday living in all facets of a person's life. It is grounded in a profound holism and an understanding of a sense of the unity of all forces of nature, something that Elisabeth Beauvoir also understands. She explains: *"Le Vodou n'est pas quelque chose qui peut s'arrêter à un pays. C'est toute une philosophie, toute une façon de vivre. On parle toujours du 'vieux continent'. L'Europe est jeune. C'est l'Afrique qui est le 'vieux continent'. C'est là qu'on trouve les vraies philosophies. Le Vodou va bien au-delà des frontières d'Haiti."* (Vodun does not stop within one country. It is a whole philosophy, a whole mode of living. People talk about "the old continent." Europe is young. It is Africa which is "the old continent." That is where real philosophies are found. Vodun goes farther than the boundaries of Haiti.)

Understanding Family Tradition and Gender

Vodun functions as a *region of refuge,* a place of security for women in the statements of all those we interviewed. Margaret Armand stated that "the world is a man's world," and that Vodun "provides women with that extra edge for overcoming obstacles." She went on to say: "The experiences I have had with Vodun made me stronger; Vodun is the culture and the tradition that empowers [me]." She added, later on, *"Ou pa poul san mèt"* (No chicken is without an owner). In other words, the traditions fashion the culture from which we spring. "[But] the outside world looks more at the *houngan* [male priest] because he is a man, though on the inside, in Vodun, there is no special or different training that distinguish men from women, though women may be more intuitive," she explained.

The tradition Margaret Armand spoke of was lived by Carole Desmesmin. Her father's grandmother, a *manbo* who specialized in the healing arts, was a *selibe* (clairvoyant) and a midwife. She made sure that everyone in her family went to school. She was also a businesswoman who owned a boat that sold sea salt, plying the waters between the port cities of Gonaïves and Petit-Goâve. Her own great-grandmother was an enslaved woman on a Petit-Goâve *habitation* (plantation). Carole Desmesmin concludes that "*istwa dayiti tout kout*" (Haiti's [500–year] history is brief, when viewed through the lenses of passing generations).

Carole's mother, however, did not practice Vodun because of the persecutions against the religion during the years of the U.S. occupation (1915–1934), when Vodouisants were killed. The traditions spoken of by Carole Desmesmin, went "*de femme en femme*" (from woman to woman), illustrating their role and presence in religion, commerce, and education albeit circumscribed by intrusive external factors such as the American occupation, the Protestant missions it brought in, and Haiti's French-controlled Roman Catholic church.[6]

Carole De Lynch, whose *manbo* grandmother was imprisoned under the U.S. occupation, came from a family that always practiced Vodun. Her grandmother's mother was a *manbo* born in Africa who was enslaved in colonial Saint Domingue. Though both Carole Desmesmin and Carole De Lynch argue that their priesthood seemed inevitable, we find in Desmesmin's case a rupture in the practice of Vodun, while with De Lynch, whose "first memories were in the *peristyle*" (the temple's courtyard), we see that her family's tradition provided an uninterrupted path, "*une voie toute tracée*," as she said (a well-defined path). Margaret Armand's paternal grandmother was a healer. When she was nine, that grandmother took her to an Ezili (the deity of love) ceremony. Her great-grandmother was a *manbo* from Petit-Goâve, and one grandfather was a *houngan* from the region of La Gosseline, near the city of Jacmel. Her immediate family, perhaps because it was in the throes of *embourgeoisement*, did not practice Vodun.

Carole De Lynch said that when an important Vodun priest from the Republic of Benin visited Haiti for fourteen days a few years ago, "He found the music and the ritual intact." De Lynch added, "In Vodun chants, one sings the [events of] Haiti's history, and [at times] predict[s] its future." Family stories and national history never seemed far removed for these women. This seems generally true in smaller societies.

Understanding the Vodun Religion within the Class System

A popular saying says *bourik travay pou chwal galonen* (the donkey works but the horse gets the honors). The juxtaposition of the (European) horse and the (African) donkey gave the mule (*mulâtre*, mulatto) a chance to govern after the defeat of the French military in 1803. The *mulâtre* was an intermediary being who became a social category and then a social class. The *manbo* we spoke to came from di-

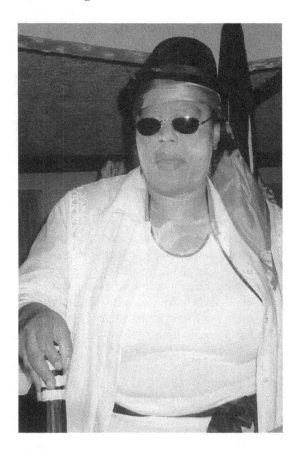

Manbo mounted by Gédé.
Individual in photo: Nostalie
(Minou) Placide. Photograph
by Claudine Michel.

verse class backgrounds, sometimes representing in their person a class in transition. The *bourgeoises* were the ones who resisted public identification as *manbo,* unable or unwilling to take the risk. Margaret Armand, who self-identifies as a *bourgeoise,* explained that some *manbo* are in the "closet," using the English concept in her Haitian Creole speech. "Lots of *manbo* are in the closet, *moun ki pè, wont*" (those who are afraid and ashamed). She referred to their fear of social retribution at the hand of judgmental social elites, to their fear of ostracism and the ridicule they think they might have to face. Social classes in Haiti seem to have meted out a different sense of self to its female adherents, a topic we shall broach at a later date.

Armand wanted to distinguish between environment and milieu and what the religion demands. She spoke against the "mystification" that is cultivated almost as an art form by many priests who jealously guard secrets that may not be secrets or that should be shared with fellow priests and of the abuse of power dishonest priests exhibit. Margaret, who is seen as a *ti-bourgeoise* by those from the peasantry and the urban working class, experienced resentment, she says, if not envy and jealousy, from these quarters. She added, "*Yo pe mwen ta depase yo*" (They are fearful that I may go beyond them [spiritually]).

Carole De Lynch faced social disgrace during her schooling by the sisters of the Sacred Heart in Port-au-Prince and when she transferred for her secondary-level education to two well-respected schools owned respectively by Madame Durocher and Madame Castel. When she was seventeen years old, her family took the unusual step, she says, of proceeding with her initiation as a *manbo*. It was unusual because of her young age; most people are not ready spiritually to make such a lifetime commitment. A committee of aged *houngan* and *manbo* volunteered to assist, intrigued by the initiation and wanting to be helpful. She had already proven herself to be a healer. Carole had suffered no interruptions in a family devoted to the Lwa, and she completed the circle by going public on national television in the late 1970s. The words of Georgette Roger, "*Se pou nou femin sèk la*" (We must close the circle) come to mind. Carole's daughter, Anastasia De Lynch, a nineteen-year-old *manbo*, continues the tradition; she was initiated at the age of seventeen, as her mother had been, and represents a new generation of Haitian *manbo*, one raised largely in the United States.

Haiti is, after all, a very small country, a bit larger than the state of Israel, with 8 million souls. People move geographically, transitioning from one social status to another, acquiring and losing wealth, and gaining a formal education if they can. But most, if not all, individuals have family that "belong" to other social classes, indicating the upward or downward movement of nuclear families within the rich networks of an extended family system. Jacqueline Epingle was born in Port-au-Prince from a father from Léogane and a mother from Jacmel. Carole Desmesmin was born in Léogane but now lives in Miami. She has family from Martinique, the Dominican Republic, and Cuba. Carole De Lynch was born in Port-au-Prince, but her parents were from the towns of Côte-de-Fer and Aquin. A (Anonymous), was born in Port-au-Prince but has roots in the city of Jérémie, in Haiti's southwest, and in Cuba.

These *manbo*, some of whom were raised in the Vodun tradition, some of whose immediate families created a psychological distance from the tradition, present a rich "broth" in terms of their perspectives on Vodun. Yet commonalities abound. However, it must be said that they are not typical of most Haitian *manbo*, most of whom live in the provinces or the slums of cities, are non-literate, and have not suffered spatial or psychological dislocation or been distanced from their religious, spiritual, or physical lives. The decision to become a *hounsi kanzo* (an initiate) or a *manbo* is part of the "normal" state of affairs for most Haitian women—which is not clearly the case for the women we interviewed, who on the surface at least, had many more choices and options.

The interaction, with all the challenges one faces, between practicing Vodouisants and the broader world is revealed in the way each *manbo* fought against her calling and resisted joining the priesthood. They ignored both the messages and

Manbo mounted by Freda.
Individual in photo:
Jacqueline Epingle. Photo-
graph by Claudine Michel.

the messengers. They ignored the Deities themselves, who would appear in in-
sistent dreams demanding that they become initiated. They shuddered at shoul-
dering the heavy responsibilities and the powers inherent in a consecrated life.
They "visited" other systems. Margaret Armand, for instance, went to New Age practitioners, who told her to go back to her faith. All religions are tribal, she said: "I
was experiencing Vodun without knowing." Most others have similar stories.
Jacqueline Epingle, despite her knowledge of the religion in a familial context,
discovered "Vodun's more universal aspects while living long-term in Canada."
Even as identity is being lost, it reasserts itself, starting with Vodun and the Kreyol
language.

Relationship with the Sacred World

Vodou *sèvite* work at finding balance and equilibrium by deriving energy from
nature's polyrhythms. Carole De Lynch asserts: "*Nous faisons partie de la nature.
Dans le Vodou, on doit se mettre en accord avec la nature. C'est le moyen de bénéficier*

de ses effets productifs." (We are part of nature. We need to put ourselves in line with nature. That is the only way to benefit from its productive effects.)

Human beings are connected with all cosmic entities and should avoid perturbing the outerworld. The goal is to stay in equilibrium with all forces of nature and to maintain social cohesion, harmony, and balance in relationships with others. Elisabeth Beauvoir explains: "*Le Vodou est une chaîne. Vous êtes un maillon de la chaîne. Si vous n'êtes pas en équilibre, vous êtes un maillon qui dérange la chaîne. . . . Quand vous êtes en parfait équilibre, les gens recherchent votre companie. C'est ainsi que vous pouvez aider les autres.*" (Vodou is a chain. You are a link in that chain. If you are not in a state of equilibrium, you are a link that messes up the chain. . . . When you are in a balanced equilibrated state, people seek you. That is when you are able to help others.)

Beauvoir shares her views on initiation into Vodou, which she considers to be a positive step in the process of restoring harmony and rhythm. She notes: "Vodun gives a person a sense of equilibrium. Initiation is a passage from '*un état désordonné,*' a disordered state, into a life of balance and equilibrium. Initiation gives you a sense of being somebody. You think more clearly. You are at a different level. . . . You continue to want to learn, but you are no longer eager to understand everything at once. Though still confronted with the everlasting problems of day-to-day living, you are no longer victims of those problems. You are now in a state where you can help others deal with their worldly problems. We are at our most powerful when we are in equilibrium."[7]

It became clear that with reference to the tenets of the religion, the *manbo* we interviewed did not sense that there were differences between male and female priests. The Lwa are sexed or engendered but within a fluid and broadly defined sexuality. These Deities typically have male or female counterparts, often identified as husband and wife, though the situation is enormously more complex than it appears to be. The male/female dualism is actually embedded *within* each Deity itself and within each human being. This bespeaks of equilibrium anchored in a context of psychic balance as "completeness." The dyad Dambala Wedo and Ayida Wedo, which represents purity and wisdom in the serpent and the rainbow, illustrate the point, as do other pairings of Lwa.

Sexual behavior shows fluidity as well, as may well be expected. It is as if heaven and earth are reflexive and reflective of the human condition and of each other, as in a mirror. The mirror is a sacred conceptual image in Vodun: when you look into the mirror, the image that looks back at you is the image of God. The human person in community, as distinct from the individualized person, is at the center of the cosmic universe in African or African-derived religions that, in turn, anthropomorphize cosmic energies, giving to Deities presence and personality and life histories. Jacqueline Epingle was asked directly about gender and sexuality and the role of homosexuality in Vodun with and for the Lwa. She is a middle-aged heterosexual woman and has been a priest for about two decades. Her responses, made without a trace of embarrassment, were as follows, in the exact form she made them, in a mix of French and Haitian languages:

Gen plis fanm pase gason, plis manbo pase houngan nan Vodou-a. La manbo s'adonne au Vodou avec plus d'acharnement et plus de charme, konsi li te fèt pou sa. Les femmes sont plus adeptes que les hommes dans les religions, toutes les religions. La societé encourage les femmes dans ce domaine. La majorité des houngans sont soit homosexuels, soit bisexuels. Gason ta pito pa pran Lwa: orgueil mâle. Gason pa rinmin pèdi kontwòl. Les femmes sont plus libres!

La spiritualité de l'homosexuel le dirige vers la religion, et certainement, la religion vodoue. Beaucoup de manbos sont bisexuelles ou lesbiennes. [Dans l'interdiction de l'homoxexualité chez les Babalawo de Cuba], la Santería agit en accord avec les systèmes européens. Aux Etats-Unis, on emmerde les Vodouisants beaucoup plus que ceux qui pratique la Santería.

(There are more women than men, more *manbo* than *houngan* in Vodun. The *manbo* gives herself to Vodun with more enthusiasm and more charm, as if she were made for this. Women are more adept than men in religions, all religions. Society encourages women in this domain. The majority of *houngan* are either homosexuals or bisexuals. Men would rather not go into trance: male pride [arrogance]. Men do not like to loose control. Women are freer!

The homosexual's [sense of] spirituality directs him toward religion, and certainly [toward] the Vodun religion. Many *manbo* are bisexual or lesbians. [In the formal demand that homosexuality not be found in *babalawo* ranks in Cuba], Santería [La Regla de Ocha/Lukumi] acts in accord with European value systems. In the United States, Vodun practitioners are harassed much more than [those who practice] Santería.)

Some of the *manbo* we interviewed commented on the importance of fostering nonconstraining and nonhindering relationships with same-sex partners, husbands, or lovers. Multilayered meanings that abide no Manichean dichotomies may give us a clue in the domain of sexuality and gender identity.

Vodun's Force/Power

To the question "*Ki fos Vodun?*" (What is the "force" or strength of Vodun?) Margaret Armand answered, "I think Vodun, I feel Vodun [every moment of every day]. I am community-oriented. [We] should work with the popular base [and] integrate Vodun in the educational system." Carole Desmesmin added, "The U.S. occupation could not control Vodun. [It] is non-hierarchical (though highly structured), autonomous, communitarian. Politics must be [re]arranged in autonomous communities." Carole De Lynch argued that "we must heal all that suffering," a theme her daughter, Anastasia De Lynch, pursued when she said that "*manbo* do receive psychological training." She went on to say that for her, a vital area is "Vodun's constructive and progressive morality." "Vodun demands respect for life," said Carole De Lynch, but "the priest can do an abortion when the situation warrants it, for instance if a woman already has four or five children." Jacqueline Epingle chose to address overarching issues concerning equilibrium and balance in what for her is "one of the world's earliest religions." In her view, the process of equilibration is what brings spirit-power and gives *fos* to the human person in community. It is also in this sense that Carole De Lynch's statement can be placed in its proper context: "Initiation demands that the person be positioned at the center, at the core, and not utilize her/his gifts recklessly *[gratuitement]*." Indeed, "the *manbo*," she continued, "lives with serenity, exercising her choice to use cosmic energetic forces in her activities." Jacqueline Epingle said, "It does us no good to rail against Vodun, against all things African, against the Kreyol language, against the very color 'black.' If Vodun had been created in Europe, its acceptance would be guaranteed." Jacqueline added with a twinkle in her eyes that "the problem [with other religions] is that they are one-way streets; Vodun has no problem with these religions, it is a two-way street. Protestantism takes issue with all other religions; this is *"a pointe de racisme"* (a bit of racism)." A (Anonymous) reminds us that the "colors [representing each Spirit in each diasporic country] change; the Lwa themselves, change" and that all is motion. Change, as adaptation, makes survival possible. Even religious tenets may change so that spirituality may live on.

Conclusion

The *manbo* we interviewed did not want to speak for all *manbo;* they reiterated that they spoke only for themselves and their understanding of their lives and their faith. They offered a reflective view from within. These *manbo* had, for the most part, received a formal education in the Western sense of the term. Their contributions were nonetheless precious, a window on an evolving Haitian religious world that is now internationalizing.

It is not new in Haitian history for women to seek their voices. The crises wrought by enslavement and dislocation and by the Revolution of 1791 made an expansion of the roles of women possible.[8] So too did the rural uprisings of the nineteenth century, the armed resistance to the U.S. occupation, and the struggle against Duvalierism. Though working-class women have developed a niche in petty commerce and religion, their impact on the politics of the country has been seen as inconsequential. Upper- and middle-class women in urban localities, albeit with some pain, organized and made some strides in accessing education and in the area of civil rights, achieving the right to vote in the constitution of 1950 that became effective only in 1957. Their demands and these gains were made in the context of Western intellectual paradigms and political philosophies and were inspired in the final analysis by what had taken place earlier in the United States and in Europe. It is in this context that one must honor the pioneering efforts of Haiti's first formal feminist movement, the Ligue Féminine d'Action Sociale (Feminine League for Social Action) of the 1930s and the more middle-class Faisceau Féminin (The Feminine Sheaf) of the 1960s. But while honoring these pioneers, one realizes that their goals and efforts were limited by the constraints of ambient conditions and that ideologically their goals reflected their allegiance to class interests and to Western definitions of personal growth and national development. None of these women were *manbo*. But demands for widespread and meaningful change cut across class boundaries, and some *bourgeoises* have now joined their sisters in wishing a new world. A paradigmatic shift has occurred.

But this shift indicates what is nonetheless real and long-standing in Haitian Vodun, though this essence is alien to the national and international norms that controlled Haiti in the past and now broadly define what passes for development in the global environment. The Haitian Revolution of 1791 came to a grinding halt in 1806. The definition of what was possible was thus circumscribed. Revolutions explode social structures, providing an *élargissement,* a widening of opportunity for change in a new dawn in society. The participation of women, whose pain was equal to or surpassed that of their male companions, was total in the Revolution. It remains unacknowledged in large measure in Haitian historiography. However, the present Haitian societal context would seem to allow for the intromission of new "indigenous" paradigms that are seemingly at odds with the previous world of Haitian politics.

Merging Ezili Dantò to Ogou Feray, male and female principle, teaches completeness. This merger is also about the (re)construction of a country and a dream of equality as expressed by ten women warriors.

Notes

When someone goes into a trance, when a Lwa possesses an individual, the Spirit is said to have mounted his/her *chwal* (horse). The visit of the Lwa to mere mortals is the apogee of any *sèvis* (ceremony). The *chwal* are the bodies through which the Lwa speak and communicate with the participants. Therefore, our title, "From the Horses' Mouths."

1. We express our appreciation to all the women we interviewed for their willingness to share their views and experiences with us and for their many insights and insiders' comments so crucial to this project. Unless otherwise indicated, these interviews took place in Miami, Florida. Margaret Armand (interview with Marlène Racine-Toussaint, April 1998; interview with Claudine Michel, January 2000); Carole Desmesmin (interview with Marlène Racine-Toussaint, April 1998); Jacqueline Epingle (interviews with Patrick Bellegarde-Smith, December 26, 1998, to January 3, 1999); Carole Lalanne De Lynch (interview with Marlène Racine-Toussaint, April 1998; interview with Claudine Michel, January 2000); Anastasia de Lynch (interview with Marlène Racine-Toussaint, April 1998; interview with Claudine Michel, January 2000); Georgette Roger (informal conversations and discussions with Patrick Bellegarde-Smith, December 28, 1998, to January 3, 1999); "Anonymous" (interviews and discussions with Patrick Bellegarde-Smith, Port-au-Prince, Haiti, starting on August 4, 1998); Elizabeth Beauvoir (interview with Marlène Racine-Toussaint, Washington, D.C., November 1997); Nicole Miller Thomas (interview with Marlène Racine-Toussaint, New York, N.Y., April 1998).

2. Elisabeth Beauvoir is a member of one of the first Haitian families to openly claim their involvement with the Vodou religion.

3. Toni Morrison, *Lecture and Speech of Acceptance, Nobel Prize for Literature, Delivered in Stockholm, Sweden, 1993* (New York: A. A. Knopf, 1993).

4. Judith Plaskow and Carol Christ, *Weaving the Visions: Patterns in Feminist Spirituality* (San Francisco: Harper, 1989), 3–5.

5. Anthropologists who specialized in the Caribbean region in the 1920s and 1930s often had to defend their regional choice, since Caribbean culture was seen as "derivative" and

not "pure," as might be the case in Africa or Asia. Sociologists, on the other hand, tended to study "developed" societies.

6. Patrick Bellegarde-Smith, *Haiti: The Breached Citadel* (Boulder, Colo.: Westview Press, 1990), 20–21.

7. For more information on the values inherent in Haitian Vodun, see Claudine Michel, *Aspects moraux et éducatifs du Vodou* (Port-au-Prince: Le Natal, 1995).

8. The Haitian Revolution of 1791 started with the Vodou ceremony of Bwa Kayiman. This is a well-accepted fact. However, the name of the female officiant, Edaïse (no last name), is unknown to most historians or is seldom mentioned. Certainly one knows that there must have been other women ignored in Haitian historiography; only wives or consorts of male leaders are typically mentioned.

8

Rainbow over Water: Haitian
Art, Vodou Aestheticism, and Philosophy

MARC A. CHRISTOPHE

During the 1940s and the 1950s, Port-au-Prince became a beacon which attracted European and Caribbean intellectuals alike. Fascinated by the vibrancy of Haitian art and its written literature, Martinican poet and *négritude* movement founder Aimé Césaire, French surrealist writer André Breton, novelist and statesman André Malraux, Cuban expressionist painter Wilfredo Lam, Cuban novelist Alejo Carpentier, and many others found themselves in Haiti in search of the *"merveilleux,"* a sense of magical realism. During that period, Haiti initiated one of the most prolific and versatile artistic phenomena of the twentieth century, one which continues to confound the experts by its exuberance and vitality.

Michel-Philippe Lerebours observed in *Haiti et ses peintres,* a two-volume study on the history and evolution of art in Haiti, that Haitian art is transcendental, that through art, the Haitian artist is able to move beyond Haiti's material poverty and connect his or her sensibility with a collective dream. According to Lerebours:

> Ce que l'artiste haitien relate, c'est une vision intériorisée qui se construit à partir du réel mais déborde le réel, l'embue et lui donne les contours du rêve. C'est une vision qui plonge le réel dans le mythique. Cette vision que l'artiste porte en lui n'est que le reflet d'une vision commune à tout le peuple haitien.

> What the Haitian artist does is to provide an interior vision which is built on reality but transcends it and gives it the contours of dreams. It is a vision which plunges the reality into the mythical. This vision that the artist has within himself is but a reflection of a vision common to the Haitian people.[1]

The vibrancy and vitality found in Haitian art are a corollary to the spirituality of the Haitian people, whose soul and artistic sensibility are informed by their contact with the universe of Vodou. In short, this is a people who escape the existential dilemma of the contemporary Western world by maintaining an equilibrium between its physical and spiritual needs and between the sacred and the profane. This concept of *equidation* and the interconnection of spiritual life and artistic sensibility is echoed in the words of Gérald Bloncourt believes that art flourishes in Haiti in many different realms:

> Within the Haitian people at every level, tapping its submerged African memory, its scars of slavery, the liberating violence of 1804, Voodoo [sic] tradition, the combites (peasants festivities centering around group work projects), the wondrousness of the imaginary in its everyday life. Its rhythms, its musical genius. Its legends. Its dream-tales, narrative countdowns of history, of a past and a destiny with

the dynamism of volcanic lava and its radiant vapors, a High Art, ancestral, visceral, dazzling.[2]

In societies still close to the world of nature and spirituality, myths and legends play a vital part in a people's effort to rationalize their existence and their place and role in the order of things. Oftentimes, these societies are characterized by the osmotic relationships between art and religion, between the sacred and daily reality. As spirits, ancestors, and the dead partake in the life of the living, likewise, Haitian artists have intrinsically meshed their inspiration with their religion, the myths and legends of their country's folklore.

In these emerging years of the twenty-first century, Haiti is still a land shrouded in myths, a land where the divine, the magical, and the sacred coalesce into a worldview that permeates the artist's mental construct as well as his or her perception and rendition of reality. Understanding the elements that impact these artists' formation should help us see their works more clearly and come to a better appreciation of their aesthetic quality.

It is around this symbiotic relation between art, religion, and philosophy and within a Haitian system of thought that I will center the discussion in this chapter. Through a thematic study of Haitian art, I hope to demonstrate how the myths, legends, and magical universe of Vodou constitute the foundations of Haiti's popular culture and how its artists have internalized philosophical themes of exile and remembrance in their artistic discourse. More important, my discussion is grounded in the existence of a Haitian aesthetic whose dynamics reside in Vodou's perception and representation of the universe and how this aesthetic is explored by Haiti's artists. This collective canon undergirds the process by which Haitian artists develop their individual aesthetic sense, their own vision of what is beautiful.

Early efforts to stimulate artistic creations in Haiti included the establishment of the Académie de dessin et de peinture under King Henry Christophe (1807–1818) and the decoration of several buildings by local artists between 1830–1860 under President Jean-Pierre Boyer. This fostering of the arts was continued by Emperor Faustin Soulouque and President Fabre-Nicolas Geffrard. However, these efforts were doomed to fail because this "high Haitian art" was rooted in European aesthetic traditions that essentially perpetuated a cultural schism and created an artistic alienation between the French-educated Haitian artist's mentality and the tangible reality of Haiti that surrounded him or her. The denial of one's own culture is tantamount to a denial of one's self, a phenomenon that Haitian social philosopher Jean Price-Mars defined as "collective bovarysm,"[3] a sort of cultural alienation that afflicted Haitian artist and writers of the nineteenth and early twentieth centuries. Bovarysm was challenged in the 1920s and in the 1930s by the indigenist literary movement, which encouraged the rediscovery of Haitian folklore and helped create a Haitian aestheticism rooted in the culture of the masses.

If art is, generally speaking, an organizing and defining process, then the Haitian artist had to create a personal pictorial discourse and sense of composition, balance, and harmony in an attempt to redefine the world. This aesthetic canon formed the basis of the revolution in art spearheaded by Le Centre d'Art, an art workshop and gallery that opened in Port-au-Prince in 1943 under the aegis of a young American teacher named Dewitt Peters.

When Peters arrived in Haiti in 1943, he was taken by the intricate beauty of the *vèvès* (ritual symbols) he saw in the Vodou temples he visited. So impressed was he by the potential of Haiti's "traditional" artists that he dreamed of opening a center where their talents could be stimulated and their works exhibited. With the help of already-established artists and the support of the Haitian government he was able to secure a site for the center, and thus Le Centre d'Art was born. In May 1944, Le Centre d'Art organized what is regarded as the first general Haitian art exhibit, to great acclaim. In the years that followed, Le Centre d'Art and Haitian painting as a whole prospered and blossomed into the artistic phenomenon that Selden Rodman called "the miracle of Haitian art."

Peters's Haitian collaborators were academically trained Haitian artists and intellectuals such as Albert Mangonès, Maurice Borno, Raymond Coupeau, Géo Remponeau, Emmanuel Lafond, Daniel Lafontant, Camille Tesserot, and Gérald Bloncourt. This first group was quickly joined by Philippe Thoby-Marcelin, Raymond Lavelanette, and Lucien Price, who helped publish Le Centre's bulletin, which appeared in November 1945. This group was augmented by the arrival of Tamara Baussan, Andrée Malebranche, Antonio Joseph, Luce Turnier, and Marie-José Nadal. Though these men and women belonged to Haiti's intellectual and social elite, they diverged from their social group, which traditionally displayed slavish admiration for France and all things Western.

The success of Le Centre d'Art and of modern Haitian art in general was due to a simple but important policy of not interfering with the artists' sources of inspiration and techniques which, in a very symbiotic way, arose from the intersection of Vodou, Haitian myths and legends, and their own individual experiences. Indeed, most of the artists who later joined Le Centre d'Art came from the peasantry and the urban working class and had received no formal education or training in art and thus were able to paint with a spontaneity and an authenticity that one does not encounter in the works of academically trained artists.

For half a century, Le Centre d'Art remained the hub of Haitian artistic creativity. Many of Haiti's great classical painters hailed from Le Centre d'Art. Among those are Philomé Obin, founder of the Aubin artistic dynasty; Hector Hypolite, a *houngan* who saw the subjects of his paintings in his dreams; and Rigaud Benoît, whose first works graced the bodies of *tap-taps* (jitneys) and taxi cabs. These painters and others, such as Wilson Bigaud or Préfète Duffaut, found their inspiration in Vodou beliefs and in the rich and complex legends and myths of Haitian folklore. Today, it is almost a truism to declare that Le Centre d'Art nurtured the artistic revolution that changed Haiti's artistic landscape and helped Haitian artists refocus their aestheticism toward a revalorization of Haiti's African roots. Also, Le Centre d'Art provided an outlet for their work and a place to meet other artists; at times, it was the only place where they could secure the basic necessities of their craft such as paint and canvases.

This movement was also linked to the political change that witnessed the overthrow of Elie Lescot, Haiti's last mulatto president, and the birth of strong cultural currents which made the 1940s one of the most effervescent periods in the history of Haitian creativity. Today, Haitian masterpieces grace the collections of major art museums such as the Musée des Arts Modernes in Paris, the Metropolitan Museum of Art, the Milwaukee Art Museum, the Figge Art Museum in Iowa (formerly the Davenport Museum of Art), and private collections all over the world.

The blossoming of Haitian pictorial art and its eminent success did not escape the analysis of critics, who have attempted to explain the reasons why this artistic phenomenon materialized with such intensity in Haiti and in no other countries in the Caribbean. My analysis of these causes through a study of the role played by Vodou aestheticism and philosophy in Haitian art is informed by the racial and social origins of the Haitian people; the migration of African mores, customs, and (particularly) religion to Saint Domingue/Haiti; and the amalgamation of these elements with French cultural elements (creolization). I also pay proper attention to the historical dynamics that gave rise to the Haitian revolution and the formation of the Haitian nation. This brief overview of Haitian history will further elucidate those points.

The war of independence in 1804 resulted in African and Creole blacks and mulattos declaring their independence from France and founding the Republic of Haiti. Unfortunately, for reasons too complex to discuss in this chapter, from the time of independence until today, Haitian history has been marred by caudillism and oppression of the masses. The leaders who were called by destiny to lead the Haitian nation soon became the new masters and treated the people not as citizens but as subjects of a state which saw itself as the supreme master. Hence, in today's Haiti, the people's fight for justice and the right to liberty and happiness bears some resemblance to the Africans' fight for recognition of human and civil rights. For the past 200 years, time has stood still in Haiti, and so has hope for a better tomorrow. Haitians still await the fulfillment of the promises of independence.

To enslaved Africans in colonial Saint Domingue, Vodou constituted a rationalizing process as well as a philosophy of remembrance that allowed memories to be kept alive, for to lose one's past is to lose oneself. As Mircea Eliade has pointed out, a function of myths is to preserve memory, and most religious ceremonies and festivities can be viewed as a memorialization of the past to prevent death (identity loss) caused by a break in the ties that link us with the ancestors.[4] In that respect, Vodou can be defined as a magical space that allowed Africans to reconnect with the land left behind—its traditions, cultures, gods, and ancestors. It is also a philosophy that brought them the strength they needed to avenge their captivity, to root their dreams of freedom in a tomorrow without misery, without tears. Accordingly, Vodou's worldview implies the destruction of the status quo (colonial Haiti) and a return to the land of origin (Lafrik Ginen). Indeed, during Haiti's war of independence, the Maroon leaders promised their warriors that if they died in combat they would return to Africa. And today, Vodou mythology and theology are inscribed with the possibility of return: the *ti-bon-anj* (soul) of a believer "returns" to En-ba-dlo (Ginen, the land below the sea); the ancestors (*lwas*) "return" through their incarnation in the believers, and finally, Vodou mythopoeia heralds a re-creation of a mythical past (the Golden Age—Lafrik Ginen re-created). As Eliade, who studied the recurrence of the Golden Age myth around the world, observed, the religious conscience of rural populations is dominated by the nostalgia for paradise, the desire to connect with a nature that is constant and perennial, protected from the turmoil of war, devastation, and conquests.[5] We see these attempts reflected in Vodou in the creation of a myth of return to a mythical Africa.

Thus, for Africans in the New World, Vodou became the holy way that connected them to the land of origin, to that place of bliss where there was no tears and no suffering. And it is not surprising that many Vodou songs speak of deliverance and of return. In fact, one could argue that as a religious system that was conceptualized in exile during a time of slavery, Vodou constituted an existential and transcendental process by which, through an intimate relationship with the spirits, one could become him/herself a spirit and escape the abject reality of plantation life. For a few minutes or hours, one could become free, could have an existence outside the master's power and dominion.

Furthermore, as a religion of remembrance and as a myth of origin, Vodou connected the African captives to Ginen and offered them a way to understand their captivity in the New World, a philosophical ground in which to anchor their humanity, the strength that allowed them to perdure and survive wretched conditions. Finally, it offered the hope that one day they would avenge their forebears and re-create Lafrik Ginen. This political agenda of the Maroons of Saint Domingue was not concretized; instead, it was replaced by a Haitian state which emulated the French model.

Our vision of Vodou eschatology as a Janus-like system, or a Gédé-like system (Gédé being spirit of death, sexual energy, and rebirth), rooted in a mythical past while simultaneously looking forward into the future, is conveyed by the two major divisions of Vodou spirits: the Rada (cool) African-inspired spirits and the Kongo/Petwo (hot) Creole-derived spirits.

Vodou's Rada side looks back to Lafrik Ginen, the ancestral and mythical land of milk and palm wine, land of peace and bliss of the ancestors, while its Kongo/Petwo, or apocalyptic, side calls for war, revenge, and destruction of the slave system, with the ultimate hope that out of its ashes a new country can emerge, purged of ills and evils.

The reconceptualization of the past, of Lafrik Ginen, what I call the anatopian vision, and the conceptualization of the future, or the utopian vision, are the two fundamental pillars of Vodou cosmogony and, by extension, of Haitian mythopoeia and theology. While Haitian cosmogony is characterized by its relativism—that is, nothing is essentially good or essentially bad—we must observe that, mythologically speaking, two major Vodou *lwas* are emblematic of Vodou's bipolarity: Ezili, spirit of love, of desire and riches, who connects with the past and Lafrik Ginen, and Ogoun Feray, spirit of war and revenge, who heralds the future and the coming of change. These two *lwas* constitute the two archetypal figures that are emblematic of Haitian collective identity, culture, and philosophy.

Yet we should not generalize by suggesting that Haitian art is influenced in all its aspects by Vodou. Indeed, Haitian art spans the full spectrum of artistic creativity and explores subjects and themes relevant to the sacred, the secular, the traditional, the fantastic, the humorous the personal, the mythological, and the purely aesthetic. Arguably one could go on to declare that in the expression of their creativity, some Haitian artists seem to have completely escaped Vodou's influence. Among this group of artists we can cite Bernard Wah, Bernard Séjourné, and Jean-Claude Legagneur, who appear to be more "modern" or cosmopolitan than "traditional" Haitian artists. However, a painting need not necessarily portray an aspect of Vodou rituals or specifically express a Vodou narrative to be influenced by the Vodou religion. An artist's style or subject matter may be Vodou-inspired or -influenced without the artist him or herself being a Vodouist, or a Vodou believer. The subject of a painting may seem to have no connection whatsoever with Vodou, yet under scrutiny one may discover that the artist's sensibility and aesthetics were influenced unconsciously by cultural factors that still emerge in the work.

Despite these cautionary remarks, I contend that Haitian painting is informed by Vodou and that an understanding of the religion is necessary in most cases to comprehend and appreciate this art form. To understand a Western/Christian nativity scene, for example, a rudimentary notion of Western hagiography or Christianity is necessary. Otherwise, the work is just another pictorial representation of the birth of a child, and the artwork's true essence escapes the viewer. The same is true of Vodou and Haitian art.

Thus, analyzing Haitian Art and Vodou aestheticism and philosophy is tantamount to unveiling the historical and cultural forces that have created the Haitian nation, molded Haitian identity, and given birth to its religiosity and artistic expression. As René Depestre observed in *Bonjour et Adieu à la Négritude,* Haitian magical realism can be defined as:

> *une manière propre à notre peuple de concevoir les rapports de l'esprit à l'imaginaire. En Haïti, même le sommeil des arbres et des pierres devient, dans l'imagination des êtres vivants, tantôt un long rêve musicien, tantôt la politesse hallucinée de quelque divinité du soir. Les éléments telluriques et sociaux de l'univers haïtien ont été, en réponse à l'apre problématique de l'esclavage, dilatés et noués en un système complexe de correspondances et de connivances symboliques ou mythiques.*[6]

our own people's way of conceiving the relationship between the mind and the imaginary. In Haiti, even the drowsiness of trees and stones becomes, in the imagination of living things, sometimes a long musical dream, sometimes the hallucinatory politeness of some night time deity. The seismic and social elements of the Haitian universe have been—in response to the problematic effects of slavery—expanded and

André Pierre, *La Sirène* (*The Mermaid*). Reprinted from Gérald Alexis, *Peintres haitiens* (Éditions Cercle d'art, 2000), p. 205.

knotted in a complex system of symbolic or mythic correspondences and schemings. (trans. Roberto Strongman)

One of the most prominent contemporary Haitian painters is André Pierre. In his *La Sirène* (*The Mermaid*), he captures the innocent joy and playfulness of a mermaid frolicking in the ocean. We admire the painting's vibrancy and the virtuosity of the artist's brushstrokes and how his almost obsessive detailing unites the pulsating motions of the sea and the energy radiating from the mermaid. Yet if we are unaware of the role Vodou myths and mythology played in André Pierre's personal life and imaginary as well as his own mysticism, we would fail to grasp the artist's metaphysical discourse. André Pierre is also a *houngan* who sometimes paints while in a trance, and thus his painting *La Sirène* immediately takes on an iconic significance. It no longer represents a mermaid, as the title apparently suggests, but Lasirenn, one of Vodou's most important female deities, who, together with Agwe, lord of the sea, rules over the oceans.

Likewise, we can draw similar inferences when viewing *The Pleasure Ship of Agwé Taroyo* by Saint Marc. Straddling the line between modernism and realism with its mix of abstract and traditional forms, the artist draws our attention to four huge triangular sails unfolded in the morning breeze. Beneath the sails, the ship's hull, which is shaped like the body of a fish, catches our eye and titillates our imagination with its rather whimsical conceptualization. The ship's arrival is acclaimed by three horn-blowing and flower-carrying mermaids. However, as in the case of André Pierre's *La Sirène,* the informed viewer will not grasp the significance of the title *The Pleasure Ship of Agwé Taroyo* if he is not aware of Agwé Taroyo and the important place he occupies in the Vodou pantheon (see plate 6).

Not every Haitian painting is directly inspired by Vodou, nor can we say whether or not a work shows definite Vodou influences. It also quite possible for an artist's work, even though it is not visibly Vodou inspired, to carry cultural undercurrents that subliminally permeate the artist's inspiration and that he or she may have acquired by what can be called cultural osmosis. The work entitled *Secrets Désirs* (*Secret Desire*) by Serge Legagneur exemplifies this possibility (see plate 7). On a dark ochre background, Legagneur depicts three working-class women as visual support for an elegantly dressed lady of the upper class. We are quick to notice the women's white headdresses that identify them as servants of the *lwas*, especially the central figure in white, who stands behind the lady and offers her a bowl of fruit. Placed at the center of the canvas, this woman is the source of a soft light which radiates from her body to illuminate with a rich glow the face of the lady, who is overwhelmed by emotion and lost in contemplation. As we delve deeper into the work's possible Vodou significance, the painting stops being an scene between a mistress and her servants and takes on a mysterious, almost liturgical meaning. This impression is intensified by the presence of the clay vessel that could represent a *govi* in the hands of the central figure. In the Vodou tradition, the *govi* is a sacred vessel that contains the spirit of the deceased. Armed with this additional information, we are able to partly unlock the painting's mystery. Could it be that the lady secretly desires the special relationship her servants maintain with the *lwas*, the ancestors? Does she think that their lives are richer than hers? As he wove his pictorial talent with a rhythmic sense of color and established a ritualistic dynamic in his work, whether willingly or unwittingly, Serge Legagneur has inscribed *Secrets Désirs* within a Vodou weltanschauung.

Sometimes one may encounter two different themes in a painting, one Vodou inspired, the other hailing from Western canons, as in Roosevelt Sanon's *Le "manger-loas," offrande aux dieux* (*The "Manger-Loas," Food Offerings to the Gods*), in which the subject of the work refers to a Vodou ritual while representing a still life (see plate 8).

Despite the possible influences from other sources, it appears that the Haitian aesthetic is above all Vodou and Creole—that is, the amalgamation of divergent racial/cultural elements into a new synthesis. As Legagneur's painting shows, we can denote these mixed elements because the artist was formally trained and exposed to the Western canon and Western styles yet continues to be inspired by aspects of Haitian folklore and religion.

This observation leads to a discussion of the socioracial and cultural forces that form the basis of Vodou and Haitian culture. The transformation of African/Kongo *minkisi* into Haitian *pakèt kongo* demonstrates how this is connected with the Haitian Vodou/Creole aesthetic. The similarity between the *pakèt kongo*'s transformation and the amalgamation of Vodou *lwas* and Catholic saints also becomes clear. The *minkisi* originated with the KiKongo people of Central Africa. Robert

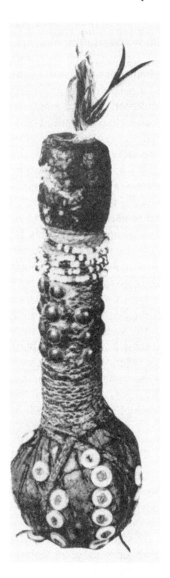

Kongo Minkisi. Reprinted from Donald J. Cosentino,
ed., *Sacred Arts of Haitian Vodou* (South Sea
International Press, 1995), p. 28.

Farris Thompson describes them as magical charms made of "leaves, shells, packets, sachets, bags, ceramic vessels, wooden images, statuettes, cloth bundles,
among other objects. They contain medicine and a soul combined to give it life
and power."[7]

Once transplanted in Haiti, the Kongo *minkisi* became *pakèt kongos.* The rough
African textile used to wrap the balls of leaves and herbs was replaced by shiny
satin, the bag itself was tied with colored ribbon and adorned with multicolored
feathers or a Christian cross instead of with raffia or rope made with vegetal fibers.

The transformation of the *minkisi* from their African/Kongo origins into the *pakèt kongo* of the New World illustrates the merging of the cultures of Africa and Europe and the birth of an aesthetic of incorporation and accumulation that is essentially Creole and Vodouist (see plate 9). The *nkisi* (singular) in our illustration expresses the potency of this creolization process which, in a gesture of bravado, added a Christian cross to an African religious object and thus created a new imagery and iconography.

This recombining of Europe and Africa, of the old to create the new, is illustrated by the aesthetic of Haitian Vodou altars, which are so inclusive that their sensibility approaches that of baroque art. In that same vein, we may theorize that Vodou aestheticism resulted from the desire of enslaved Africans to emulate the trappings of the master's life, to borrow the religious paraphernalia that the master venerated or endowed with power and associate it with his own religious or magical elements imported from Africa. Indeed, adaptation of Africans to the social dynamics of Saint Domingue went way beyond mere survival, and the emergence of Vodou expresses their spiritual and material aspirations. The influence of colonial mores and customs on enslaved Africans and the attractiveness and luxury of the colonial lifestyle and their role in the creation of a new Creole identity have not been exhaustively explored. As Donald J. Cosentino has aptly observed: "The pantheon of *lwas* who rode into Saint Domingue in the heads and on the shoulders of African captives, adapting themselves as did their horses to the existential realities of a new world is one of the consistently underrated events in world's religious history."[8]

The absorption of Catholic rituals and saints into Vodou cosmogony and liturgy also illustrates the principle of fusion. By fusion, I mean the encounter and synthesis of diverse and apparently opposed elements. In applying this concept to the so-called Catholico-Vodou syncretism, I am quite aware that my position runs counter to the one favored by most researchers. According to these scholars, the Africans in Saint Domingue "hid" their *lwas* under the guise of Catholic saints for fear of being discovered by the white colonists. I believe that this may be an inconclusive and an a posteriori conclusion of scholars who are attempting, without presenting a convincing argument, to explain the fusion of *lwas* and saints observed in Vodou.

When we consider that the majority of the Africans spent their entire lives on plantations, that they were only superficially catechized, that eighteenth-century technology did not allow for mass production of lithographs, and that it was almost impossible for the masses of African captives to be exposed to the images of Catholic saints, we can only conclude that it is preposterous to think that they were so visually familiar with Christian iconography that they would use the knowledge of the apparent relationship between an African deity and a Catholic saint to camouflage the deity under the cover of the saint. To do so would have required a certain degree of familiarity with the saints that the slaves did not possess. If, as Leslie Desmangles posits, Vodou was "born out of the difficult and oppressive conditions of slavery and the necessary adaptation to a new environ-

Vodou altar. Reprinted from Donald J. Cosentino, ed., *Sacred Arts of Haitian Vodou* (South Sea International Press, 1995), p. 59.

ment,"[9] it follows that the African deities and Christian saints could not have preserved their original characteristics in the harsh reality of Saint Domingue and that ultimately they had to merge, to fuse. Certainly today's Haitians do not perceive or venerate Catholic saints as Europeans do. Although Haitians and Europeans may be referring to the same historical characters, the truth is that in the

Vodou concept of the universe some Catholic saints are fused with Vodou *lwas,* are perceived as *lwas.*

In effect, when a Vodouist looks at a lithograph of Saint Jacques/James or the Maria Dolorosa del Monte Calvario, he does not think that Ogou or Ezili are "hiding" under the pictures of those saints. Rather, in his vision, Saint Jacques is Ogou, Ezili is the Maria Dolorosa del Monte Calvario, and the obverse statements are true as well.

Moreover, one should not see the fusion of *lwas* and saints as a "christianization" of African deities or a "paganization" of Roman Catholic saints but as a metaphysical construct to which Vodou eschatology has given cosmic dimensions and which reflects the Haitian's vision of the world. It is a phenomenon that responds to the existential needs of an uprooted people who are attempting to bring order and meaning to the chaos of their world. But, more important, incorporating and fusing such diverse cultural forms and religious experiences into a relationship of balance and equilibrium illustrates the all-inclusive and harmonizing characteristics of Haitian Vodou and of Vodou aestheticism. As Donald J. Cosentino has observed:

> To look at a Vodou altar cluttered with customized whiskey bottles, satin pomanders, clay pots dressed in lace, plaster statues of Saint Anthony and the laughing Buddha, holy cards, political kitsch, Dresden clocks, bottles of Moet-et-Chandon, rosaries, crucifixes, Masonic insignia, eye-shadowed kewpie dolls, atomizers of Anaïs-Anaïs, wooden phalli, goat skulls, Christmas tree ornaments, Arawak, Celts . . . is to gauge the achievement of slaves and freemen who imagined a myth broad enough and fabricated a ritual complex enough to encompass all this disparate stuff (see plate 10).[10]

Rather than becoming empty vessels, Africans turned the tables on Europeans and borrowed from their cultural paraphernalia. They wove them with elements of Africa's cultures, breathed a new life force into them and created a new Creole self, a Creole religion and a Creole culture that best fit their *new* being, their *new* existence in the New World.

If Vodou constituted a means of recapturing the humanity of enslaved Africans, such a project would not have been complete if it had not encompassed the full dimensions of their "humanness," with all its frailties, ambitions, and desires as well as its weaknesses and grandeurs. The Bible says that God created man in his own image and likeness, but I believe that the contrary is true, that it is man who created God in accordance with his dreams and desires. The transformation of the image of the Christian God over the centuries is ample proof of the validity of this assertion; so is the creation in Saint Domingue/Haiti of Vodou's anthropomorphic deities. In their characteristics and general tendencies, these deities express the hope, fears, phantasms, and temperament of their creators.

Though these considerations apply to most Vodou deities, the characteristics and temperament of two Vodou deities are offered here as illustrations: the two manifestations of Ezili known as Ezili Dantò and Ezili Freda.

Ezili is the deity of love, wealth, motherhood. In her manifestation as Ezili Dantò,

Ezili Dantò.

she is dark skinned, strong, and courageous and is often assimilated with the Catholic Mater Salvatoris. As Ezili Freda, she is a light-skinned mulatto who enjoys comfort and luxury and is associated with Maria Dolorosa del Monte Calvario.

In a country where the majority of the population lives in poverty, the two Ezilis exemplify the Haitian Vodouist's strength and courage (Ezili Dantò) as well as his or her aspiration to material wealth (Ezili Freda). Haitian devotees join the two deities in mystical marriages. These unions are occasions for elaborate ceremonies where rings and vows are exchanged for a lifetime commitment between the newlyweds.

As mother, Ezili embodies continuity, repose, and the bliss of the maternal womb that some interpret as Lafrik Ginen. According to Leslie G. Desmangles, Ezili "symbolizes Ginen's cosmic womb from which the released ancestral *gwo-bon-anjs* (souls) are reclaimed." As Desmangles posits: "Ezili is therefore the embodiment of human longing for an ideal in which human fantasy transcends the limitations of mundane reality."[11]

Another archetypal deity in Vodou mythopoeia is Ogou Feray, who symbolizes strength and valor; he slays the enemy and rights the wrongs. In ritual songs, the *sèvitè* (Vodou believer) portrays him as a general who is said to have contributed heavily to the war of independence. It is no accident that Ogou's emblematic *vèvè*, which includes two crossed swords and a stylized central palm tree, is an abstracted version of the Haitian coat of arms and that Ogou's ritual colors, blue and red, are the same as those of the Haitian flag. In addition, leg-

Ezili Freda.

end has it that Ogou was the *mèt tèt* (personal spirit) of Jean-Jacques Dessalines, Haiti's liberator.

When one looks at Haitian history and the long list of dictators who have ruled since independence in 1804, one could argue that the oppression suffered by modern-day Haitians echoes, to some extent, the conditions of Africans in Saint Domingue who hoped for a better life for Haiti. It mirrors their ancestors' quest for Ginen, "land of milk and palm wine." Haitian artists, faced with Haiti's harsh realities, responded to the violence and destruction around them by recapturing in their works the vision of a past long gone, conceptualized as Lafrik Ginen/Eden/ Earthly Paradise, and by also projecting their dreams of a peaceful and prosperous future Haiti.

Indeed, the anatopian (Lafrik Ginen) and utopian (Haiti reborn/remade) currents that emerge repeatedly from the pictorial discourse of Haiti's artists are prevalent in Haitian art. They illustrate the two mythical divisions: the theme of Eden,

Ogou.

or paradise lost, that can be connected to Vodou's mythical representation of Lafrik Ginen (Rada) and the theme of paradise re-created that permeates Vodou's messianism (Petwo) and its search for a land without misery, without sufferings.

In the Lafrik Ginen current, the artist turns time and again toward the past to recapture an ideal moment of the mythical history of the Haitian people, the supreme and fundamental moment before the Atlantic crossing represented by the earthly paradise theme. Oftentimes, this type of work portrays an Eden-like space, a pristine garden filled with flowers and fruit-bearing trees, refreshed by silvery streams and waterfalls and inhabited by "African" animals that do not exist in Haiti's fauna. The viewer is left to wonder about the strength of the atavism and collective memory that cause Haitian artists, five centuries after the first African arrived in the New World, to attempt to reconnect with the land of their ancestors and rediscover its paradisiacal splendor.

Some critics may argue that the presence of the earthly paradise theme in Haitian painting is connected to the story of Adam and Eve in the biblical Garden of Eden, that Haitian artists must have seen illustrations of the biblical paradise, and that they are influenced by such illustrations. Perhaps. However, this association should not shock us since it falls within the scope of the concept of fusion discussed earlier, and one can readily understand why the artists would merge the myth of Lafrik Ginen/Earthly Paradise with the biblical myth of Eden (see plate 11). Indeed, both concepts spring from the same myth of return that Mircea Eliade studied. This process of combining old and new, profane and sacred, Christian and African is essential to Vodou. In this instance, Christian and Vodou beliefs and traditions are recombined so as to express the multiple dimensions of the historical and mythical reality of the Haitian people.

The other paradigm that is encountered in Haitian art and that calls for more probing inquiry is the utopian current that springs from the artist's attempt to reconceptualize his or her reality by painting images of a new, vibrant, and peaceful Haiti (see plates 12, 13, 14). Although this a common theme in Haitian art as a whole, the utopian theme is particularly favored by a group of artists that Marie-José Nadal-Gardère and Gérald Bloncourt call the Jacmel School. The works produced by these artists are notable for their portrayal of calm and rainbow-colored landscapes by which they express their dreams of a green and prosperous Haiti. This group is represented by such painters as Murat Saint-Vil, Jean-Louis Sénatus, Roosevelt Sanon, Rémy Paillan, Camille Torchon, and Henri-Robert Brésil.

In contrast to the anatopian vision and its reproduction of Lafrik Ginen/Eden, which often portrays a primordial couple surrounded by an exuberant and overpowering jungle, the utopian paintings present a well-controlled space characterized by a geometrical sense of harmony. They reveal the will of humanity to impose order on the world and rebuild it through its own effort. No longer will reality be abandoned to chance; rather, it will obey the rules of logic, order, and social harmony.

It is evident that the paintings of the Jacmel School bear no resemblance to the actual Haitian countryside, which is now barren and worn as a result of deforestation and erosion. Moreover, when one contemplates the sociopolitical quagmire facing Haiti today, one would certainly tend to discard these pastel-colored paintings as flights of fancy, frivolous expressions of art for art's sake. Yet in spite of their sometimes fanciful or fantastic approach, these paintings should not be rejected as escapism. They are not windows opening into a fantasy world but mirrors that reflect the artists' will to re-create their land and adorn it in the most careful fashion. What we see represented in these works is the crystallization of a dream deferred for almost 200 years, a dream that has given Haitian art one of its most defining themes: the utopian landscape.

If anatopia is the other side of utopia, if indeed they are the two sides of the

Wilson Anacréon, *L'Age d'or* (*Golden Age*). Reprinted from Jean Marie Drot,
La Rencontre des deux mondes (Edizioni Carte Segrete, 1992), p. 49.

same reality, perhaps it may still be possible to re-create the past in the future. In
this instance, the past becomes a guide, a framework onto which the future will
be built. The future becomes a reconstructed, modified image of the past. Haitian utopian paintings may be viewed as a futuristic expression of the archetypal
concept of and quest for Ginen, the Haitian/Vodou lost paradise.

In other examples, such as in the paintings of Préfète Duffaut, the will to reconstruct and rebuild Haiti is so powerful that his art may be perceived as the
most potent expression of the aesthetic of fusion and repossession. Even a cursory look at Duffaut's works reveals that, in contrast to other artists who reconstruct Haiti's natural environment and grant it the same pristine quality of Lafrik
Ginen/Eden, Duffaut builds cities of bridges, spiraling staircases, and towers that
seem to defy heaven (see plate 15). His fantastic cities, which emerge with one
singular thrust from beneath the sea, are literally out of this world. Yet though
Duffaut's cities are outlandish, they are not that distant from the Haitian collective consciousness. His reconstruction brings to mind the fabulous city of
Vilokan, the city below the water in the land of Ginen which, according to Vodou
tradition, is inhabited by the *lwas* and ancestors of the Haitian people.

The painting by Wilson Anacréon entitled (aptly enough) *L'Age d'or* (*Golden
Age*) illustrates in the most striking fashion the artist's personal vision as well as
the messianism that lies at the core of Haitian art and of Haitian philosophy.
Anacréon's presents his vision of the New Haiti coming out of darkness, bathed
in the glorious morning light and still fresh with the morning's dew. Dividing the
canvas's space almost perpendicular to the horizontal plane, a stream cuts a sil-

very, meandering line and water gushes from the distant blue mountains dotted with small flower-like peasant huts. On the right side of the canvas, a man on a prancing horse, hat raised, salutes the new dawn. Yet Anacréon's painting is ambiguous. While the title, *The Golden Age,* points towards the past (Ginen), the principal figure on the horse salutes the rising sun, a metaphor for a new day and a new beginning. Thus, the painting straddles two spaces and two times. It stands, as in a Vodou crossroad (*kalfou*), at the junction of utopia and anatopia, between Lafrik Ginen and utopian/futuristic Haiti. It encapsulates the cosmogonic and eschatological tension of Haitian society, historically and mythically caught between a return to the past and the construction of a future utopia.

What to make of Haitian art? How to characterize it? From the inception of Le Centre d'Art, these questions have baffled critics. Incapable of understanding its intricacy and intrinsic qualities, these critics have often categorized it as naïve or primitive. Some have even gone so far as to deplore its lack of engagement, its lack of political content, or its dearth of redeeming social qualities. With the exception of a few decidedly ideological artists such as Rigaud Benoît (*Boat People,* 1965), Valcin II (*Le Cyclone Flora*), Edouard Duval-Carrié (*Mardi Gras at Fort Dimanche,* 1993; *Incident in a Garden,* 1994), Haitian artists generally appear to be aesthetes more interested in *l'art pour l'art* than in what Jean-Paul Sartre called *engagement.* However, while Haitian utopian painting does not outwardly question Haiti's political systems or governmental policies, it does convey, albeit in an indirect fashion, the alienation of the nation's artists and their rejection of Haiti's general state of decay.

The two visions of reality as perceived in Haitian painting essentially convey the same message, that of the Haitian people's desire to reconnect their ancestors' dream of an African/Eden with their own dream of a modern comfortable Haiti.

Haiti's artists are not as "naïve" as they are perceived to be by the critics; indeed, their thematic and aesthetic concerns reveal great sensitivity to their world, to its myths as well as its history. With both retrospective and progressive elements, an accumulation of details and ornaments, an abundance of polyphonic elements, the expressive qualities of its coloring and hues, Haitian art can be deemed as essentially humanistic and, to some extent, baroque. It is an art that rejects the rigidity and the soberness of academism, an art situated at the junction of passions, intellect, and spirituality. Like the Vodou that grants it its intensity and depth, Haitian art expresses all the tension, paradoxes, and vibrancy of Haiti's Creole culture.

As does the history of invasion, wars, slavery, and paradise lost and regained in the Antilles, Haitian aestheticism represents the quest for a balance between opposites. It is the linear espousing the sensuousness of the curve, it is the circular mirroring the rigidity of the vertical, it is the effervescent blossoming of life itself in all its antithesis and oxymoronic equilibrium. And this is the real miracle of Haitian art, a reflection on the Haitian will to survive in body and spirit in spite of enslavers and oppressors. It is the desire to create beauty out of misery, to build a culture out of suffering, to develop an aestheticism grounded in the belief that Haiti will one day blossom like the garden of Ginen and will stand upright like the towers of Vilokan.

The past 200 years of Haitian contributions to art and culture perhaps constitutes the greatest monument the Haitians have built to their survival in a hostile and alienating environment. Rather than accepting the inhuman conditions imposed upon them by slavery and years of oppression, Haitians have created an existential philosophy of fusion and repossession that granted them the demiurgic qualities of re-creating their selves and asserting their humanity. And out of the chaos of the plantation system and the cultures that were brought into Saint Domingue by the Atlantic currents, they conceptualized a world and an aesthetic that expresses the multipolarity of Haitian culture and identity.

Notes

1. Michel-Philippe Lerebours, *Haiti et ses peintres,* vol. 1 (Port-au-Prince: L'Imprimeur II, 1989), 275. All translations are mine unless otherwise indicated.

2. Gérald Bloncourt, *La Peinture haïtienne* (Paris: Nathan, 1986), 22.

3. Jean Price-Mars, *So Spoke the Uncle,* trans. Magdaline Shannon (Washington, D.C.: Three Continents Press, 1983), 8.

4. Mircea Eliade, *Aspects du mythe* (Paris: Gallimard, 1963), 150–163.

5. Ibid., 213.

6. René Depestre, *Bonjour et adieu à la Négritude* (Paris: Robert Laffont, 1980), 236–237.

7. Robert Farris Thompson, *Flash of the Spirit: African and Afro-American Art and Philosophy* (New York: Vintage Books, 1984), 117.

8. Donald J. Cosentino, ed., *Sacred Arts of Haitian Vodou* (Los Angeles: UCLA Fowler Museum of Cultural History, 1995), 25.

9. Leslie G. Desmangles, *Faces of the Gods: Vodou and Catholicism in Haiti* (Chapel Hill: University of North Carolina Press), 15.

10. Ibid., 27.

11. Ibid., 133.

9

A Reading of the *Marasa* Concept
in Lilas Desquiron's *Les Chemins de Loco-Miroir*

FLORENCE BELLANDE-ROBERTSON

The Haitian intellectual elite, steeped in the literary traditions of France and else-where, has nonetheless utilized Haitian religion and folklore as fodder for its in-spiration in recent years. One recalls the excellent peasant novels of Jacques Roumain, Pierre Marcelin, Philippe Thoby-Marcelin, and Jacques Stephen Alexis that mined the subterranean currents of a "real" Haiti that has otherwise been unknown or ignored altogether by the westernizing elite.[1]

Lilas Desquiron's novel *Les Chemins de Loco-Miroir* is yet another effort to con-nect Haiti's two halves to make it whole again.[2] The novel is woven around the Haitian social tapestry, sisterhood, and the symbolism of the *marasa*[3] concept. Of all the Vodou elements that permeate the text, the *marasa* concept is of par-ticular significance because it plays a determining role in establishing Violaine and Cocotte's spiritual and mystical bond. This notion is the *potomitan* of *Les Chemins de Loco-Miroir,* the central pillar which supports the novel's structure. The idea of *marasa* illuminates Haiti's social and racial problematic, intimating a path toward healing through the acceptance of its twin-ness, and thus the notion that its hybridity could lead to a creole culture. In each of the novel's three parts, a Vodou ceremony constitutes the paroxysmal moment; these ceremonies shoul-der the progression of the novel's narrative.

The French word "*miroir*" in the novel's title, which translates as "*miwa*" in the creole language, is associated with the deity Loko in the expression "*Loco-miroir,*" a term that refers to one of Vodou's most venerated Lwa, Loko-Miwa—the healer. This choice of language indicates the author's intent to direct an inquisitive gaze, as in a mirror, into the depth of the Haitian psyche and to invoke Loko's healing power in order to unravel the Haitian problematic.

If we delve further in the Vodou arcanum, we discover other religious sym-bolism attached to Loko-Miwa and other Lwa. Leslie Desmangles observed that "the lwas are often referred to as mirror images."[4] Desmangles pursued this con-cept by underlining Vodou's dual characteristics and the unity existing between humans and Lwa: "During Vodou ceremonies the mirrored image of the world of the living is symbolized by a number of ritual observances. Then the houngan greets his assistant. . . . The two face each other while holding hands, bow to each other (reflecting the inverse of the motion of the other) and then perform a num-ber of turns . . . to represent the profane world of the living as reflected in the sa-cred, cosmic mirror of the lwas."[5] Thus, at the outset, Lilas Desquiron has in-scribed her novel both within the realm of Vodou and its Lwa and within Haitian history. Ceremonies, rituals, and manifestations of the Lwa help elucidate the tragedy that befalls the life of the two spiritual twin sisters, the *marasa,* Violaine and Cocotte.

The novel opens with the retrospective musing of eighty-year-old Cocotte, who is sitting in front of her house on a hill in the southern town of Jérémie. Cocotte, the novel's primary narrator, is mesmerized by the ebb and flow of the Caribbean Sea, and unfolds the tragedy of her *marasa*-sister Violaine in a flashback. Violaine Delavigne (De-la-vigne, of the root, of the earth) is emblematic of the tragic history of Haiti's disunity, a disintegration attributable to the presence of disparate cultural influences.

Throughout the novel other voices join Cocotte to recount the story of the young vibrant heiress who was born in a *cocon de dentelle* (a lace cocoon) but destined by the Lwa to be the *marasa*/mystical twin of Cocotte, a peasant girl from their common ancestral village.[6] These girls symbolize the fragile balance of two worlds, the European and African worlds and the color and class divide. Far from adhering to the values and mores of her class, Violaine revels in her hybridity and internalizes her cultural and genetic heritage. She transcends the schizophrenia of her class, accepting her *créolité.*[7] She is perceived as a threat to her world and to her own mother, who decides that she must be zombified. Desquiron nevertheless infuses hope in the unfolding of the story since Violaine also undergoes a process of dezombification and triumphs over her fate. She is reunited with her *marasa,* symbolizing the union of Haiti's separated halves.

Before proceeding further, it is important to look at the significance of the social and spiritual realities behind the concept of twin-ness/*marasa.* The *marasa,* biological twins, may be of the same or mixed gender. However, in Haiti, where the reality of life is intertwined with religious elements, when this type of birth occurs, mythical, spiritual, and symbolic significance is implied. For a simple set of twins, Haitians speak of *marasa de,* while a set of three is *marasa twa.* A male child born after a set of twins is called a *dosou,* and a female, a *dosa.* The *dosou* or *dosa* complements the twins and is reputed to have more power than the twins themselves. This trilogy refers to the *marasa* trinity mentioned by Maya Deren.[8] The three main divisions of Violaine's life and the three cultural currents, the African, European, and Amerindian, converge and coincide to give birth to the Haitian people and culture.

Haitian anthropologist Michel Laguerre observed that because the *marasa* "are young orphaned spirits, the twins cannot provide for themselves; they are mostly dependent on their devotees. . . . The congregation guarantees the twin spirits that it will continue to take care of them. This is a guarantee for life."[9]

They incarnate the notion of the segmentation of some original cosmic totality that must regain wholeness. It is specifically this aspect that Desquiron plays with in order to reconstruct her vision of a Haiti capable, at last, of recuperating its wholeness. Maya Deren wrote that "twins . . . are understood as two parts of a whole, hence shar[e] one soul. . . . Since the twins are, essentially, one, that which affects one part affects the other and whatever disease or accident may beset one twin is understood to threaten the other; and their violent separation may lead to disaster."[10]

Moreover, for the Vodou believer, *marasa* symbolizes abundance, plurality, wholeness, healing, innocence, and newness, thus their representation as children. *Marasa* are also referred to as *kalfou marasa,* for they are guardians in control of the crossroads and are linked to the *Lwa*-spirit Legba, who opens the gate to the crossroads. We therefore see the linkage between *marasa,* Legba, and Loko-Miwa, from whence derives the title of the novel: Legba guards the crossroad of life, and Loko, who is the one who sees into the future and into the souls of beings, guards the *ounfò.*

One further appreciates the richness of the metaphor and the message of hope it conveys when it is applied to the Haitian reality. It is a fusion of opposite elements that create an opening, *l'ouverture,* not only in terms of the discourse on identity and *créolité* but also in terms of a new vision where both parts of the Haitian melting pot might come together.

The novel opens in an unspecified time, with Cocotte reminiscing and lamenting on the past and the general state of decay of Jérémie, which, after the tragic events in the lives of Cocotte and Violaine, appears to be on the brink of disintegration: "*Ay, ma soeur Violaine est partie depuis longtemps rejoindre ses ancêtres de l'autre côté de l'eau et moi mes cheveux sont blancs comme la mer Caraibe. . . . Mes yeux infatigables sont un cadeau empoisonné des Loas.*" (Violaine, my sister, left some time ago to join our ancestors on the other side of the great water. As for me, my hair has turned as white as the Caribbean glistening in the sunlight. . . . My tireless eyes are an accursed gift from the Lwa.)[11]

As the story unfolds, we learn that a calamity has fallen on the region, that a political massacre has occurred, and that at the center of it all were Cocotte and Violaine. Years ago, these two young girls from the mountains *morne Macaya* and from the town of Jérémie, respectively, were consecrated as spiritual sisters at a Vodou ceremony.

Violaine Delavigne was a member of a prominent *mulâtre* family, and Cocotte, daughter of peasants, was born *dans le canal, à la lisière des plantations caféières. Dans le canal où toutes les femmes se sont toujours retirées pour accoucher*" (in the canal on the edge of the coffee plantations, in that canal where all the women went to give birth).[12] Yet in spite of their class differences, both children's births were marked by the same Vodou ceremony, which consecrated their *marasa*-ness. So it was at the age of eight that Cocotte went to live in the Delavignes' home to be near Violaine, her *marasa* sister. One wonders what role Cocotte played in the drama that engulfed Violaine Delavigne's life. Is it possible that Cocotte influenced Violaine's preferences for the culture of the peasantry over her class snobbery and cultural alienation?

Violaine's natural inclinations were reinforced when she discovered that she herself was the living reincarnation of Chimène, her paternal great-grandmother, a beautiful peasant woman "*noire, noire, sans équivoque toute noire!*" (black, black as black can be. No doubt about it, she is completely black!).[13] Like Cocotte,

Chimène had come down from the hills at a young age to live in the Delavignes' home. As Chimène blossomed, Violaine's great-grandfather fell passionately in love with her. Chimène returned this love and gave him "*trois fils à l'arrière-grand père, trois superbes garçons couleur tabac*" (three sons, three superb-looking sons the color of tobacco).[14] This blood link with the past brought Violaine closer to Cocotte. Moreover, she came to realize that the elite of Jérémie had built their public life on the rejection of their racial origins, from the moment when the blood of European ancestors mixed with the blood of their African ancestors. "*Et j'ai découvert, moi, enfoui au fond d'une malle, le secret de ma famille, le même secret que toutes les familles mülatresses de Jérémie cachent farouchement au fond de la même vieille malle*" (And I discovered all by myself, buried at the bottom of the trunk, my own family's secret, which is in fact the same secret all mulatto families from Jérémie fiercely hide at the bottom of a similar old trunk).[15]

As Violaine uncovers the hypocrisy of her class and its racial and cultural alienation, she becomes aware of her own *métissage*, and that links her to Cocotte and to the people in the mountains:

> *Rebelles très tôt échappés au fouet et à la canne . . . pour se réfugier dans la montagne libre. . . . Leur sang, ce sang-là coule en nous. Je regarde Cocotte de toute mon âme, et je vous le dis, notre lien n'est pas seulement mystique, nous sommes soeurs de sang.*

> Our ancestors were rebels who escaped the whip and cane early on . . . to find refuge in the freedom of the mountains. . . . The blood that coursed through their veins back then flows in us today. As I continue to watch Cocotte with every fiber of my being, I can tell you here and now that our bond is not just mystical. We are blood sisters through and through.[16]

The story might have ended with Violaine's acceptance of the cultural and racial *marasa*-ness at the level of the collectivity, but Violaine's discovery of the hypocrisy of her class marks a turning point in the character's growth in becoming a new person. As the story progresses, the thematic evolution and architecture of the text shifts. Indeed, as Violaine reaches the point of self-realization, the character of Cocotte loses importance. Whereas in Part I, Cocotte was at once actor and interlocutor; beginning with Part II, she becomes an observer and a spectator of Violaine and her unfurling tragic love story. Violaine falls in love with Alexandre, a young dark-skinned and vibrant man not of her class who completes the circle; he plays the *dosou* to the two *marasa*.

As Cocotte becomes less an actor and more a spectator, her role shifts to that of a confidant, that of a "reporter." Accordingly, the *we* that punctuated her representations in Part I, that symbolized her spiritual connection with Violaine, is gradually replaced by the he/she/they of the marginal observer. She distances herself, and her life is reduced to telling or reporting the troubles in Violaine's life. Alexandre, the *dosou*, looms larger than ever. Cocotte is indeed a spectator, as the story shifts from the union of these twins to the story of the passion of a *marasa* for her *dosou*. Cocotte re-enters the novel at the end of Part III.

As for Violaine, she crystallizes her being, because the more she actualizes her will and affirms her personality, the more she begins to distance herself from her childhood twin. She is no longer simply Cocotte's *marasa.* She becomes within her *self* a *marasa;* that is, a being who biologically and culturally synthesizes two strong currents—African and European[17]—that gave birth to her and her nation. She voices this in a triumphant affirmation: "*Je suis Violaine Delavigne, métisse et foissonnante. Tu comprends, je ne renie rien*" (I am Violaine Delavigne, of mixed blood but bountiful all the same. As you see, I deny nothing).[18] Once her awareness becomes a profound inner reality, Violaine is on a collision course with the world. Alexandre reappears from Port-au-Prince. His reappearance in Violaine's life marks another stage in the development of the novel.

Although we know that Alexandre, in the biological sense, is not Violaine's twin, the feelings she expresses when she sees him lead us to believe that on a spiritual plane, Violaine found in Alexandre a soul as complementary as the one that linked her to Cocotte. It is apparent to the reader that the same fate that joined Violaine and Cocotte is inexorably pushing Violaine and Alexandre toward each other. Cocotte expresses this when she says:

> *Et pourtant, en y pensant bien, rien n'était plus possible, rien n'était plus dans le droit fil du tissu de la vie. Car, enfin, les conventions, les tabous, les préjugés, c'est un, et les lois se-crètes qui font qu'un homme et une femme ont été crées l'un pour l'autre de toute éternité comme le canari pour l'eau claire, c'est bien autre chose.*

> And yet, when thinking about it more intently, nothing is more possible, nothing more inevitable, more natural, more compelling, more understandable. Nothing was more in line with the fabric of life itself. Because after all, customs, taboos, preju-dices are one thing, but the secret laws decreeing that a man and a woman have been created for each other for eternity, like the canary for the clear water, is an-other matter altogether.[19]

Indeed, more than anyone else, Alexandre, a lightning rod, becomes for Vio-laine a crystallizing element that allows her to posit her creole being, to facilitate her sense of balance and equilibrium against her class alienation and chaotic ex-istence. Whereas in the case of Violaine and Cocotte, the issue Desquiron is rais-ing is the spiritual linkage; in the case of Violaine and Alexandre, the issue that the author raises is the problematic of race and color and how it might be re-solved in Haitian society.

Marasas materialize in different guises. They are children, they are siblings, but they can also be a primordial ancestral couple. *Tout marasa pa memm* (not all *marasas* are the same). In Vodou beliefs, ancestral *marasas,* according to Laguerre, "get their energy from Africa where they were born. Africa is a center of spiritual and material energy . . . mythological or real."[20] Alfred Métraux states that "any family which includes twins, either among its living members or in one of its an-cestral lines[,] must, under pain of 'chastisement,' serve them with offerings and sacrifice. Sometimes a family reeling from a series of misfortunes learns from a *houngan* that it has been neglecting twins far back in its ancestry at the time of Guinea" (*Toute famille qui compte des jumeaux . . . dans une de ces lignées ancestrales doit, sous peine de 'châtiment', leur faire des offrandes et des sacrifices. Parfois, une famille frappée par une succession de malheurs apprend de la bouche d'un hougan qu'elle est punie pour avoir négligé les Marasa appartenant à sa lointaine parenté, 'au temps de la Guinée).*[21]

Within Vodou's cosmogony, the *marasa* are considered to be "the first children of God" and the "childhood of the race."[22] In fact, the first and most important characteristic of the "divine twins" is that they incarnate the notion of the segmentation of some original cosmic totality that must regain wholeness. Maya Deren advances this perspective: "The worship of the Marasa, the Divine Twins, is a celebration of man's twinned nature: half matter, half metaphysical; half mortal, half immortal; half human, half divine."[23] It is specifically this aspect upon which I play in order to reconstruct the novel's narrative into a vision of a Haiti capable, at last, of recuperating its wholeness.

Cocotte's devotion to her *marasa* is strong and explains her compulsion to carry Violaine's mission to the ultimate, even when she is called to sacrifice her virginity in exchange for the release of a jailed Alexandre.

We can further appreciate the richness of the *marasa* metaphor and the message of hope it conveys when it is applied to the reality of Haiti's *créolité*. It is as if the text as a whole moves from a literal analysis of the relationship between the two *marasa* to a metaphorical study of Haiti's class and color conflict and the nation's apparent inability to merge its cultural and racial elements. After all, although Mme Delavigne accepted Violaine's relationship with Cocotte, she violently opposed Violaine's love for Alexandre. Haiti's sexual politics would not allow it. The mother's wrath is such that she decides to zombify her child—to cause a spiritual death.

She is "killed" and brought back to life as a zombie. Then she is entrusted to Philippe Edouard, to whom she had been promised as a child and whose class and color prejudice have reached such a frenzy that he would rather have Violaine zombified than accept seeing her with Alexandre. And so Violaine is turned into Philippe Edouard's "toy," a living corpse who is the object of his sexual whims and libido.

While Alexandre lingers in a Port-au-Prince jail, Philippe Edouard descends into insanity as he repeatedly rapes the zombie that his "wife" has become. The constant scenes of rape—"*viol*" in French—mirror the first letters of Violaine's name (Viol-aine). Alexandre seems to describe what he imagines to be happening. He describes it with disgust:

Et je contemple effrayée . . . Cet homme qui bascule chaque jour un peu plus dans la démence. Je le regarde te couvrir de son grand corp frissonnant, habiller ton corps endormi de baisers brûlants. Je le regarde enduire sans relache tes membres inertes de ton parfum préféré, t'appeler comme un fou, sangloter la tête sur ton ventre, te serrer à t'étouffer. Mais tu es inaccessible à sa quête. Tu ne te défends même pas. Je le regarde t'aimer tout seul, si seul.

And I'm rather frightened, Violaine, as I watch this man possessed by you and whom you're unable to see. He's a man who leans a bit more each day toward insanity. I watch him cover you with his huge quaking frame, lavish your sleeping body with passionate kisses. I watch him coat your inert limbs with your favorite perfume without ever seeming to tire. He calls out to you like a madman, sobs over you with his head on your stomach, and squeezes you so hard it could smother you. Despite all this attention, you remain inaccessible, beyond his grasp. You don't even make an effort to defend yourself. I see him trying to love you all alone, so completely alone.[24]

In the last pages of the novel, the story moves from the province of Grande-Anse, where the town of Jérémie is located, to Port-au-Prince, as if to indicate that changes in the Haitian sociocultural and political spectrum must take place in the capital city first. Earlier in the novel, readers got a glimpse of the capital as the place where Alexandre resided as a university student and activist. In Port-au-Prince, all three main characters reconverge: the *marasas;* Violaine and Cocotte, who reappear as "actors"; and Alexandre, the *dosou.* Cocotte's plan to help free Alexandre is foiled.

In the meantime, Cocotte builds a coalition with the market women of the Iron Market, where she attempts to make a living by selling small household items. Two years after the zombification that seemed to have ended Violaine's life and as Cocotte muses painfully about her *marasa,* she sees Violaine in the midst of a group of market women! At the sight of Violaine, disheveled and haggard and still not completely back, Cocotte is renewed.

For Cocotte and Violaine, life is beginning anew and it is together that they will struggle as united *marasa* sisters; this time, however, it is with a new resolve that they are challenging the future. Cocotte formulates this resolve in those terms: "*nous allons nous mettre debout. . . . Et nous irons notre chemin pour nôtre compte*" (we are both going to stand tall. . . . And we'll make our way along our own trail all by ourselves).[25]

This usage of the personal pronoun "*nous*" is significant, for it implies a oneness found again, a union of shared strengths which this time may transcend all obstacles. More markedly, Violaine and Cocotte are no longer alone in their struggle. They have the support of the other women at the portals of the Marché en Fer, the main market in the city, who sympathize with the two *marasas'* pain, telling them: "*Non, Vous n'êtes pas toutes seules. On est là aussi nous-mêmes, ne l'oublie pas!*" (No, you two are not alone. We're all here for you, and don't forget it!).[26] It is on this note of rebirth, of union and solidarity between Violaine and Cocotte, between the *marasa* and the women of the Marché en Fer, that Lilas Desquiron ends the story of *Les Chemins de Loco-Miroir.*

The novel was written on two levels: first, as the tragic story of two female *marasa* and their *dosou,* and second, as a passionate metaphor to envision the possible oneness of Haitian culture and mixed identity.

The notion popularized by Melville Herskowitz that "symbolism is the essence of myth" applies to the *marasa* concept as a metaphor for Haiti. He purported that "myth . . . implies a social acceptance of approved symbols that by transcending the generations, are at once the instrument of identification with the past, and with the continuation of present and future."[27] In particular, Desquiron's use of myths and of religio-philosophical elements in the novel echoes the importance granted to myth in the molding of culture and society.

As we look at Desquiron's literary representation of the *marasa* concept, we realize that she takes liberties to deconstruct and reassemble her vision of how *marasa*-ness can be crystallized into a powerful, unifying metaphor—the harmonious union of Haiti's separate halves, a union the forefathers of the Haitian nation understood and hoped would be lasting. Such a vision of Haiti's creole society is one that would be the synthesis of the two worlds that co-exist in a fragmented Haiti.

It is from that prism that I have analyzed Lilas Desquiron's masterful use of myth and symbols that unify the many themes presented. Weaving myths and reality, Desquiron is able to connect Haiti's past and present and, through the acceptance and affirmation of Haiti's *pluriculturalité,* multiculturalism, and *créolité,* point the path, *les chemins,* that could lead the country out of its quagmire.

Through the myth of the *marasa,* inherited from Africa and re-interpreted with variations in Haiti, Lilas Desquiron presents a model of reunification for the whole nation which must transcend class interests, must combine the efforts of all Haitians regardless of class, color, and gender. Like a magician or a master storyteller patterned after Haiti's oral culture, she incorporates these aspects of the novel, taking as superstructure the life of the two sisters. She presents not only a bleak portrayal of the past and of contemporary Haiti but also a hopeful picture of a Haiti yet to come, *"une Haiti en devenir."* This future can take place, the author infers, only if the country accepts the merging of its twin-ness, the two sides of its warring cultures. This window of hope suggests quite an undertaking since the interests of those from the light-skinned and dark-skinned upper class and the governing power do not coincide with those of the darker-skinned lower-class Haitians.

The answer lies within the problem. Desquiron traced paths from which the protagonists could chose to escape. My faith for Haiti's future is equally positive and similarly grounded in self-acceptance and renewed tradition. The ultimate metaphor is that the *marasa* are the children of Haiti; Loko, the healer, is the guardian of the sacred space that is Haiti.

Notes

1. See Jacques Roumain, *Gouverneurs de la Rosée* (Port-au-Prince: Imprimerie de L'Etat, 1944); Pierre Marcelin and Philippe Thoby Marcelin, *La Bête de Musseau* (New York: Rinehart & Company, Inc. 1946); and Jacques Stephen Alexis, *Compère Général Soleil* (Paris: Gallimard, 1955), among others.

2. This study of *Les Chemins de Loco-Miroir* is based on the 1990 Stock Edition published in Paris. English quotes are from English translation by Robin Orr Bodkins, *Reflections of Loko Miwa* (Charlottesville: University Press of Virginia, 1998).

3. The word "*marasa*" is the Creole-language translation of the French "*gémellité*" and the

English "twin." However, the concept conveyed by the word "*marasa*" is specific to Haitian culture, where it has mystical connotations that are not present in other cultures.

4. Leslie Desmangles, *The Faces of the Gods* (Chapel Hill: University of North Carolina Press, 1992), 103.

5. Ibid.

6. The ancestral village, the Village Racine, is the village in the Macaya hills of Jérémie from whence originated Violaine's paternal great-grandmother, Chimène, whom the heroine resembles, except that Violaine is light skinned and Chimène was "noire, noire"; that is, very dark.

7. *Créolité* is the interactional or transactional aggregate of Caribbean, European, African, Asian, and Levantine cultural elements, united on the same soil by the yoke of history. *Créolité* is the world diffracted but recomposed. It is an annihilation of phased universality, of monolingualism, and the necessity of accepting ourselves as complex, for complexity is the very essence of our identity. See also Patrick Chamoiseau and Raphaël Confiant, *Lettres Créoles: Tracées Antillaises et Continentales de la Litérature 1635–1975* (Paris: Hatier, 1991).

8. Maya Deren, *Divine Horsemen: The Living Gods of Haiti* (1953; reprint, New Paltz, N.Y.: McPherson and Co., 1983), 40. Page citations are to the later edition.

9. Michel S. Laguerre, *Voodoo Heritage* (Beverly Hills, Calif.: Sage Publications, 1980), 58.

10. Deren, *Divine Horsemen,* 39.

11. Desquiron, *Les Chemins,* 9; Desquiron, *Reflections,* 5.

12. Desquiron, *Les Chemins,* 14; Desquiron, *Reflections,* 9.

13. Desquiron, *Les Chemins,* 58; Desquiron, *Reflections,* 42.

14. Desquiron, *Les Chemins,* 60; Desquiron, *Reflections,* 43.

15. Desquiron, *Les Chemins,* 58; Desquiron, *Reflections,* 41–42.

16. Desquiron, *Les Chemins,* 62; Desquiron, *Reflections,* 44–45.

17. Africa and Europe are named as the two strongest currents, but we must not obliterate the Amerindians (Taino and Arawaks) who were the native inhabitants of Ayiti. Even though the population of 1 million or so were decimated by the Spaniards within fifty years, a few of them took refuge in the remote hills and thus became the first "maroons," who later mixed with the African Maroons.

18. Desquiron, *Les Chemins,* 83; Desquiron, *Reflections,* 63.

19. Desquiron, *Les Chemins,* 76; Desquiron, *Reflections,* 57.

20. Laguerre, *Voodoo Heritage,* 62.

21. Métraux, *Voodoo in Haiti,* trans. Hugo Charteries (New York: Schocken Books, 1972), 146, 129–130.

22. Deren, *Divine Horsemen,* 38.

23. Ibid.

24. Desquiron, *Les Chemins,* 181; Desquiron, *Reflections,* 138.

25. Desquiron, *Les Chemins,* 236; Desquiron, *Reflections,* 182.

26. Desquiron, *Les Chemins,* 237; Desquiron, *Reflections,* 182.

27. Melville J. Herskovitz, *Dahomean Narratives* (Evanston, Ill.: Northwestern University Press, 1967), 82.

10

Herbs and Energy: The Holistic
Medical System of the Haitian People

MAX-G. BEAUVOIR

From the beginning of time humanity has suffered disease and illness as part of daily existence. Both are viewed as deficiencies, making people momentarily or permanently incapacitated, and for that reason, they open the door for thoughts from all those who feel directly or indirectly concerned about human health.

Disease is not exclusively a human plight; it is observed in the vegetal, mineral, and animal kingdoms. Virus, bacteria, and fungi develop on rocks and prey upon them. Botanists and agronomists have observed infectious diseases in plants and the immunological reactions plants develop as defense mechanisms. Other scientists have studied the role of natural selection in reducing the impact of pathologies in animals and plants. Naturalists have observed some animals grooming (bathing in mud, dust, and sand) and using friction as forms of treatment; others ingest particular leaves or tree bark that is not part of their ordinary diet. Some birds even succeed in reducing limb impairments with a "dressing," as it were, bandaging wounds and sores.

Nevertheless, human disease is different in that the social conditions of existence which develop within all societies create the context into which disease can be inserted. Colonialism and neocolonialism, for instance, have given rise to a number of endemic diseases which have been perpetuated by the conditions of squalor in which populations that are the victims of such worldwide forces and processes are required to live. Like poverty and illiteracy, certain illnesses are products of the social structure.

The Haitian nation faced grave political and economic difficulties from the beginning. Isolated from the international arena for half a century after its independence, the country was subjected to assaults that increased political strife and created renewed conditions for poverty after Haiti was "allowed" to rejoin the world created by the dominant international powers in the 1860s.

It is within this difficult context that the Haitian population developed its indigenous system of healing. University (Western) medicine has only recently been introduced in the country and has not been able to attend to the population's health care needs. Concentrated in the capital of Port-au-Prince and the major towns, this medical body depends on expensive imported therapeutic ingredients and complex physical installations. At present, one hospital bed exists for every 1,400 Haitians, and there are only eleven hospital centers in cities and towns spread throughout the national territory. Each physician attends to a population of 10,000.

The holistic medical system of the Haitian people has emerged from the thoughts and practices of earlier generations. It fills the void left by the absence of formal medicine, but it does so only partly. Non-Western healing arts are entities sui generis. I refer to this form of healing as holistic because it consistently connects all parts of the human being, systems and subsystems, to the whole. The fact of the matter is that in the Haitian context, the individual cannot be understood well without reference to his/her totality: mind, spirit, body, society, and universe. It is a system that consists of interconnected and interrelated parts that form an organic whole.

The thought that gave rise to this indigenous medical system has continuity with the knowledge and the understanding of Haiti's African ancestors. Contributions to its evolution may have also come partly from Native American sources and partly from European elements. The neotraditional medical system of Haiti is part of the culture of a people that has found within its own heritage the principles, methods, and medical knowledge that would appear to be appropriate to its needs and worldview.

Previous Research and Considerations

The limited bibliography on this method of healing suggests that very little scholarly work has been done in this domain. Much of it is biased, and much remains to be done. This chapter relies partly on a doctoral thesis presented in 1985 by Bernard Weniger of the School of Pharmacy and Toxicology at the University of Metz, France. Weniger showed the results of qualitative chemical or biochemical studies. When applicable, I will make use of these studies.

Having been personally involved in treating a large number of patients by the traditional method for over a quarter of a century, I take the liberty of offering what seems to me to be a systematic categorization of medical practices in Haiti. I also indicate methods used to bring about cures and the principles behind the cures. My aim is to go beyond the descriptive level, highlighting the meanings and values embedded in the system. I seek to avoid the nuances and subtleties of religious, philosophical, medical, and biological jargon, arguments, and controversies in order to best serve the interests of those who want introductory knowledge of this domain.

Since there has never been official recognition of the existence of the field of traditional medicine by the governments of Haiti or tests to check the knowledge and competence of its professionals, I cannot suggest that the practice of neotraditional or indigenous medicine is understood by all *oungan* and *manbo* who practice it or that the practice is similar everywhere. I know that *oungan* and *manbo* in different regions of the country often function within specifically defined ecosystems, and their knowledge is restricted to the herbs of one area. I mention this because this has often been overlooked or has been interpreted as ignorance by outsiders and scientists. In reality this shows a form of specialization. Additionally, in this field, as in most others, degrees of competency exist.

I state with some pride that the knowledge I have acquired came from lengthy and patient tutoring by a number of pre-literate doctors of Haiti known as *oun-gan* and *manbo*. Throughout the centuries, such healers have accumulated a large corpus of knowledge in the practice of traditional healing. The ones I worked with generously agreed to pass their knowledge on to me. This is why I apologize for errors, shortcomings, or omissions that come from my own limitations.

Categorization

I divide the practice of holistic healing in Haiti into three different categories:

First, a *Phytotherapeutic Social System,* which is unique in that this type of healer is not expected to be a professional. Having learned the positive outcome of a recipe through past experience, he or she is able to recommend it to a sick person only as a suggestion. In so doing, that healer performs both a cultural and medical act, though he or she may not feel concerned with matters of methodology or principles. It is understood, in this case, that the treatment is making use of a simple, a type of social medicine generally described as "the simple method of healing," or "*medsin senp.*" The Haitian people probably refer to it by this expression because of the limited scope of this activity.

Second, a *Phytotherapeutic Medical System,* which is only practiced by a professional. As a recognized healer, he or she may bear the title of *oungan* (man) or *manbo/hugbonn* (female). The *oungan* and *manbo,* guardians of the ancestral tradition, are fully equal in the exercise of those functions. A number of other healers also exist, such as the *doktè fèy* (leaf doctor), *fanm chaj* (midwife), and *ganga* (healer).

Third, a *Masterly Medical System.* The principles of this system are based on the dynamism of a life concept named "energy," a force that has no mass but has "potentialities." Divinity is seen as the source of life, thus of all energies. Ultimately these professionals always tap into that divine energy to bring about cures. The human being is seen as energy of a lesser dimension, as are animals, plants, and everything else that possess life. All function well within normal ranges. When a person is out of the norm, outside the normal range of energy, he or she is recognized as sick and feels that way.

All three systems are used side by side in Haiti. They fit together, they are complementary to each other and to Western medicine. The population appreciates these three systems and turns to them nine times out of ten, out of necessity, reducing the crushing load for hospitals and physicians. No Haitian government has recognized the presence of a parallel form of medical practice, as is the case in China and India, with traditional Chinese and Indian Ayurvedic medicines, and no encouragement has yet been given to the traditionalists.

The Phytotherapeutic Social System

This medical system is loosely organized and seems to have been present from the dawn of humanity. The system is flexible in its structure, and the person who does the treatments does not necessarily have to be recognized as a healer or professional. Most of the time the healer is a member of the extended family. The person recalls, at the appropriate moment, the appropriate leaf, the correct infusion, or the right recipe that is supposed to bring about relief.

I have given this type of medicine a place in this presentation because it seems to be used more frequently than all the other systems put together. It is the first line of defense in emergencies. Its accessibility has made it so popular that it cannot be missed. Haitians and foreigners have written about it as if it was the only system used in Haiti alongside the Western medical system. Based on similar principles and methods of treatment as the phytotherapeutic medical system, it is described as *medsin senp,* the simple method of healing. When a person is ill, someone is sent to the marketplace where leaves are sold. Those leaves are combined, infused, and ingested. I label this system "social" because there is no exchange of money between the patient and the healer. There is no contract binding them, not even a moral one. The recipes are only offered as a benevolent suggestion and the healer is not required to see to the success of the treatment.

However, it is quite an attractive system of medicine, for it tends to popularize medical knowledge and make medicine accessible to all, rich and poor. Leaf markets, which sell their products inexpensively, are present all over the country. Biologists, botanists, ethnobotanists, chemists, and biochemists, as well as *santeros* and *santeras* who own *botanicas* elsewhere in the world, run to Haiti all year long to gather leaves and roots. (*Santeros* and *santeras* are priests in the neo-African-derived religion of La Regla de Ocha, or Santería.) Though seemingly an amorphous structure, this socioethical system responds to the needs of the Haitian people. As a social and ethical arrangement, its goal is to find ways to adequately and realistically respond to the needs and well-being of the person. It also tries to define the kinds of relationships that should exist between various individuals as they function in society. Altruistic responsibility toward others seems to be its primary moral principle. This ethic encourages each member of the society to show concern for the needs and interests of others. Like the Vodoun religion, the medical aspect of the phytotherapeutic social system is one part of that culture that hopes to emphasize features such as hospitality, brotherhood, tolerance, and simplicity.

The Phytotherapeutic Medical System

More commonly known in the Haitian Creole language as *medsin fèy* and in English as herbal or botanical medicine, phytotherapy can best be described as a type of medicine that makes herbs an integral part of the treatment. The word "herb" is understood to mean plants and animals, or any parts of plants and animals, that are used for medicinal purposes. An herb may be a leaf, a flower, a stem, a seed, a root, a fruit, or the bark of a tree or it might also be part of an animal or the animal in its entirety. It could, for instance, be the liver of a fish or the wool of a lamb. Certain plants that are used to flavor food such as thyme, chives, or parsley *woucou* (*parwah—Bixa orellana*) are also considered herbs when they are used for medicinal purposes, as are certain peppers such as *pwav potorik, pwav ginen,* or *pwav a manje* (Piperacea family), *reseda* (henna), and allspice. Oils are also extracted from avocado, coconut, sesame, peanuts, castor beans, almond, and many others. All of these substances fit into the category of herbs.

It should be noted that in phytotherapeutic medicine, those herbs work in a somewhat similar fashion to the pharmaceutical drugs used in conventional Western medicine; that is, via a chemical action or reaction that affects human physiology. The World Health Organization has stated that approximately 25 percent of all prescription drugs are still derived from trees, shrubs, or herbs. Others are made from extracts, and still others are synthesized chemically to mimic a natural plant compound. Of 119 plant-derived pharmaceutical medicines that are on pharmacy shelves today in the United States, 74 percent correlate directly with their traditional uses.

When involved in the field of phytotherapeutic medicine, it is not sufficient to purchase herbs at the marketplaces, where people sell leaves that are too often dry, tired, old, and lifeless. One must collect them under the proper conditions, "according to the *règleman*," as it is said in the Vodoun culture, meaning in accordance with the proper protocol. According to that protocol, collecting herbs should always imply a certain degree of respect for the plant to guarantee its cooperation. That respect is translated by the songs, dances, and method of approach and the fact that the harvest must be "purchased." One must buy the herbs from the plants, and one must deposit the money to pay for it, like a sacrifice, at the foot of the tree while singing the appropriate songs. One must also take into account the influences of the moon and the sun at the moment of collection and the prevailing weather conditions or atmospherics at the time.

Most species of herbs must be harvested before the plant flowers and preferably during an ascending moon. It is better to collect roots and the tubercles before the flowering time, even before the new leaves or buds come out, and during a descending moon. When the moon is waning, the vitality of the plant, meaning the biologically active principles it contains, is greater at the roots. At the end of November and at the beginning of December, the potency and curative power of a plant is almost absent. Most leaves should be harvested before sunrise. That is the optimum time when the plants hold the totality of their curative powers. But when the sun shines or is high in the sky, the plants are said to be "at work" and consequently lose a significant portion of their active principles.

During the preparation of certain mixtures, some of the ingredients reach their full potentiality only after the clapping of thunder or only when lightning strikes. This is why certain types of preparation should be set aside and done only periodically, when the weather is acceptable. The best times of the year are the second half of December, May, and August. Healers often prefer wild vegetables and plants over the cultivated varieties since they are frequently found to be richer in nutrients. This was noted when studying an improved process for obtaining sapogenin, mainly hecogenin, a chemical substance of the steroid family, from the plant known as *pite,* or sisal. It seemed that in the wild, the hormonal glands of the plant were stimulated more vigorously by its competition with weeds. When they were tested in the laboratory, the wild plants yielded a much higher quantity of that particular compound than the cultivated plants did. But it takes dedication to follow the behavior and strength of each species of animals and plants, including those that live in water, land, or air; those that strive in the mountains; and those that grow at sea level.

POTENCY, TOXICITY, AND DOSAGES

In the field of biochemistry, herbs are generally classified as natural products and are considered in themselves to be naturally diluted. The concentration of the biologically active substances they contain is low most of the time, on the order of the microgram and even the picogram. That simply means that only one gram of active material is contained in 1 ton or in 1,000 tons of the whole plant. Under such a condition, the need to use a scale or a balance to weigh the raw materials at the time of preparation of a *te* (an infusion) is superfluous. Some plants, however, must be viewed as very toxic or potent. Such is the case, for instance, of the *kokomb zombi* (thorn apple or Devil's apple—*Datura stramonium*). The flowers are usually sun dried, rolled up in paper, and smoked as cigarettes as an effective treatment for asthma.

Laboratories have shown that the entire datura plant is powerful, containing some strong alkaloids of the tropane family. The concentrations of hyoscyamine, atropine, and scopolamine it contains are in the order of 0.2 to 0.45 percent; that is, almost 5 grams of these substances are contained in 1 kilogram of the plant. Hyoscyamine is a parasympatholytic substance which causes heart accelerations and dilation of the bronchioles; it has a general antispasmodic effect on the individual. The toxin provokes an easily reached state of hallucination and loss of control of oneself, and it may even lead to death.

The range in potencies of an herb may vary widely among parts of the same plant—its flowers, leaves, and roots. The range varies from plant to plant in the same family and from one species to another, depending on the season of the year, whether or not the season is rainy, or when conditions of humidity change or with altitude. There are quite different degrees of potency ranging from the from extra-mild "activities" of watercress and the *bab-mayi* (corn husk), which are used as a *rafrechi* or as a *te* for cleansing, for instance, to the very potent *konkonb zombie.* Laboratories have produced evidence, though, of the presence of very valuable alkaloids, saponin, polyphenols, salicylic acid, allantoin, and potassium salts in the various styles of corn, while the watercress seems to be rich in iodine, iron, and vitamins A and C.

Haitian *oungan* and *manbo* recommend that the corn's "beard"—the hair ad-

Kouche yam. Feys pou remed. Photograph by Claudine Michel.

joined to corn cobs, be used as a *rafrechi,* or "detox," as one might say it in English, even when the person doesn't appear to be sick, just as a method of prophylaxis or for internal hygiene. This is recommended particularly when a person lives in places that are infested with parasites and mosquitoes, when that person eats alone or at hours that are irregular, when his or her diet includes too many fatty substances and/or spices, when the quality of the water he or she drinks is has not been confirmed, or when the person has a weak liver. Weakness in the liver may be due to spiritual, emotional, or physical stress or it may follow a previously cured hepatitis, malaria, typhoid, amoeboid, or viral infection. This condition may be noticed only when that person starts abusing alcohol or drugs. However, individuals may very well live with only a fraction of their liver, not knowing that they have a liver condition at all. A *rafrechi* is then used to alleviate such conditions. This is an extra-mild process of internal cleansing that involves the boiling of two to three fistfuls of corn "beards" for about twenty to thirty minutes in a large volume of water (about one gallon or three to four liters). When cooled and strained, this extract is kept in the refrigerator and drunk ad libitum throughout the day and for a number of days thereafter, typically seven.

Depending upon the person's health condition, one may wish to increase the potency of the broth by adding some of the following herbs: a few leaves of lettuce; a few buds of squash or pumpkin (*joumou*; about seven to ten buds); a few young leaves of okra; the inside white coat of a bitter orange, or *chadèk* (*Citrus grandis*); some leaves of sweetsop (*Annona squamosa*); and a little pinch of table salt. These add to the power or efficacy of the detox. Each one of these additions brings to the whole thing new chemicals whose effects multiply the effect of the *bab mayi*.

The plants in the *bab mayi* have many healing ingredients. Laboratories have shown that the leaves of *joumou* contain a p-hydroxy benzoic alcohol; the leaves of the *calalou* (okra) contain phosphorus, a flavonoid called gossypine, and some amino acids; the *zoranj si* (orange) contains an essential oil rich in limonene, linalool, nerol, stachydrin, a tri-terpene lactone amaroid, and vitamin C; and the leaves of *kachiman* contain dopamine and a substance called reticulin, which is a spasmolytic and analgesic. The general effect of the salt precipitates some of the important ingredients (the salting-out effect), and its overall action is also spiritual.

A different process is suggested when one wants to further increase the strength of the *rafrechi* to bring about not only a general cleansing that will affect the digestive tract, intestinal tract, and liver but will also cleanse the blood, lungs, heart, and kidneys. It is called *"bay moun nan you lòk,"* meaning "giving the person a lock," a process that involves adding to the above-mentioned leaves some or all of the following herbs:

a few branches of *lamitie;* that is, dodder or love-vine (*Cuscuta americana*)
twenty-one leaves of *twa zòm fò* (*Stemodia durantifolia*)
twenty-one leaves of *ti sanit;* small senna leaves (*Cassia obovata*)
twenty-one leaves of *vulnerè;* sage or clary (*Salvia occidentalis*)
a few branches of *dèyè do;* quinine, or gale of wind (*Phyllanthus niruri*)
twenty-one leaves of *medsiyen barachen;* bellyache bush (*Jatropha gossypifolia*)
some scrapings of *muscat;* nutmeg (*Myristica officinalis*)

After twenty minutes of heavy boiling, the broth is strained and then reduced further by boiling to the approximate volume of a couple of glasses, or a pint. Two parts of this concentrate are then combined with one part of extracted castor oil and brought back to a boil for about five to ten minutes and then cooled overnight. The mixture is gently warmed up the following morning and the patient drinks it while still fasting. It is customary for the patient to eat an orange or a grapefruit immediately after ingesting the lock. No other food should be served to that person until he or she has two or three bowel movements.

Lamitie, as a Convolvulaceae, contains some resin and it is well known to be an anti-icteric, an anti-dysenteric, a purgative, and a depurative. The *twa zòm fò* is a scrofulariacea that contains alkaloids, steroids, terpenoids, quinones, and flavonoids. The *ti sanit* acts against worms and larvae; it contains an oxymethyl-anthraquinone. The *vulnerè,* also called *ti bom mawon* in Haitian Creole, acts against flatulence, gas, and abdominal pain through its active principles, which are fumaric acid and an essential oil that contains camphor, borneol, and cineol. The *dèyè do* acts against flatulence and fever; it is a febrifuge and antispasmodic. Its active principles are mainly a phyllantin and an hypophyllantin. The *medsiyen barachen,* or "*ti medsiyen,*" also acts against abdominal pains with its jatrophin and diterpenic derivative esters. The *mascriti* oil is purgative because of the ricinoleic acid liberated by the pancreatic lipase, which increases the peristaltic movement of the intestine. It also contains gallic, shikimic, ellagic, ferulic, and p-coumarinic acids.

The *rafrechi* and the *lòk* are not the only methods of treatment that use boiled and ingested herbs. Among others, one should mention the *te,* or tea (infusion), and the decoction. Other means are the bath; the *ralman,* or direct rubbing of the body with crushed herbs and herbal extracts; and the cataplasm, or poultice, a warm, moist mass that is made with tubercles and applied to a sore part of the body. Smoking is also an efficient means of treatment when flowers are dried, rolled up in paper, and smoked as a cigarette, as in the case of the treatment of asthma. A small red bean called *wari* and a larger one named *je bourik*—that is, horse-eye bean, or *Mucuna urens* L.—are simply put into one's pocket or hung around the neck as a necklace. This proves to be a very efficient treatment for hemorrhoids.

The *te* is also an infusion. It is prepared by steeping the selected leaves and flowers in hot water for three to five minutes. In the case of denser materials such as roots and barks, it becomes a decoction when they are put for fifteen to twenty minutes in water at a rolling boil. Due to the higher water content of fresh herbs, three parts fresh herbs replaces one part of the dry ones.

Infusions are most appropriate for tender plant parts such as leaves, flowers, or green stems, where the medicinal properties are easily accessible. To infuse barks, roots, or seeds, it is best to powder them first in a mortar in order to break down some of their cell walls before adding them to the water. Seeds should be bruised to release the volatile oils from the cells. Any aromatic herbs should be infused in a pot that has a well-sealed lid to reduce the loss of the volatile oils through evaporation.

Becoming a phytotherapeutic healer thus requires not only a good knowledge of the herbs and their classification but also an awareness of their compatibilities and incompatibilities when blending and mixing them. Furthermore, it calls for a fair appreciation of the environment and the immediate surroundings and an acceptable knowledge of the human being's body and its functioning.

The student of phytotherapeutic medicine, though, is not required to know as much anatomy and physiology as his university counterparts. The level of knowledge in those fields is definitely not comparable, and it would be absurd to weigh them on the same scale. He or she must understand, however, that a phytotherapeutic student is not authorized to perform autopsies in order to comprehend the functioning of the human body. The systematic encounter between these two types of medicine with the abnormalities found at the autopsies in Europe and North America allowed the symptoms and the syndromes to be understood and became the basis for modern medicine. Young *oungan* and *manbo,* who are limited to what they can observe from dissecting animals at the time of ritual sacrifices and must adjust their knowledge by comparing what they have learned that way with what they know about human anatomy, reach a point of understanding where they realize that the body of a person is a unit, indeed a complex piece of machinery.

A skeletal connection of bones and cartilage wrapped inside the skin gives the body its shape, its architecture, and its possibilities of action. The bones are attached to one another by muscles, which have the ability to contract and stretch to allow various movements to take place easily. Though much less flexible than the muscles or the skin, which themselves are much less elastic than the body fluids, all bones show a certain degree of springiness when the person is alive. In a living person everything is somewhat supple and flexible. That potential of tractability decreases with age and maturity. At the time of death, the bones completely lose that property because the person loses a spirit named Dan, born from Dan-Ballah Wedo and Ayi-Da Wedo, the snake Gods. The word "*da*," or "*dan*," signifies "Life," "the Life Force," or "the condition of movement" in English.

A collection of organs constitutes the human being's substructure. They function most of the time independent of the person's will. Of particular relevance are the brain, heart, *biskèt,* lungs, belly cavity, kidneys, and lower part of the stomach cavity (*anba ti vant*—pelvic cavity), which is the seat of the sexual organs.

The important organ named *biskèt,* which doesn't seem to be the thymus, doesn't seem to have an equivalent in the anatomy books. Located behind what is understood to be the xyphoid appendix, it acts like a gland that will habitually "fall" after excessive effort. When it does, a condition called "*biskèt tonbe*" or "*fallen biskèt*" occurs, generating all sorts of perturbations in the physiology of the person, male or female, young or old. Redressing an abnormally inverted or retroverted "*biskèt* which has fallen" calls for painful and elaborate manipulations and treatment.

There is, and should always be, complete harmony in the body. That is why it is believed that skin, bones, organs, blood, blood vessels, hair, nails, teeth, and muscles are all made up of the same fundamental substances, though each compound may be present in a particular area in a different concentration. Just as the crust of the bread is basically the same as the crumb, the tough tissue called skin is but an oxidized and a concentrated form of muscle or blood, made of the same things.

Waters fill up all the empty spaces in the body's cavities. Never pure, even when very clear, they contain a few ingredients that are more or less diluted depending upon where one looks in the various parts of the body. When red, that water is called blood; when pink or salmon-colored, it is called serum; and when white, it is called milk. When totally clear, it may be called tears or cerebrospinal fluid. Whenever it is yellow or yellowish-green, it is called pus, and its presence is a clear sign of an infection.

The function of the cerebrospinal fluid is greatly magnetic and sexual; its goals are reproducing the species and maintaining contact with the spiritual world. Unlike the circulation of the blood, this subsystem of clear liquid functions inside the cerebrospinal cavity without a pump. The circulation of that liquid is maintained by the movements back and forth of the pelvis. This is why, in order to maintain the efficiency of this subsystem, dancing is considered a prophylactic activity, especially for young persons.

The principal function of the blood is to serve as a vehicle for the life force. It constantly flows in all parts of the body. The redder it is, the better one feels. To give away some of it, voluntarily or accidentally, is considered equivalent to losing a part of one's vital energy or vitality.

Any impairment in the functioning of the structure, one of the substructures, or the organs of a person automatically generates disease and possible complications.

DISEASES

This kind of knowledge seems sufficient to illustrate that a body is not a simple machine that is designed to become ill. On the contrary, the machine is intelligent and heals itself in most instances. As a matter of fact, it does so constantly, and that is why one remains healthy most of the time in spite of the fact that the equilibrium of life is unstable. Even when researchers in university medical laboratories state that a particular condition is incurable and that the only option is to endure a lifetime of dependency on drugs that have troublesome side effects, the phytotherapeutic student knows that there is always hope that a sick condition can be improved upon or reversed.

So good health takes on a different meaning that is significantly broader than what is usually comprehended by that term in the modern Western world. It becomes something quite different from just the absence of disease. The definition of good health is stretched to include the fact that the organism is in good condition and that all the subsystems of the body are in good shape, that the many organic functions are harmoniously balanced and integrated with each other, that there is a total equilibrium, which is the basis of the feeling of well-being. Although the defense mechanisms and the immune system of one's body are in a constant fight against the many hazards that life presents, one feels confident that the healthy organism is able to answer positively and efficiently to the aggressions of disease-causing or pathogenic organisms, toxic substances, and stress factors of various kinds.

To regain one's lost health, then, requires generally the very same inputs that were needed to keep one healthy in the first place. One must reverse all the processes that negatively impacted upon that health and over which one has a certain amount of control most of the time. This includes taking responsibility for stopping the lifestyle choices one knows are harmful; one needs to positively address the real needs that such behavior masks.

All expenses of energy that aim at maintaining and preserving our life ought to be perceived as being "good," but those that create disturbances in the equilibrium of our system, subsystems, or organs will invariably lead to the degradation of our life and of our health and must be rejected as being "bad." This principle is simply stated in Vodoun culture as the basis of good health and moral law.

The basis of Vodoun ethics would then be to live as much as possible with the ultimate goal of conserving and developing one's life and health. The most evident corollary is to do this while taking into account the respect one owes to the life and health of others in our surroundings, in our family, in our society, and in the life of all the many species of living beings that exist around us in the universe.

Depending upon the nature of one's health problems, this might simply involve keeping peace around oneself, sleeping better and enough hours every day, eating more regularly and in a more balanced way, making sure to receive a reasonable exposure to fresh air and sunlight, and so on. It may furthermore include one's hygiene, such as regular cleansing of the body, inside and outside; addressing any structural or mechanical causes of imbalance; learning how to properly cope with stress; and learning how to deal with our mental and emotional needs.

Of course, at the beginning one might require help from a competent person, and that help should always come in the form of the treatment that is most appropriate. Let me mention, as examples, just a few of the diseases identified by phytotherapeutic medicine and some of the herbs that have been selected by the tradition to balance them. A comparison of these examples with the data that come from pharmaceutical laboratories will make my arguments more clear.

Phytotherapeutic medicine defines, at the level of the structure, diseases of nails, hairs, teeth, skin, bones and muscles; and, at the level of the substructures, diseases of the organs and of the mind:

> Sensory organ diseases: *maltèt,* or headaches; *la grip,* or cold, cough, and laryngitis; *malozye,* or eye infections; *malzorèy,* or ear infection and earaches; *malgòj,* or sore throats and throat infections; *maldan,* or toothaches . . . and many more.

> Body diseases: *fèblès,* or general weaknesses and asthenia; *anemi,* or anemia; *dyare,* or diarrhea; *lafyèv,* or fevers; *bra kase, pye kase,* and *tèt fann,* or fractures of the limbs or the skull with inflammation; *boule,* or burns; *rimatis,* or rheumatism; *maladi po,* or skin diseases; *abse, bouton,* and *absedlen,* or abscesses and boils, and so forth.

> Organic diseases: *maladi kè,* or heart disease; *tansyon,* or high blood pressure; *pwatrinè* or *maladi poumon,* or pneumonia, tuberculosis, asthma; *sik,* or diabetes; *disantri,* or dysentery and liver conditions; *vè,* or worms; *dlosi ak asidite* and *gaz,* or gastralgia and stomach problems; *pa ka monte lèt,* or inability to produce breast milk; *maladi vesi ak ren,* or bladder and kidney problems; *fredi,* or frigidity and decrease of libido; *sida,* AIDS; *kansè,* or cancer; *chanpiyon,* or fungus; and hemorrhoids

> Emotional and mental diseases: *sezisman,* or emotional shocks; *lèt pase,* or a mental disturbance that follows delivery; distractions; attention disorders; conscious and

unconscious thoughts; interpretation of perceptions; memory problems; and problems with instability or imbalance of mind, desire, and changes in intellectual power or capacity

All of those diseases find their appropriate answer or treatment in the phytotherapeutic medicinal aspect.

TREATMENTS

To name just a few, phytotherapeutic medical practice suggests the following remedies:

Abscesses or boils: *zonyon dilin,* or white amaryllis (spider lily) juice (*Hymenocallis caribaea*); *siwèl* leaf juice, or hog plum (purple mombin, *Spondias purpurea*); steeped calabash-gourd pulp (*Crescentia cujete*) or *kòk souri* root pulp (snowberry, *Chiococca alba*). Laboratories have found the presence of a pyrolophenanthrenic alkaloid in the roots of the *kòk souri* that is also present in the *zonyon dilin.* This alkaloid has a strong antibiotic activity, particularly against Staphylococcus aureus and Bacillus subtilis. *Kalbas* pulp contains steroids, polyphenols, and alkaloids.

Asthma (*opresyon*): *degonfle*-leaf decoctions (*Acalypha alopecuroida*); the flower of *konkonb zombi* (jimsonweed, *Datura stramonium*); tea from the leaves of the tomato and *bonbonyen* (wild sage). *Degonfle* leaves contain cyanogenic derivatives and steroids; *konkonb zonbi* contains hyoscyamine, atropine, and scopolamine; and tomato leaves contain nitro-steroids such as tomatidin, solanidin, furocoumarin, and tryptamin. *Bonbonyen* contains b-sitosterol, lantaden, and terpenic acids.

Emotional shocks: vervain (*Stachytarpheta jamaicensis*), *langichat,* or thoroughwort (*Eupatorium odoratum*) or thyme-leaf teas; the juice of kidney-bean leaves; cashew-tree leaves, or *fèy doliv* (*Moringa oleifera*); coffee leaves (*Coffea arabica*); and *fèy koray,* or scarlet-bush leaves (*Hamelia patens*). All of these should be taken as decoctions, and all should be taken with the addition of salt. Vervain leaves have gamma-amino butyric acid and dopamine; thoroughwort leaves contain chalcon, odoratin, flavonoid, isosakuratin, salvigenin, and some sesquiterpenic and triterpenic acids such as eupatol, lupeol, and b-amyrin; thyme is an essential oil rich in thymol, carvacrol (20–70%), cymen, pinene, borneol, and linalool, among others. In addition to their bactericidal and fungicidal activities, they are also antispasmodic. Kidney-bean leaves contain some very efficient cyanogenetic derivatives; *pom kajou* leaves contain juglon, cycloartenol, and cycloeucalenol; *fèy doliv* leaves contain carotenoid, benzylsevenol, and pterygospermin; coffee leaves contain methyl salicylate and caffeine, which is well known to excite the nervous system and at the same time to be tonicardiac. Furthermore, it accelerates the respiratory processes.

Bladder and kidney conditions: leaf decoctions of *fèy kas dou,* or golden shower-tree (*Cassia fistula*), *fèy zorèy bourik* (*Sansevieria guinensis*), *fèy marigouya/bonbon koulèv* (love-in-a-mist, *Passiflora foetida*), and *fèy lougawou* (*Bryophillum pinnatum*). Laboratory research has found certain glucidic derivatives, pectin, rheine, and sennosides A and B in *kas dou* leaves and anthocyanate glucosides, hydroxy-5-tryptamin, and salicylic acid in *marigouya* leaves.

Hypertension: *rafrechi* made of the decoction of the wooden part of the coconut to which is added leaves from the following plants: almond (*Terminalia catappa*); *fèy a kè* (sun bush, *Lepianthes peltata*); *kenèp,* or honeyberry (*Melicocca bijuga*); and *pòpòt lam veritab,* the male fruit of the breadfruit tree (*Artocarpus incisa*). Studies have found that the entire almond tree is rich with ellagin, quercetol, leuco-cyanidin, kaempferol, and some flavonoids; *fèy à kè* is rich in anethol.

Diabetes (diagnosed by the attraction of ants to the patients' urine): decoction of bark of *pom kajou,* or cashew tree (*Anacardium occidentale*) or *dèyè do,* or niruri (*Phyllanthus niruri*); decoction of the leaves of *trompèt,* or trumpet tree (*Cecropia peltata*) or *twa zòm fò* (*Stemodia durantifolia*). Daily diet should include millet or sorghum (instead of rice) and *pwa congo,* or Congo or pigeon pea (*Cystisus cajan*). Laboratory studies have found vitamin C, cardol, and anacardol in the bark of the *pom kajou* and a leucocyanidin, some steroids, and an ursolic acid in the leaves of the trumpet tree. The *pitimi* is a glucide that contains some cyanogenetic derivatives. The *pwa congo* has been found to show the presence of an isoflavone, which is a fungicide called cajanon. It is also a good source of protein.

One could continue, ad infinitum, to compare the data from phytotherapeutic medicine to what is given by the pharmaceutical laboratories. Hundreds of herbs are used in Haiti, and such a study would certainly prove to be interesting. So interesting, in fact, that in 1983, according to the director of the United States Information Agency in Haiti, more than a thousand anthropologists, ethnologists, biochemists from the United States alone were roaming around the country. Some of them, indeed, had found the gems they were looking for. I will mention for the record what one remarkable discovery: *Bwa lèt,* or snakeroot or bitter bush (*Rauwolfia serpentina*) was commonly used by the people of the mountain town of Kenscoff, thirty kilometers north of Port-au-Prince. It provides the biochemically active principle recognized as reserpine, which has become a classic all over the world for the treatment of heart diseases.

Around 1940–1950, Dr. Gregory Pincus came to Haiti to research certain plants such as *Chapo kare,* or iron wood (*Sloanea domingensis*) and shallot, *chalòt mawon.* In these plants, he discovered the active principles of the birth control pill which changed life and social behavior around the globe. The country most often mentioned in conjunction with his work is Puerto Rico, where he later performed experiments using his birth control pill. However, Dr. Pincus did most of his research and experimentation in Haiti with the authorization, facilities, and moral support of the Haitian government.

III. Masterly Vodoun Medicine

Addressing health through a complicated mix of specific personal spiritual entities in dynamic interaction (which, for the sake of convenience can be called "nanm," or soul) falls within the purview of another form of medicine concerned with the effect of the soul on the body and on the mind. Only here can one see the linking of the somatic and the psyche, the blending that needs to occur in the process of healing, now understood to be more than the mere treatment of mechanical pathological disease processes.

Masterly Vodoun medicine is the spiritually most sophisticated level in the Haitian people's holistic medical system. Intrinsically located within Vodoun's culture, worldview, and religion, its operations include both the phytotherapeutic social and medical systems. However, Vodoun medicine goes beyond the other two systems in linking the individual to his and her global, social, and cosmological environment.

SPIRITUAL STRUCTURE OF THE HUMAN BEING

The concept of the human soul in Haitian Vodoun is complex. There is no synthetic term to designate its whole, since its manipulation is highly specialized. The word "*nanm*," which refers to a specific part of this conglomerate, is sometimes used, roughly translated by the English word "soul." This *nanm* is understood to be the seat of several spiritual entities, a *ti bon anj*, a *gwo bon anj*, a *nanm*, a *lwa mèt tèt*, the *wonsiyon*, and a set of *lwa rasin* (maternal and paternal) that is also called *lwa eritaj*. One entity, the *zetwal*, is not even located in the physical body; it resides in a star. Clan ancestors also belong to these influencing forces; they are honored and recognized for their continued interaction with and impact on human activity. Consequently, it is impossible to refer to the individual person as one who has mere corporal unity. The body is viewed as only a part of the whole person. This is why the person is perceived and defined as a psychosocial entity who needs to be in a continuous state of energetic equilibration.

All these entities act as forces and energies that function at the level of the individual, to whom they confer a particular sense of appreciation for the fundamentals of existence. However, they are still only a fraction of the individual's motivating and inhibiting forces. Other electromagnetic forces exist that are defined as external to humans: they are the 401 *lwa*. Even though those *lwa* are perceived as anthropomorphized forms of the Sacred, they sometimes act in groupings known as escorts. Together they help orient human beings in society and societies in the environment; they establish guidelines and direction for issues related to logic, ethics, morals, and aesthetics. They help humans devise the codes of conduct that are understood to be the mores of Haitian civilization. Their primary function is consequently to serve as guides to life in society, in nature, and in the universe.

The vision Vodounists have of all those many forces or immaterial energies acting in concert may not in fact be very distinguishable from what other peoples in other societies refer to as God. I hesitate, though, to use the word, because it is a conceptual issue of enormous complexity and I am not certain that I am fully cognizant of what such a concept represents for others that are not Vodounists.

Illness, then, results from a breach within this complexity that engenders conditions of disequilibrium, disharmony, chaos, and disorder. It may translate into simple injuries, accidents, or dysfunctions in the structure of the individual or of his or her organs; dysfunctions of the mind; or in total collapse, which suggests an inability to function efficiently within oneself, in one's society, or in the world.

Different from the mind, from which evolves conscious and unconscious thoughts processed by the brain, the soul can best be defined as that which engenders the rational, emotional, and volitional faculties in the human being; hence, it determines all behavior. It involves the very essence of who we are and is conceived as forming an entity distinct from the body and from the mind.

The soul, which does not have any physical or material reality, is regarded as the immortal and spiritual part of the person that survives physical death. Acting as the true axis of life, the *nanm* is thus perceived as being perpetually in motion. It turns around its own axis, vibrating continuously, as it does in everything else that has life. The differences that exist between living things are the vibrations that are generated differently, qualitatively, and in terms of intensity. Those vibrations are different one from the other, each one having its particular rate, amplitude, and mode of vibration.

The manifestations and influences of those movements extend to the mental activities of the human being and account for the bewildering succession of moods, feelings, and other changes that one notices in all lives. In a harmonious context, the soul carries along with it the other two components of the human person— the body and the mind. When the soul goes well, everything else goes well. Conversely, when there is disorder, disharmony or disequilibrium, everything else follows.

Masterly Vodoun medicine identifies seven internal spiritual entities, particles, energies, or forces.

• The first is the *gwo bon anj,* which translated into English means "big good angel." In the language of the Haitian people, it is called *sè mèdo,* as it is also for the Fon people of the Republic of Benin in Africa. Undifferentiated from one person to another, the *sè mèdo* is the divine particle that exists in each person. Essentially, the function of the *sè mèdo* is to keep that person alive, and it is viewed as the breath of life that everyone possesses. That is why everyone commands respect and, one hopes, the love of others for the simple fact of their existence.

• The second component is a *ti bon anj,* which translated into English means "small good angel." It is also known as the *sè lido,* in West Africa as in Haiti. Immortal and indestructible, it is the spiritual principle of the person that could be referred to as the intellect. Its function is to allow the person to know, to understand, to reinforce his or her attention, and to develop his or her aptitudes. This holistic system includes a belief in sixteen reincarnations and the belief that the experiences of the person in previous lives are retained and fill the bag of the unconscious. The *sè lido* is the seat of intelligence, knowledge, reflection, memory, and will. It enables the individual to make comparisons and judgments and to set him or herself up in a state of equilibrium. Very autonomous, this spirit is able to leave the body at any given time, to liberate itself temporarily, and to act freely. In moments of trance, the *ti bon anj* is displaced and gives way to the intercession of the Vodoun spirits.

• The *nanm,* often referred to as the *"nyam," "djam,"* or *"djanm,"* may be translated into English as the soul proper. It is that vital energy in a person whose forces are localized in each cell of the anatomical structure and in the various organs of the substructure of the body. As a perfect watchdog, it controls the functioning of these cells and structures. It may thus be viewed as also being the seat of genetics, and at its command, one transmits one's biological inheritance.

• The *zetwal,* translated into English as the *"star"* of a person, is also known in Africa as the *"sè kpoli."* In contrast to the other *sè,* or spirits, of the person, this one is believed to reside outside the body in a star, as a star in the ocean of stars. It is from that belief that one usually says that one is born on a good or shiny star or on a dimly lit or bad star. Shooting stars indicate the death of someone or the fact that someone has left his or her corporal body behind to change spiritual condition. The role of the *zetwal* is to serve as the guardian of the "spiritual calabash." This means that all the many events, good and bad, that should enrich the wisdom of a person fall from it as coming from an inverted spiritual gourd. Acting in a manner somewhat analogous to what people in the Western world might call fate, the *zetwal* provides persons with what is helpful for their spiritual advancement.

• The *lwa mèt tèt,* or the " spirit master of one's head," is one of the spiritual forces that vibrates in harmony with one of the 401 pulsating forces that sustain the universe, generally referred to as *lwa.* Everyone functions under the influence of a set of *lwa,* and one in particular, called *lwa mèt tèt,* vibrates at frequencies that are characteristic of the person. As an archetype, it provides the individual with his or her major character traits, making some persons calm and peaceful and others fiery and combative. Still others may have a changing and stormy disposition, or others will have totally different basic tendencies, making them tender, sentimental, or full of passion. The *lwa mèt tèt* gives some people an abundant sense of humor and some the trait of generosity.

• The *lwa rasin,* or *lwa eritaj,* binds the individual to his or her ancestors, those who are near in time as well as to those who are far away, therefore guaranteeing the lineage. They influence the behavior of the individual by establishing the link with those near and distant ancestors who enter the path of the unconscious to talk to him or her in dreams, to warn of danger, and to intervene at the many levels of his life.

• The *wonsiyon* are a series of spirits that accompany the *lwa mèt tèt* and modify somewhat the amplitude and the frequencies of its vibration or presence. Perceived as energies of very close vibrations, they add their own frequencies to the frequency of the *lwa mèt tèt* in order to generate new vibrations and frequencies. Consequently, they modify the amplitude or the character of individuals by their presence. It is due to the contribution of the *wonsiyon* that everyone attains ultimately what may be called "the irreducible personality," or the uniqueness of the individual.

The English language has a saying: "When it rains, it pours." The disordered state of a person is the best guarantor of illness for that person. "Illness" may translate as a physical or a mental condition or it may be an accident; it may also translate as the sudden loss of a job or good fortune, the lack of stability, or the total absence of peace in one's life.

The *wonsiyon* affect the normal functions or the health of the individual, his or her household, and his or her society. Thus, to say that someone's life is in disorder includes notions that are linked to more than just health. This is why it is said that the person, as it may also be said for a society, is sick because they are disordered.

PRINCIPLES

The Vodoun masterly medical system reduces to a simple principle: that of the dynamism of a certain conception of life, called energy. The mythical genesis of Vodoun teaches that the universe includes two worlds, the visible world and the invisible world. These two worlds are by no means seen to be distinct; quite the contrary, they are assumed to interpenetrate one another, mingling continually. Much larger than the visible world, the invisible one is replete with energies, including the spirits of all those who have existed since the beginning of time. It also includes the forces of the universe. These 401 spirits constitute what one might call "God," or even the "spirits of the ancestor." They constantly intervene in human matters and "mount" people by a process which is defined as trance or possession. These spirits play a very important role in the diagnosis of illness, which is often revealed through dreams, along with the appropriate treatments.

The 401 facets of the divine referred to as *lwa* are systematically categorized as the elements of earth, water, air, and fire (Petwo divinities). The individual *lwa mèt tèt* belongs to these 401 divinities. Possession by the *lwa* most commonly occurs during Vodoun ceremonies; but it may also take place at any time—especially in stressful situations. Furthermore, a frequent type of possession is associated with the sleep state. Recognized as a valid and legitimate form of cultural expression, possession is seen as a way to free the individual of inhibitions and frustrations; it acts as a psychic outlet.

Typically, there are two sorts of possession. The first is called *bosal* (or rough). Here, the person releases all excess energies built up within him or herself, often through violent thrashing of the body and generally disorganized, "wild" behavior, which is nevertheless understood, interpreted, and considered to be of great significance to all. The second, more controlled possession implies a reorganization of the self to achieve harmony within the self and with the various forces of nature in the universe. In this case, the individual *ti bon anj* is understood to be displaced and replaced by one of the 401 *lwa*. The person is re-equilibrated by the very process of his or her absorption within these higher forces. Indeed, at this moment, individual identities disappear, making way for the total affirmation of the divinity, who may choose to soothsay, sing, dance, carry out amazing feats such as glass- or fire-eating, or cure illnesses.

The human being is also seen as a force, or as an energy of a lesser dimension, which explains why each possession is specifically modulated according to the individual's personal *nanm*. At times these personal energies need to be synchronized so as to fit within the range which is considered to be harmonious and balanced.

Animals, plants, and everything else that possesses life are also seen as energy. Herbs are used in phytotherapeutic medicine for their chemical contents, but herbs used in masterly Vodoun medicine are seen as energy channelers, though they also contain biologically active substances.

Masterly medicine should be viewed as an energetic system of medicine since the human being is considered to be a cosmic or energetic force constantly swimming in a cosmic "soup," an energetic world. The herbs act as energy providers or retrievers that may be absorbed by the skin in the form of ointments, baths, or frictions or taken internally as food, an infusion, or tea.

Of course, in these particular situations, the knowledge a healer may have acquired of anatomy and physiology becomes rather irrelevant. All that matters is learning how to recognize a state of disorder and energetic disequilibrium and learning the appropriate manner to act upon this imbalance in order to increase or decrease the energy level of that person—that is to say, to re-equilibrate the person. Nevertheless, usually this medical system is adjoined to the phytotherapeutic system for optimal results. These combined treatments are carried out by the same person who, as we stated earlier, is considered to be a professional healer.

This type of medicine is based upon the belief that a normal range of energy exists within which each person functions well and that this range depends upon the spirit or spirits which give everyone his or her character. Under ordinary circumstances, the standard limits of normalcy in a person are recognizable by the person's demeanor, outward behavior, and emotional stability. Within the normal range, a person feels good, comfortable, and in perfect health. When depletion of energy occurs, he or she feels lethargic, weak, and/or listless. Incapable of normal activity, the person tends to experience the unpleasant sensation of being ill at ease and somewhat depressed, discouraged, and perhaps rejected. When the level of energy becomes excessive, a person can become excited, hyperactive, and nervous. In this state, he or she may seem hyper-agitated, happy but not in a relaxed way, borderline euphoric, or supercharged or in an overexcited state. These are signs of poor health. They are capable of degenerating into very serious conditions.

When a person is sick, those situations last significantly longer than what could be called a normal duration, meaning beyond three to five days. Those fuzzy limits are qualitative indeed and are ill defined. They vary with the individual, but they become manifest when deterioration of the patient's quality of health and vitality occurs. When health degenerates, the sickness evolves to the point where impairments in spiritual, intellectual, or physical functioning take place. Suicidal or homicidal tendencies are not excluded from this portrait as the energy of the person collapses.

Being of a masterly nature, this medicine is not reducible to formulas or recipes. The individual is to be seen in his or her entire complexity within each component (body, mind, and soul), viewed in his or her unique aspect. The individual's specificity is thus taken into account and treated accordingly. Each treatment is unique.

TREATMENTS

Modes of treatment emphasize specific aspects of the universal forces—water, air, fire, earth—based on an individual's illness. But treatment also considers the energetic forces represented by his or her *lwa mèt tèt.*

The first element of the treatment therefore consists of a *chandèl,* or *leson* (consultation), in which the healer determines if indeed there is illness, what its nature and causes are, which spirits are involved, and what options are open to the individual. Often, this is carried out in a state of possession and it is the spirit possessing the healer that speaks instead of him or her. In contradistinction to clinical medicine, in which the patient is expected to reveal his or her medical history to the physician, here it is the possessed healer who talks mostly, while the role of the patient is to approve or frown. A patient who disapproves of the diagnosis pays the standard amount for the consultation and is authorized to go to another healer. Shopping around is considered legitimate.

Once the patient is satisfied with the diagnosis, the treatment begins in earnest and the patient, accompanied by family members, confides in the healer at once. All aspects of the illness are covered. The healer's principal task at this point is to uncover the predominant aspect(s) of the individual's imbalance in order to determine the therapy.

He or she may then decide to "pass the patient in the earth," which implies a close communication with the soil (treatments dominated by such *lwa* as Legba, Ayizan, Zaka, Linglesou, Baron, Gede, and so forth). These treatments use clay, ashes, and earth; sometimes the patient is even temporarily buried (with the means to breathe). Or the healer may decide to proceed with an air technique (here the consulting spirits would be Sobo, Badè, Kebyesou, Shango Lwa): these may imply simple energy transfers such as fanning (*vantayaj*) and spraying (*foula*), which are its most common forms. In the first, a fowl (or occasionally a broom), accompanied by rock salt (for Lwa Avadra), is passed over the individual's body; in the second, he or she is sprayed with water or alcohol solutions understood to convey the spirits' energy and provide re-equilibration with those elements. Additionally sacrifices are commonly carried out, the animals' blood being considered an excellent energetic medium.

Fire dominants are treated by the "passing of flames" (*pase flanm*): here the individual is literally "bathed" with a fire, leaf, and alcohol mixture. Particular care is given to the application of this lit mixture to his/her articulations (feet, knees, elbows, shoulders, hands, neck) and to the forehead.

Water dominants, finally, represent one of the most commonly encountered forms of treatments. Baths of a great diversity of types are applied. Odors are of utmost significance and they are produced by the vigorous macerating action of leaf-tearing. Each of these is carefully selected according to the illness concerned. Immediate results emerge from the energy charge which flows from these herbs and the energy used to macerate them.

Some illnesses are believed to result from the individual's inappropriate social behavior. For instance, some cases pertain to inheritance disputes in which the individual is perceived to have wrongly appropriated common family land. Other examples involve lack of respect, lack of courage, and/or lack of generosity, which may in themselves constitute a weakness of character that reflect on the individual's health. In these situations it is said that the individual is persecuted by the spirit of a dead person (mò), sent to him or her by neighbors or relatives. In these cases it is necessary to have the patient redeem him or herself. Pilgrimages, charity visits to hospitals, contributions of food to prisoners and to the poor, coffee for the ancestors, masses for the deceased, and such other actions constitute elements that may bring about a remedy. Furthermore, the invading mò can be chased away by resolute means, such as a good flogging with pigeon pea stems (Cystisus cajan L.), considered one of the most radical and efficient means of expulsion.

Most serious treatments end with the application of a gad (guard), a protection destined to preserve the individual from further harm. The African tradition of scarring is in order here; generally a small mark is applied to the upper arm.

Singing and dancing, the common forms of Vodoun expression, are themselves considered a prophylaxis, promoting a healthy distribution of the dan throughout the body. Annually, herb baths are held at the end of the year, which corresponds to the first rise of sap after herbal hibernation at the rising moon. These baths are known for their invigorating capacities, charging all participants for a new year full of promise.

Non-Vodounists also partake (and thus often benefit) from energy transfers. Though Vodoun is not apostolic and never seeks conversions, repeated treatments can call for initiation which, in and of itself, is considered a final treatment. Here the individual recognizes his or her ancestral traditions and his/her lineage lwa. This is the ultimate re-equilibrating function, which is why healers consider it to be the masterly Vodoun medicine: the supreme form of medical treatment.

Because the breadth of Vodoun healing has seldom been considered in the literature or in present-day research, this chapter has attempted to present the basic elements of Vodoun healing, each separately, in an effort at systematization. It is important to recall, however, that the system functions in terms of synergies. Understanding this totality demands a recognition of the different parts; it is necessary that further research of a multidisciplinary nature be carried out in order to shed more light on this shadowy domain.

Note

Max-G. Beauvoir is one of the most prominent *houngan* within the Haitian community. He also practiced in the United States for about ten years. He was one of the first to go to the media, starting in the 1970s, in Haiti and abroad to argue that Vodou was indeed a legitimate religion and healing system. From very early on, he made no attempts to hide that he was an initiate and active practitioner in the religion. As a *houngan-therapeute,* a priest whose specialty is in the traditional healing arts, and as one who apprenticed for many years with elders in the priesthood, he is allowed to speak on these matters with authority. Specific levels of treatment correspond to different levels of understanding of Vodou mysticism. The right to treat within this metaphysical system is granted in accordance with the gradations achieved in the priesthood. Beauvoir has reached those highest levels that confer access to the most sophisticated healing practices as well as the privilege of teaching those practices to others—practitioners and scholars from various milieux and communities. He also trained as a chemist at the Sorbonne in Paris and at New York University. He has a large, well-known temple, Le Pérystile, in the Port-au-Prince suburb of Mariani, and in the 1990s he ran the first Haitian Vodou temple in the United States, The Temple of Yehweh, in Washington, D.C.—Eds.

Conclusion

PATRICK BELLEGARDE-SMITH AND CLAUDINE MICHEL

In this multicultural and multinational world—"worlds," to be precise—it is enormously important to allow multitudinous voices to reveal themselves, particularly if they have been violently silenced down through the centuries. The emic perspective, that of the insider, continues to be cherished as a means of preserving a sense of "authenticity." The old adage that absence makes the heart grow fonder no longer holds in new ethnographies. Of all African American religions, Haitian Vodou is still the most denigrated and disparaged. Of course, this is merely a matter of degree, for they all receive this treatment. Some religious expressions have been declared beyond the pale by racism.

The authors of this book have gone beyond familiar analytical categories to look into a pervasive neo-African system. In this enterprise, they are clearly innovative and bold. Their categories, analyses, and conclusions will not endear them to established academic scientific cultures rooted in Western Europe and North America. In this regard, they have eschewed the safety afforded them and the rewards those who stay within the norms earn, *les bornes* of accepted discourse. At the same time, the scope of that paradigm and ideological discourse has been diminished in the context of a world politics where one superpower exists, and these ten Haitian scholars are daring enough to suggest that Haitian sociocultural, political, and economic development can never occur when indigenous and popular intellectual systems are ignored or not taken seriously—and then applied. A carbon copy—*le pale reflet d'une pensée blanche*—an imitation of Western developmental thought and models, democracy even, is destined to fail. What can be more democratic, ultimately, at least in theory, than the century-long social constructs that have allowed a culture to survive and thrive? Neither polemical nor controversial, the authors have sought to delineate what they consider to be accurate in terms of their own culture and society, providing fair prescriptions for what ails the Haitian body politic.

After 500 years of a witch's brew, both editors and contributors of the present work have remarked that it was perhaps time to illuminate facets of Haitian Vodou from those described by previous ethnologists, ethnographers, anthropologists, and sundry others, fully recognizing these predecessors as intellectual ancestors. The authors in this volume undertook this book because they were Haitian themselves and because the views they would present were markedly absent from the scholarly record. We wrote this book collectively, as if our lives depended on it. Religion was but one of our interests; Vodou is not so much a religion as it is a system and a discipline that absorbs and swallows all other systems, fields, and universes. In much the same way that one accepts the many implications of a Christian, Islamic, or Buddhist worldview, one observes that the Vodou world-view extends beyond vision to incorporate other senses. And in much the same way that Christian, Jewish, or Muslim scholars dove into the minutiae of their traditions, we have sought to do exactly the same, by highlighting, by bringing accuracy, by exposing worlds mostly unknown to outsiders. Some critics may argue that few Vodou practitioners will see themselves reflected in our prose and our analyses. One answer is that few Roman Catholics find themselves mirrored in the splendiferous works of Saint Augustine or Saint Teresa of Avila, two "doctors" of the church. But some will recognize themselves in our work and will better understand the broad scholarly import of what, for most Haitians, is simply a way of life.

Our outlook is as fresh as it is new. The contributors offer many dimensions of analyses of Vodou epistemology, theology, and aesthetics. Each of the chapters links to the next one, but ultimately all of the chapters create a bridge to a complex world and cosmic reality. Some have been initiated as priests and practice the ancestral traditions they analyze. Largely trained at American colleges and universities, they have learned new tricks, and now they turn their bag of tricks on themselves and upon Haitian society.

The issues raised so dramatically by Guérin C. Montilus and Réginald O. Crosley—the first, a Haitian scholar with a D.Phil. from the Sorbonne and many years of field research in Dahomey/Benin, Nigeria, Haiti, and Cuba; the other, a medical doctor, a Protestant, hence a semi-outsider in the Haitian firmament—highlight the sophistication of the African and Haitian intellectual scientific corpus. Though this was done recently with respect to some selected African societies, that sort of study has never been done in connection with Haiti. The "big picture" they provide will illuminate the particularities illustrated in subsequent chapters. Notwithstanding the strength and the inherent logic of the African worldview, conditions and circumstances somewhat unique to Haiti forced it to amalgamate, to join, as it were, traditions culled from various religions in West and Central Africa, a situation not as readily observed next door in Cuba or in Brazil. In those countries, the Haitian religion is seen with a modicum of fear, as more potent, more effective, and "darker."

Patrick Bellegarde-Smith, who provides another big picture, has developed scholarly notoriety for having analyzed the immense complexity of both the evolution of the Haitian historical discourse and the fractured nature of competing ontological assumptions of different formulations of Haitian national identity. He has located his analysis within the context of a international political system controlled by the Western powers and the social classes that found their genesis in the colonial world that gave birth to Haiti. No one else had done this to date, and no one had declared unambiguously that the road to democratization in Haiti would be an Africanizing process. Professor Claudine Michel's contributions locate themselves in the novel arguments introduced by the preceding scholars when she describes the methods by which the tenets of Haitian culture as expressed in the Vodou religion could be incorporated in the areas of education, instruction, and knowledge. Her approach has never been tried before, save perhaps for a small school in the Republic of Trinidad and Tobago in the eastern Caribbean. Her methodology is unique, powerful, and uncompromising; the pedagogical and political implications of the work are formidable. No school in Haiti has yet followed Dr. Michel's model in its entirety, though some prescriptions made in her work have been put into place in some grassroots schools and projects in Haiti. It is a pedagogy of liberation.

The Haitian genius is seen in the work of anthropologist Rénald Clérisme and musicologist Gerdès Fleurant, who find in music a path to political transformation through defense of the rights of the peasantry and the urban working class. Though field research is not new in Haiti, Fleurant and Clérisme bring to the fore their personal connections with the Haitian countryside. Certainly there are risks in this kind of work: the insider's knowledge they share with others can and might be used to suppress further an already oppressed population by endogamous as well as exogamous elites. Such is the cost and the price of social science.

In the absence of "modern" medicine, which is prohibitively costly, the Afro-Haitian medical system has served Haiti relatively well. Though trained in chemistry in France and the United States, Max-G. Beauvoir has turned his powers of observation inward. His mentors were all so-called illiterate peasants who were nonetheless full of knowledge. They transmitted the kind of knowledge that transcends academic Western science and moves into increasingly complex realms of multidimensional realities. No one else has yet been able to describe the healing arts in Haiti with such engrossing details. And no one else has written about the subject.

The work of Marc A. Christophe and Florence Bellande-Robertson is marked by what the world has come to know as the apotheosis of Haitian "high" culture, the plastic arts and literature. The first is still the domain of a collective ethos rooted in the multidimensionality of mass-based popular culture, the appanage of working-class and rural Haiti. The other, the tool of the upper class, Haiti's lasting achievement, is its written literature. Upper-class Haitians, who patterned themselves after the French, produced more books on a per capita basis than any other country in Latin America well into the 1950s. Haitian arts, which were disparaged for decades by the upper classes, placed the country on the world map. In his essay, Christophe, himself a gifted artist and a professor of French and Caribbean literature, teases the philosophical substrata, the ideological superstructure that undergirds most Haitian art. It is perhaps his personal *engagement* as an artist and his academic training that led him to this confluence between art and philosophy, that broke the dam, allowing the waters to flow.

Bellande-Robertson is the first to look at a novel by anthropologist and minister of culture Lilas Desquiron; she turns her perceptive powers of analysis toward and upon the intense, solid, unacknowledged connection that has always existed between the peasantry and the erstwhile aristocracy. Although the novel plays itself out through the trope of the discourse of social class in Haiti, it is also about an ancestral spirituality in which Haitians either find their essence or have their essence foisted on them by circumstances and the Deities even as they reject it. While the first chapters of Desquiron's novel addressed the African sense of the world as it applied to Haiti, the last chapter is about the fusion that has already taken place between Africa and Haiti, the upper and lower classes, between gods and (wo)men, even as little of this is ever perceived by the protagonists. *We are,* and have completed, the circle.

The collective essay that delves into the realities of Haitian female priests at home and abroad examines the ultimate disconnect between cosmic reality in which the female principle is paramount and a daily reality in which sexism reigns. The preeminence of female deities in the Haitian pantheon and the preponderance of female priests in Haiti contrasts sharply with the arduous conditions, the travails under which Haitian women labor. Working-class women and *bourgeoises* mingle their voices and speak out as they are interviewed for the first time. Their odes of joy and their lamentations are most precious.

This is the first time that ten Haitians have come together to write a book that, they hope, will allow others to glimpse their complex and complicated world, a world that remains unseen and unknown and unacknowledged by most others.

Appendix: Table of Haitian Lwa

Names	Description	Colors	Days	Trees	Symbols	Offerings	Roman Catholic names
Legba (Rada/ Petwo)	Chief of Crossroads and gates	Red, brown, and white	Friday and Saturday	Calabash and Cirouellier	Crosses, crutches, old man in rags, keys, and walking sticks	Cassava, mottled roosters, tobacco, and pipes	St. Anthony, St. Peter, and Jesus Christ
Avelekete (Rada)			Friday and Saturday				
Dambala (Rada)	Wise Serpent	White and light green	Thursday		Snakes and eggs	Almond syrup, white flour, and eggs	St. Patrick, Jesus Christ, and Moses
Ayida Wedo (Rada)	Wise Rainbow	White and light blue	Monday and Tuesday	Cotton	Rainbows	Milk and white chickens	Our Lady of Immaculate Conception
Marasa (Rada/ Petwo)	Twins				Palm leaves	Rice pudding, popcorn, and cola	St. Cosme, St. Damian, and St. Nicholas
Hevioso (Rada)	Stones, fire and wind				Thunder and lightning		St. Jerome
Ezili Freda (Rada)	Love, sensuality, and beauty	Pink, gold, and light blue	Tuesday and Thursday	Laurel	Hearts, pink cakes, and perfume	Wine, perfume, and liqueurs	La Mercie
Ezili Danto (Nago/ Pewto)	Mother/ Warrior	Dark blue and red	Tuesday and Thursday		Daggers and black dolls	Fried pork, perfume, red wine, and barbancourt rum	Lady Czesto-chowa, Lady of Mount Carmel, and St. Rose

Names	Description	Colors	Days	Trees	Symbols	Offerings	Roman Catholic names
Ogou (Nago)	Warrior family and Justice	Red	Saturday	Calabash	Machetes	Cigars, red roosters, rum and, machetes	St. James the Elder, St. James the Minor, St. John the Baptist, St. Philippe, St. Joachin, St. Michael, St. Georges, and Joan of Arc
Lasirenn (Rada)	"mermaid" and the ocean	Light blue and blue-green			Shells, combs, and mirrors	Wine and perfume	St. Caridad, Star of the Sea, and St. Peola
Agwe (Rada)	Sea Captain	Blue, white, and green	Thursday		Boats, oars, and fish	Champagne, liqueurs, cakes, and white hens	St. Ulrich and St. Expedit
Azaka (Rada)	Patron of agriculture	Blue, green, and red	Friday and Saturday	Avocado and Banana	Lizards, machetes, pipes, and straw bags	Kleren, tobacco, corn, unrefined sugar, and cassava	St. Isidore and St. Andrew
Klermezinn (Rada)				Haitian Cherry	Lizards, machetes, pipes, and straw bags	Kleren, tobacco, corn, unrefined sugar, and cassava bread	St. Claire

Names	Description	Colors	Days	Trees	Symbols	Offerings	Roman Catholic names
Simbi (Rada/ Petwo)	Fresh water and healer	White and green			Snakes, wells, ponds, and streams	White, black, and gray animals	Sacred Heart, St. John the Baptist, and Jesus Christ
Loko (Rada)	Gives power to priests	Yellow		Mapou	Red roosters	Roosters	St. Joseph
Ayizan (Rada)	Guardian of the temple	Cream		Palm	Palm leaves	Roosters	St. Ann, Altagracia and Jesus Christ
Gran Brigit (Gede)	Death and cemeteries	Purple, black, and mauve	Monday and Friday		Coffee	Peppers and black coffee	St. Catherine
Bawon (Gede)	Death and cemeteries	White and black	Monday and Friday		Skulls, crosses, cadavers, phalluses, and coffins	Cigarettes, black goats, and sunglasses	St. Gerard, St. Ives, and St. Expedit

PREPARED BY KYRAH M. DANIELS 1/3/2003

Bibliography

Aborampah, Osei-Mensah. "Family Structure in African Fertility Studies: Some Conceptual and Methodological Issues." *A Current Bibliography on African Affairs* 18, no. 4 (1985–1986): 319–335.

Alexis, Jacques Stéphen. *Les arbres musiciens.* Port-au-Prince: Ateliers Fardin, 1957.

———. *Compère Général Soleil.* Paris: Gallimard, 1955.

Amadiume, Ifi. *Re-inventing Africa: Matriarchy, Religion, and Culture.* New York: Zed Books, 1997.

Anglade, Mireille Neptune. *L'autre moitié du développement: A propos du travail des femmes en Haïti.* Pétion-Ville: Editions des Alizés and Paris: Karthala, 1986.

Antoine, Paul. "Place du palma-christi dans la culture populaire." In *Cahier de folklore et des traditions orales,* ed. Max Benoît. Port-au-Prince: Imprimerie des Antilles, 1980.

Aspect, Alain, J. Dalibard, and G. Roger. "Experimental Test of Bell's Inequalities Using Time-Varying Analyzers." *Physical Review Letters* 49, no. 25 (December 1982): 1804–1807.

Averill, Gage. *A Day for the Hunter, a Day for the Prey: Popular Music and Power in Haiti.* Chicago: University of Chicago Press, 1997.

Barnes, Sandra T., ed. *Africa's Ogun: Old World and New.* Bloomington: Indiana University Press, 1989.

Barthes, Roland. *Poétique du récit.* Paris: Seuil, 1977.

Bastide, Roger. *African Civilizations in the New World.* Trans. Peter Green. New York: Harper & Row, 1971.

———. *The African Religions of Brazil: Toward a Sociology of the Interpenetration of Civilizations.* Trans. Helen Sebba. Baltimore: Johns Hopkins Press, 1978.

———. *Les amériques noires.* Paris: Petite Bibliothèque Payot, 1967.

———. "Color, Racism and Christianity." In *Color and Race,* ed. John Hope Franklin, 34–49. Boston: Houghton-Mifflin, 1968.

———. *Les religions africaines au Brésil; vers une sociologie des interpénétrations civilisations.* Paris: Presses Universitaires de France, 1960.

Bastien, Rémy. *Religion and Politics in Haiti.* Washington, D.C.: Institute for Cross-Cultural Research, 1966.

Beauvoir, Max G. "Foreword." In Reginald Crosley, *The Vodou Quantum Leap: Alternate Realities, Power and Mysticism.* St. Paul, Minn.: Llewellyn Publications, 2000.

Bellegarde, Dantès. *Dessalines a parlé.* Port-au-Prince: Société d'Editions et de Librairie, 1948.

———. *La nation haïtienne.* Paris: Editions J. de Gigord, 1938.

———. *Histoire du peuple haïtien.* Port-au-Prince: Collection du Tricinquantenaire, 1953.

Bellegarde-Smith, Patrick. *Haiti: The Breached Citadel.* Boulder, Colo.: Westview Press, 1990.

———. *In the Shadow of Powers: Dantès Bellegarde in Haitian Social Thought.* Atlantic Highlands, N.J.: Humanities Press International, 1985.

———. "Rum as Cognac: Fluidity of an Etho-Cultural Crisis—Haiti." *Kaleidoscope II* (Spring 1994): 13–18.

Blaut, James M. *The Colonizer's Model of the World: Geographical Diffusionism and Eurocentric History.* New York: Guilford Press, 1993.

Blier, Suzanne Preston. *African Vodun: Art, Psychology, and Power.* Chicago: University of Chicago Press, 1995.

Bloncourt, Gérald. *La peinture haïtienne (Haitian Arts)*. Paris: Nathan, 1986.

Bodkins, Robin Orr. *Reflections of Loko Miwa*. Charlottesville: University Press of Virginia, 1998.

Bohm, David. *Quantum Theory*. New York: Prentice Hall, 1951.

Bourguignon, Erika. *Possession*. 1976; reprint, Prospect Heights, Ill.: Waveland Press, 1991.

Boyer, Ernest. "Teaching Religion in the Public Schools and Elsewhere." *Journal of the Academy of Religion* 60, no. 3 (Fall 1992): 515–525.

Brandon, George. *Santería, from Africa to the New World: The Dead Sell Memories*. Bloomington: Indiana University Press, 1997.

Brodwin, Paul. *Medicine and Morality in Haiti: The Contest for Power*. London: Cambridge University Press, 1996.

Brown, Karen McCarthy. "Alourdes: A Case Study of Moral Leadership in Haitian Vodou." In *Saints and Virtues*, ed. John Stratton Hawley. Berkeley: University of California Press, 1987.

———. *Mama Lola: A Vodou Priestess in Brooklyn*. Berkeley: University of California Press, 2001.

———. "Plenty Confidence in Myself: The Initiation of a White Woman Scholar into Haitian Vodou." *Journal of Feminist Studies in Religion* 3, no. 1 (Spring 1987): 67–76.

———. "The Vèvè of Haitian Vodou: A Structural Analysis of Visual Imagery." Ph.D. diss., Temple University, 1976.

Brutus, Timoléon, and Arsène Pierre-Noël. *Les plantes et les légumes d'Haïti qui guérissent: mille et une recettes*. 3 vols. Port-au-Prince: Imprimerie de l'Etat, 1959–1966.

Capra, Fritjof. *The Tao of Physics: An Exploration of the Parallels Between Modern Physics and Eastern Mysticism*. Boston: Shambhala, 1991.

Césaire, Aimé. *Discourse on Colonialism*. Trans. Joan Pinkham. New York: Monthly Review Press, 1972.

Chamoiseau, Patrick, and Raphaël Confiant. *Lettres créoles, tracées antillaises et continentales de la litérature 1635–1975*. Paris: Hatier, 1991.

Chancy, Myriam J. A. *Framing Silence: Revolutionary Novels by Haitian Women*. New Brunswick, N.J.: Rutgers University Press, 1997.

Chomsky, Noam. "The Tragedy of Haiti." In *The Haiti Files: Decoding the Crisis*, ed. James Ridgeway. Washington D.C.: Essential Books and Azul Editions, 1994.

Cinéas, Jean Baptiste. *L'héritage sacré*. Port-au-Prince: Ateliers Fardin, 1937.

Claude-Narcisse, Jasmine. *Mémoire de femmes*. Port-au-Prince: UNICEF, 1997.

Conniff, Michael, and Thomas Davis. *Africans in the Americas: A History of the Black Diaspora*. New York: St. Martin's Press, 1994.

Cosentino, Donald J., ed. *Sacred Arts of Haitian Vodou*. Los Angeles, California: UCLA Fowler Museum of Cultural History, 1995.

Courlander, Harold. *The Drum and the Hoe: Life and Lore of the Haitian People*. Berkeley: University of California Press, 1973.

———. *Haiti Singing*. 1939; reprint, New York: Cooper Square, 1973.

Coveney, Peter, and Roger Highfield. *The Arrow of Time: A Voyage through Science to Solve Time's Greatest Mystery*. London: W. H. Allen, 1990.

Dash, Michael J. *Literature and Ideology in Haiti, 1915–1961*. Totowa, N.J.: Barnes and Noble Books, 1981.

Dauphin, Claude. *La musique du vaudou: fonctions, structures et styles*. Sherbrooke, Québec: Naaman, 1986.

Davis, Wade. *Passage of Darkness: The Ethnobiology of a Haitian Zombie*. Chapel Hill: University of North Carolina Press, 1988.

———. *The Serpent and the Rainbow*. New York: Warner Books, 1985.

Dayan, Joan. *Haiti, History, and the Gods.* Berkeley: University of California Press, 1995.

Déita. *La légende des loa. Vodou haïtien.* Port-au-Prince: n.p., 1993.

———. *Mon pays inconnu.* Port-au-Prince: L'Imprimeur II, 1997.

Delbeau, Jean-Claude. *Société, culture et médecine populaire traditionnelle: étude sur le terrain d'un cas.* Port-au-Prince: Imprimerie H. Deschamps, 1990.

Denis, Lorimer. "Rituel observé en vue de la protection du nouveau-né contre les maléfices des sorciers, le mauvais oeil ou maldiocre, les mauvais airs ou loup-garous." [*Bulletin*] *Bureau d'Ethnnologie* 2 (1947): 5–6.

Depestre, René. *Bonjour et adieu à la Négritude.* Paris: Robert Laffont, 1980.

Deren, Maya. *Divine Horsemen: The Living Gods of Haiti.* 1953; reprint, New Paltz, N.Y.: McPherson & Co., 1983.

De Saint-Méry, Moreau. *Description topographique de l'isle de Saint-Domingue, physique, civile, politique et historique de la partie française de l'île de Saint-Domingue.* 1797. New edition ed. Blanche Maurel and Etienne Taillemite. Paris: Société de l'histoire de la Colonie Française, 1958.

Desmangles, Leslie G. *The Faces of the Gods: Vodou and Roman Catholicism in Haiti.* Chapel Hill: University of North Carolina Press, 1992.

Desquiron, Lilas. *Les chemins de Loco-Miroir.* Paris: Stock, 1990.

———. *Les racines du vodou.* Port-au-Prince: Editions Henri Deschamps, 1990.

———. *Reflections of Loko-Miwa.* Trans. Robin Orr Bodkin. Charlottesville: University Press of Virginia, 1998.

DeWitt, Bryce, and Neil Graham, eds. *The Many-Worlds Interpretation of Quantum Mechanics.* Princeton: Princeton University Press, 1973.

Diop, Cheikh Anta. *Civilization or Barbarism: An Authentic Anthropology.* Trans. Yaa-Lengi Meema Ngemi. Brooklyn, N.Y.: Lawrence Hill Books, 1991.

Douglas, Paul H. "The Political History of the Occupation." In *Occupied Haiti,* ed. Emily Greene Balch. New York: Negro University Press, 1969.

Dunham, Katherine. *Dances of Haiti.* 1947; reprint, Los Angeles: Center for Afro-American Studies, UCLA, 1983.

———. *Island Possessed.* 1969; reprint; Chicago: University of Chicago Press, 1994.

Einstein, Albert, B. Podolsky, and N. Rosen. "Can Quantum-Mechanical Description of Physical Reality Be Considered Complete?" *Physical Review* 47, no. 10 (May 15, 1935): 777–780.

Eliade, Mircea. *Aspects du mythe.* Paris: Gallimard, 1963.

Fanon, Frantz. *Black Skin, White Masks.* Trans. Charles Lam Markmann. New York: Grove Press, 1967.

———. *Peau noires, masques blancs.* Paris: Editions du Seuil, 1995.

Farmer, Paul. *The Uses of Haiti.* Monroe, Maine: Common Courage Press, 1994.

Fatunmbi, Awo Falokun. *Ibase Orisa: Ifa Proverbs, Folktales, Sacred History and Prayer.* Bronx, N.Y.: Original Publications, 1994.

Fernadez-Olmos, Margarite, and Lizabeth Paravisini-Gebert, eds. *Sacred Possessions: Vodou, Santería, Obeah, and the Caribbean.* New Brunswick, N.J.: Rutgers University Press, 1977.

Fick, Carolyn E. *The Making of Haiti: The Saint Domingue Revolution from Below.* Knoxville: University of Tennessee Press, 1990.

Fleurant, Gerdès. *Dancing Spirits: Rhythms and Rituals of Haitian Vodun, the Rada Rite.* Westport: Greenwood Press, 1996.

———. "The Ethnomusicology of Yanvalou: A Study of the Rada Rite of Haiti." Ph.D. diss., Tufts University, 1987.

————. *Haitian Pilgrimage*. Videocassette. Dir. Robin Lloyd. Script by Greg Guma. 29 mins. Burlington, Vt.: Green Valley Films, 1991.

Freedman, S., and J. Clauser. "Experimental Test of Local Hidden Variable Theories." *Physical Review Letters* 28, no. 14 (April 3, 1972): 938–941.

Ford, Kenneth. *The World of Elementary Particles*. New York: Blaisdell, 1963.

Fouchard, Jean. *The Haitian Maroons: Liberty or Death*. Trans. A. Faulkner Watts. New York: Blyden Press, 1981.

————. *La méringue: Dance nationale d'Haiti*. Québec: Léneac, 1973.

Gaillard, Roger. *Les blancs débarquent*. 7 vols. Port-au-Prince: Imprimerie Le Natal, 1974–1984.

Galembo, Phyllis. *Vodou: Visions and Voices of Haiti*. Berkeley, Calif.: Ten Speed Press, 1998.

Gates, Henry Louis, Jr. *The Signifying Monkey: A Theory of African-American Literary Criticism*. New York: Oxford University Press, 1988.

Gleason, Judith. *Oya: In Praise of the Goddess*. San Francisco: Harper San Francisco, 1992.

Gleick, James. *Chaos: Making a New Science*. New York: Viking Press, 1987.

Gouraige, Ghislain. *La diaspora d'Haïti et l'Afrique*. Sherbrooke: Editions Naaman, 1974.

Hall, James. *Sangoma: My Odyssey into the Spirit World of Africa*. New York: Putnam, 1994.

Hamilton, Cynthia. "A Way of Seeing: Culture as Political Expression in the Works of C. L. R. James." *Journal of Black Studies* 22, no. 3 (March 1992): 429–443.

Hecht, David, and Maliqalim Simone. *Invisible Governance: The Art of African Micropolitics*. Brooklyn, N.Y.: Autonomedia, 1994.

Herskovits, Melville J. *Dahomean Narrative*. Evanston, Ill.: Northwestern University Press, 1967.

————. *Life in a Haitian Valley*. 1937; reprint, Garden City, N.Y.: Anchor Books, 1971.

Honorat, Lamartinière. *Les dances folkloriques haïtiennes*. Port-au-Prince: Imprimerie de l'Etat, 1955.

Hood, Mantle. "The Challenge of Bi-Musicality." *Ethnomusicology* 4, no. 2 (Winter 1960): 55–59.

Hurbon, Laënnec. *Le barbare imaginaire*. Port-au-Prince: Editions HenriDeschamps, 1987.

————. *Culture et dictature en Haïti: l'imaginaire sous controle*. Paris: L'Harmattan, 1979.

————. *Dieu dans le vaudou haïtien*. Port-au-Prince: Editions Henri Deschamps, 1987.

————. *Les mystères du vaudou*. Paris: Gallimard, 1993.

————. *Voodoo. Search for the Spirit*. Trans. Lory Frankel. New York: Harry N. Abrams, 1995.

Hurston, Zora Neale. *Tell My Horse: Voodoo and Life in Haiti and Jamaica*. 1938; reprint, New York: Perennial Library, 1990.

Jahn, Janheinz. *Muntu: The New African Culture*. New York: Grove Press, 1961.

James, C. L. R. *The Black Jacobins: Toussaint l'Ouverture and the San Domingo Revolution*. New York: Vintage Books, 1963.

James, Joel, José Millet, and Alexis Alarcón. *El vodú en Cuba*. Santiago: Editorial Oriente, 1998.

Jones, A. M. *Studies in African Music*. 2 vols. London: Oxford University Press, 1959.

Kalupahana, David J. *The Principles of Buddhist Psychology*. Albany: State University of New York Press, 1987.

Kochman, Thomas. *Black and White: Styles in Conflict*. Chicago: University of Chicago Press, 1984.

Kolinski, Mieczyslaw. "Haiti." In *New Grove Dictionary of Music and Musicians*. London: Macmillan, 1980.

La Belle, Thomas. "An Introduction to the Nonformal Education of Children and Youth." *Comparative Education Review* 25, no. 3 (1981): 313–329.

Laguerre, Michel S. "Haitian Americans." In *Ethnicity and Medical Care,* ed. Alan Harwood. Cambridge: Harvard University Press, 1981.

———. *Voodoo and Politics in Haiti.* New York: St. Martin's Press, 1989.

———. *Voodoo Heritage.* Beverly Hills, Calif.: Sage Publications, 1980.

Lataillade, Edith. *Le dernier fil: ou les sanctions au quotidian.* Port-au-Prince: Le Natal, 1998.

Léon, Rulx. "Médecine et superstitions locales." *Relève* 4 (October 1934): 7–12.

Lerebours, Michel-Philippe. *Haiti et ses peintres.* Vol. 1. Port-au-Prince: L'Imprimeur II, 1989.

Lesne, Christian. *Cinq essais d'ethnopsychiatrie antillaise.* Paris: Editions L'Harmattan, 1990.

Leyburn, James G. *The Haitian People.* New Haven: Yale University Press, 1966.

Locke, David Lawrence. "The Music of Atsiagbeko." Ph.D. diss., Wesleyan University, 1979.

Madiou, Thomas. *Histoire d'Haïti.* 4 vols. Port-au-Prince: Imprimerie J. Courtois, 1847–1848.

Marcelin, Milo. "Cent croyances et superstitions." *Optique* 7 (1954): 48–56.

Marcelin, Pierre, and Philippe Thoby-Marcelin. *La bête de Musseau.* New York: Rinehart & Co., 1946.

Maximilien, Louis. *Vodou: Rite Rada-Kanzo.* Port-au-Prince: Imprimerie de L'Etat, 1945.

Mbiti, John S. *African Religions and Philosophy.* Garden City, N.Y.: Doubleday, 1970.

McAlister, Elisabeth. *Rara! Vodou, Power, and Performance in Haiti and Its Diaspora.* Berkeley: University of California Press, 2002.

Menkiti, Ifeanyi A. "Person and Community in African Thought." In *African Philosophy: An Introduction,* ed. R. A. Wright. Washington, D.C.: University Press of America, 1979.

Memmi, Albert. *Portrait du colonisé précédé du portrait du colonisateur.* Paris: Editions Buchet/Chastel, Correa, 1957.

Métraux, Alfred. "Médecine et vodou en Haïti." *Acta Tropica* 10 (1953): 28–68.

———. *Le vaudou haïtien.* Paris: Gallimard, 1958.

———. *Voodoo in Haiti.* Trans. Hugo Charteries. New York: Schocken Books, 1972.

Michel, Claudine. *Aspects éducatifs et moraux du vodou haïtien.* Port-au-Prince: Imprimerie Le Natal, 1995.

———. *Tapping the Wisdom of the Ancestors: An Attempt to Recast Vodou and Morality through the Voice of Mama Lola and Karen McCarthy Brown.* Research Report No. 27. Boston: William Monroe Trotter Institute, 1996.

———. "Women's Moral and Spiritual Leadership in Haitian Vodou: The Voice of Mama Lola and Karen McCarthy Brown." *Journal of Feminist Studies of Religion* 17, no. 2 (2001): 61–85.

Mintz, Sidney. "Introduction." In Alfred Métraux, *Voodoo in Haiti.* New York: Schocken, 1972.

Montilus, Guérin. "Africans in Diaspora: The Myth of Dahomey in Haiti." *Journal of Caribbean Studies* 2, no. 1 (Spring 1981): 73–84.

———. *Dompim: The Spirituality of African Peoples.* Nashville, Tenn.: Winston-Derek Publishers, 1991.

———. "Haïti: un cas témoin de la vivacité des religions africaines en Amérique et pourquoi." Ph.D. diss., University of Zurich, 1972.

Morrison, Toni. *Lecture and Speech of Acceptance, Nobel Prize for Literature, Delivered in Stockholm, Sweden, 1993.* New York: A. A. Knopf, 1993.

Moskin, Robert. *The U.S. Marine Corps Story.* Boston: Little, Brown and Co., 1992.

Murray, Gerald Francis. *Folk Healers of Petit-Goave: A Model for Incorporating Traditional Healers into the Modern Delivery System.* Port-au-Prince: International Development Research Center, 1977.

Nketia, J. H. Kwabena. *African Music in Ghana.* Evanston: Northwestern University Press, 1959.

Nord, Warren A. "Public Schools Should Teach Religious Studies." In *Education in America: Opposing Viewpoints,* ed. Charles Cozic. San Diego: Greenhaven, 1992.

Olupona, Jacob K. "Major Issues in the Study of African Traditional Religion." In *African Traditional Religions in Contemporary Society,* ed. Jacob K. Olupona. St. Paul, Minn.: Paragon House, 1991.

Pantaleoni, Hewitt. "The Rhythm of Atsia Dance Drumming among the Anlo (Eve) of Anyako." Ph.D. diss., Wesleyan University, 1972.

Paul, Emmanuel C., and Lorimer Denis. *Essai d'organographie haïtienne.* Port-au-Prince: Imprimerie Valcin, 1948.

Paris, Peter J. *The Spirituality of African Peoples: The Search for a Common Moral Discourse.* Minneapolis: Fortress, 1995.

Parrinder, Geoffrey. *Religion in Africa.* New York: Praeger, 1969.

Planson, Claude. *Le vaudou.* Paris: MA Editions, 1987.

Plaskow, Judith, and Carol Christ. *Weaving the Visions: Patterns in Feminist Spirituality.* San Francisco, Calif.: Harper, 1989.

Plummer, Brenda Gayle. *Haiti and the Great Powers, 1902–1915.* Baton Rouge: Louisiana State University Press, 1988.

Pocock, J. G. A. *Politics, Language and the Time: Essays on Political Thought and History.* New York: Atheneum, 1971.

Price, Hannibal. *De la réhabilitation de la race noire par la République d'Haiti.* Port-au-Prince: Verolot, 1900.

Price, Richard, ed. *Maroon Societies: Rebel Slave Communities in the Americas.* Garden City, N.Y.: Anchor Press, 1973.

Price-Mars, Jean. *Ainsi parla l'oncle: essais d'ethnographie.* Paris: Imprimerie de Compiègne, 1928.

———. *So Spoke the Uncle.* Trans. Magdaline Shannon. Washington, D.C.: Three Continents Press, 1983.

Polk, Patrick A. *Haitian Vodou Flags.* Jackson: University Press of Mississippi, 1997.

Primack, Joel R. "The Case of the Dark Matter." In *Science Year: The World Book Annual Science Supplement.* Chicago: World Book, 1990.

Ray, Benjamin C. *African Religions: Symbol, Ritual, and Community.* Englewood Cliffs, N.J.: Prentice-Hall, 1976.

Renda, Mary A. *Taking Haiti: Military Occupation and the Culture of U.S. Imperialism, 1915–1940.* Chapel Hill: University of North Carolina, 2001.

Rigaud, Milo. *La tradition voudoo et le voudoo haïtien: son temple, ses mystères, sa magie.* Paris: Editions Niclaus, 1953.

———. *Secrets of Voodoo.* Trans. Robert B. Cross. 1969; reprint, San Francisco: City Lights Books, 1985.

———. *Vèvè: Diagrammes du vaudou.* New York: Trilingual Edition, 1974.

Rimbaud, Arthur. *Illuminations.* Neuchatel: La Baconniere, 1986.

Roumain, Jacques. *Gouverneurs de la rosée.* Port-au-Prince: Imprimerie de l'Etat, 1944.

———. *Masters of the Dew.* Trans. Langston Hughes and Mercer Cook. London: Heinneman, 1978.

Seabrook, William B. *L'île magique: les mystéres du vaudou.* Trans. France-Marie Watkins. Paris: J'ai Lu, 1971.

———. *The Magic Island.* New York: Harcourt, Brace and Co., 1929.

Smucker, Glenn R. "The Social Character of Religion in Rural Haiti." In *Haiti, Today and Tomorrow: An Interdisciplinary Study,* ed. C. Foster and A. Valdman. Washington D.C.: University Press of America, 1984.

Somé, Malidoma Patrice. *Of Water and the Spirit: Ritual, Magic, and Initiation in the Life of an African Shaman.* New York: Putnam, 1994.

Taylor, Patrick. *The Narrative of Liberation: Perspectives on Afro-Caribbean Literature, Popular Culture, and Politics.* Ithaca: Cornell University Press, 1989.

————. *Nation Dance: Religion, Identity, and Cultural Difference in the Caribbean.* Blooming-ton: Indiana University Press, 2001.

Telda, Elleni. "Indigenous African Education as a Means for Understanding the Fullness of Life: Amara Traditional Education." *Journal of Black Studies* 23, no. 1 (Fall 1992): 7–27.

Thompson, Robert Farris. *Flash of the Spirit: African and Afro-American Art and Philosophy.* New York: Random House, 1984.

Trouillot, Michel-Rolph. *Silencing the Past: Power and the Production of History.* Boston: Bea-con Press, 1995.

Turner, Michael S. "The Universe." *Science Year: The World Book Annual Science Supplement.* Chicago: World Book, 1994.

Turner, Victor. *The Ritual Process: Structure and Anti-Structure.* Ithaca: Cornell University Press, 1969.

Vansina, Jan. *Oral Tradition as History.* Madison: University of Wisconsin Press, 1985.

Verger, Pierre. *Orisha: Les dieux Yorouba en Afrique et au nouveau monde.* Paris: Editions A. M. Métalié, 1982.

Voeks, Robert A. *Sacred Leaves of Candomblé: African Magic, Medicine, and Religion in Brazil.* Austin: University of Texas Press, 1997.

Wilcken, Lois, featuring Frisner Augustin. *The Drums of Vodou.* Tempe, Ariz.: White Cliffs, 1992.

Williams-Yarborough, Lavinia. *Haiti-Dance.* Frankfort: Brooners-Druckerei, 1964.

Wilson, Edmund. *Red, Black, Blond, and Olive; Studies in Four Civilizations: Zuni, Haiti, Soviet Union, Israel.* New York: Oxford University Press, 1956.

Wolf, Fred Alan. *Taking the Quantum Leap: The New Physics for Nonscientists.* New York: Harper & Row, 1989.

Yih, David. "Music and Dance of Haitian Vodou: Diversity and Unity in Regional Reper-toires." Ph.D. dissertation, Wesleyan University, 1995.

Young, Robert J. C. *Colonial Desire: Hybridity in Theory, Culture, and Race.* London: Rout-ledge, 1995.

Contributors

Patrick Bellegarde-Smith is Professor of Africology at the University of Wisconsin, Milwaukee. He is a *houngan asogwe,* a priest of Vodou. He is author of *In the Shadow of Powers: Dantès Bellegarde in Haitian Social Thought* (1985) and *Haiti: The Breached Citadel* (1990, 2004), editor of *Fragment of Bone* (2005) and co-editor (with Claudine Michel) of *Invisible Powers: Vodou and Development in Haiti* (forthcoming) and *Woman: Gender, Power, and Politics in Haitian Vodou.*

Claudine Michel is Professor of Black Studies at the University of California, Santa Barbara. She is author of *Aspects Educatifs et Moraux du Vodou Haïtien* (1995), and co-author of *Théories du Développement de l'Enfant: Etudes Comparatives* (1994), among other works. Her research has been published in many scholarly journals and other academic venues. She is currently editor of the *Journal of Haitian Studies* and a founding member of KOSANBA, a scholarly association for the study of Haitian Vodou.

Max-G. Beauvoir holds advanced degrees in biochemistry. He is a *hougan,* a Vodou priest and healer. He had a major Vodou temple in the United States, the Temple of Yehwe in Washington, D.C., and is the owner of the Peristyle of Mariani. He is author of the only known version of *La Prière Dior.* In 2005 he became president of BRODE, the national organization of Haitian houngan and manbo.

Florence Bellande-Robertson holds a Ph.D. in comparative literature from UCLA and is President of the foundation Hope for Haiti and Vice-President of the Multicultural Women's Press consortium. She is author of *The Marassa Concept in Lilas Desquiron's Reflections of Loko Miwa* (1999) and *Perhaps Tomorrow* (1983). She is co-editor (with Claudine Michel and Marlène Racine-Toussaint) of *Brassage: An Anthology of Haitian Women's Poetry* (2004).

Marc A. Christophe is Professor of French Language and French and Francophone Literatures and assistant chair of the Department of Languages and Communication Disorders at the University of the District of Columbia. He is author of two books, *Le Pain de l'exil* (1988) and *La Gloire de l'Arc-en-ciel* (1998). His work has appeared in many scholarly venues, including *The Journal of Haitian Studies, The College Language Association's Journal, Phylon,* and *The Literary Griot.*

Rénald Clérismé is former ambassador of Haiti at the United Nations in Switzerland and at the Ministère des Affaires Etrangères in Haiti. He has published a number of articles on issues of community organizations and development in Haiti. He is author of *Main d'Oeuvre Haïtienne, Capital Dominicain—Essai d'Anthropologie His-*

torique (2003). He runs a nonprofit cultural and medical center in Chateau, near Les Cayes.

Réginald O. Crosley is a poet, a scholar of religion and physics, and physician who practices medicine and nephrology in Baltimore, Maryland. He is author of *Immanences* (1988), *The Second Coming of Christ May Be Postponed Again* (1991), *Vodou Quantum Leap* (2000), *Harmoniques* (2002), and *Alternative Medicine and Miracles* (2004).

Gerdès Fleurant is Professor Emeritus of Music Culture at Wellesley College. He is author of many articles in scholarly books and journals as well as *Dancing Spirit: Rhythms and Rituals of Haitian Vodun, the Rada Rite* (1996). He is also a *houngan* and the president and founder of the Léocardie and Alexandre Kenscoff Cultural Center in Mirebailais, Haiti.

Guérin C. Montilus holds a Ph.D. from the Sorbonne and is Professor of Anthropology at Wayne State University. He is author of *Les Lwa haïtiens et les Vodun du Royaume d'Allada* (1987) and *Dompim: The Spirituality of African Peoples* (1988). He has pioneered research on the African roots of Haitian Vodou.

Marlène Racine-Toussaint is President of the Multicultural Women's Press consortium. She is author of *Ces femmes sont aussi nos soeurs* (1999). She is the author of "Perspective historique du role de la première dame de la République d'Haïti," which appeared in 2004 in the *Journal of Haitian Studies*. She is co-editor, with Florence Bellande Robertson, of *Brassage: An Anthology of Haitian Women's Poetry* (2005) and author of a book on Haitian first ladies (forthcoming).

Index

Lightning Source UK Ltd.
Milton Keynes UK
UKHW02f1932110118
315984UK00005B/239/P